MW01181606

Solaris 9 Network Administrator

John Philcox

CERTIFICATION

Solaris 9 Network Administrator Exam Cram 2 (Exam CX-310-044)

International Standard Book Number: 0-7897-2870-2

Library of Congress Catalog Card Number: 2003100982

Printed in the United States of America

First Printing: August 2003

06   05   04   03   4   3   2   1

Que Publishing offers excellent discounts on this book when ordered in quantity for bulk purchases or special sales. For more information, please contact

U.S. Corporate and Government Sales
1-800-382-3419
corpsales@pearsontechgroup.com

For sales outside the U.S., please contact

International Sales
1-317-581-3793
international@pearsontechgroup.com

Trademarks

Warning and Disclaimer

Publisher
Paul Boger

Executive Editor
Jeff Riley

Acquitions Editior
Carol Ackerman

Development Editor
Grant Munroe

Managing Editor
Charlotte Clapp

Project Editor
Tonya Simpson

Copy Editor
Margo Catts

Indexer
Mandie Frank

Proofreader
Juli Cook

Technical Editors
Ross Brunson
Philip LaVoie

Team Coordinator
Pamalee Nelson

Multimedia Developer
Dan Scherf

Interior Designer
Gary Adair

Cover Designer
Anne Jones

Page Layout
Cheryl Lynch
Michelle Mitchell
Heather Stephenson

Que Certification • 201 West 103rd Street • Indianapolis, Indiana 46290

A Note from Series Editor Ed Tittel

You know better than to trust your certification preparation to just anybody. That's why you, and more than two million others, have purchased an Exam Cram book. As Series Editor for the new and improved Exam Cram 2 series, I have worked with the staff at Que Certification to ensure you won't be disappointed. That's why we've taken the world's best-selling certification product—a finalist for "Best Study Guide" in a CertCities reader poll in 2002—and made it even better.

Best Study Guides

As a "Favorite Study Guide Author" finalist in a 2002 poll of CertCities readers, I know the value of good books. You'll be impressed with Que Certification's stringent review process, which ensures the books are high-quality, relevant, and technically accurate. Rest assured that at least a dozen industry experts—including the panel of certification experts at CramSession—have reviewed this material, helping us deliver an excellent solution to your exam preparation needs.

We've also added a preview edition of PrepLogic's powerful, full-featured test engine, which is trusted by certification students throughout the world.

As a 20-year-plus veteran of the computing industry and the original creator and editor of the Exam Cram series, I've brought my IT experience to bear on these books. During my tenure at Novell from 1989 to 1994, I worked with and around its excellent education and certification department. This experience helped push my writing and teaching activities heavily in the certification direction. Since then, I've worked on more than 70 certification-related books, and I write about certification topics for numerous Web sites and for *Certification* magazine.

In 1996, while studying for various MCP exams, I became frustrated with the huge, unwieldy study guides that were the only preparation tools available. As an experienced IT professional and former instructor, I wanted "nothing but the facts" necessary to prepare for the exams. From this impetus, Exam Cram emerged in 1997. It quickly became the best-selling computer book series since "...*For Dummies*," and the best-selling certification book series ever. By maintaining an intense focus on subject matter, tracking errata and updates quickly, and following the certification market closely, Exam Cram was able to establish the dominant position in cert prep books.

You will not be disappointed in your decision to purchase this book. If you are, please contact me at etittel@jump.net. All suggestions, ideas, input, or constructive criticism are welcome!

Ed Tittel

Taking You to the Solaris 9 System Administrator Finish Line!

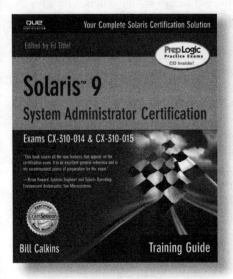

Solaris 9 System Administrator Certification Training Guide
Bill Calkins
ISBN 0-7897-2922-9
$49.99 US/$77.99 CAN/£36.50 Net UK

Before you walk into your local testing center, make absolutely sure you're prepared to pass your exam. In addition to the Exam Cram2 series, consider our Training Guide series. Que Certification's Training Guides have exactly what you need to pass your exam:

- Exam Objectives highlighted in every chapter

- Notes, Tips, Warnings, and Exam Tips advise what to watch out for

- Step-by-Step Exercises for "hands-on" practice

- End-of-chapter Exercises and Exam Questions

- Final Review with Fast Facts, Study and Exam Tips, and another Practice Exam

- A CD that includes PrepLogic Practice Tests for complete evaluation of your knowledge

- Our authors are recognized experts in the field. In most cases, they are current or former instructors, trainers, or consultants – they know exactly what you need to know!

I would like to dedicate this book to Dad, Cecil Philcox, who loved books and reading. I wish he could have been here to see this achievement.

About the Author

John Philcox is owner and director of Mobile Ventures Limited, a computer consultancy based in Cheltenham, Gloucestershire, in the United Kingdom, specializing in Unix systems and networks. He has more than 20 years experience in IT, 15 of those with SunOS and Solaris environments. He is a certified Solaris administrator, as well as a professional member of the Institution of Analysts and Programmers and the Institute of Management of Information Systems, both in the U.K. John is also a member of Usenix and SAGE. He has worked in a number of large multi-vendor networks in both the public and private sectors of business.

John was the author of *Solaris System Management* (New Riders Publishing, ISBN: 073571018X) and a contributing author of *Solaris 9 System Administration Training Guide (Exam CX-310-014 and CX-310-015* (Que Publishing, ISBN: 0789729229).

John has also been a technical editor/reviewer on the following books:

➤ *Solaris 2.6 Administrator Certification Training Guide Part II* (New Riders Publishing, ISBN: 1578700868)

➤ *Solaris 7 Administrator Certification Training Guide: Part I and II* (New Riders Publishing, ISBN: 1578702496)

➤ *Solaris 8 Security* (New Riders Publishing, ISBN: 1578702704)

➤ *Solaris 8 Training Guide (310-011 and 310-012): System Administrator* (New Riders Publishing, ISBN: 1578702593)

➤ *Inside Solaris 9* (New Riders Publishing, ISBN: 0735711011)

About the Technical Reviewers

Philip LaVoie is an SCSA and SCNA working for Dow Jones & Company, Inc. Not believing that system administration ends with the operating system and hardware, he has experience programming Java, PERL, PHP, C, C++, and PostScript. With a love for his wife Kate and an affinity for logic and attention to detail, Phil maintains and designs Oracle and MySQL databases and is a long-time supporter of Linux and free software.

Ross Brunson is currently the director of Linux/Unix education for The Training Camp and an LPI-US (Linux Professional Institute) board member. He has the following certifications: LPIC1, SCSA, SCNA, LCI, LCA, Linux+, CCNA, MCSA, MCP+I, MCSE4, MCT, and Inet+.

He began his IT career in the U.S. Army in the 1980s working with battlefield simulation systems running on Unix platforms. Before joining The Training Camp, Ross authored several books about UNIX/Linux Integration with Window, including the *Linux and Windows 2000 Integration Toolkit*.

Ross began his formal training and consulting career with Learning Tree International as a courseware technical editor and his area's second-highest scoring instructor.

After a number of years conducting TCP/IP, UNIX, Linux, and Networking courses for Learning Tree, Mastering Computers of Scottsdale and other companies, he took a courseware and development position at Computer Associates developing and delivering Windows 2000 and Linux courses for many USA and International companies.

Ross then took a position with Thomson Learning's Sair Linux certification and courseware division as the Director of Courseware Development and Instruction. He built an excellent instructor force spanning 13 countries and 110 instructors in little over a year, delivering many "train-the-trainers" to current and prospective instructors in the U.S. and overseas. Ross has conducted certification seminars at four consecutive Linuxworld shows, with over 2,500 people attending and testing as a result of his team's efforts.

He lives in Coeur d'Alene, Idaho, with his wife, baby daughter, and dogs, and enjoys canoeing, fishing, and hiking in between teaching and consulting gigs.

Acknowledgments

With my office being at home, Tracey, my wife, and our two boys, Nathan and Lewis, have gotten used to me working until 2:00 a.m. Your support has been unconditional and deserves a special mention.

I'd like to thank Bill Calkins, who got me into the whole writing and editing arena. We've worked together on a number of books for almost four years—let's hope there are many more.

Thanks to the technical reviewers, Ross Brunson and Philip LaVoie, for providing such thorough reviews and suggestions. This book wouldn't be the same without your valuable input.

A special mention to Grant Munroe, development editor, who really knows his business and has provided helpful comments throughout the writing process.

Finally, thanks to all the people at Que who put it all together and somehow made this finished book emerge at the other end—especially Carol Ackerman and Margo Catts.

We Want to Hear from You!

As the reader of this book, *you* are our most important critic and commentator. We value your opinion and want to know what we're doing right, what we could do better, what areas you'd like to see us publish in, and any other words of wisdom you're willing to pass our way.

As an executive editor for Que, I welcome your comments. You can email or write me directly to let me know what you did or didn't like about this book—as well as what we can do to make our books better.

Please note that I cannot help you with technical problems related to the *topic* of this book. We do have a User Services group, however, where I will forward specific technical questions related to the book.

When you write, please be sure to include this book's title and author as well as your name, email address, and phone number. I will carefully review your comments and share them with the author and editors who worked on the book.

Email: feedback@quepublishing.com

Mail: Jeff Riley
           Que Certification
           201 West 103rd Street
           Indianapolis, IN 46290 USA

For more information about this book or another Que title, visit our Web site at www.quepublishing.com. Type the ISBN (excluding hyphens) or the title of a book in the Search field to find the page you're looking for.

Contents at a Glance

Table of Contents

· ·

Introduction

. . . .

Welcome to *Solaris 9 Network Administrator Exam Cram 2*. This book will help you get ready to take—and pass—the *Sun Certified Network Administrator for the Solaris 9 Operating Environment (CX-310-044)* exam required to obtain the Sun Certified Network Administrator for Solaris 9 certification. This chapter discusses Sun's certification program in general and how the *Exam Cram 2* can help you prepare for the Solaris 9 certification exam. It doesn't matter whether this is the first time you're going to take the exam or you've taken it previously; this book is going to give you the necessary information and techniques to obtain certified status.

Exam Cram 2 books help you understand and appreciate the subjects and materials you need to pass Solaris certification exams. The books are aimed strictly at test preparation and review. They do not teach you everything you need to know about a topic. Instead, they present and dissect the questions and problems that you're likely to encounter on the test.

Nevertheless, to completely prepare yourself for any Solaris test, I recommend that you begin by taking the self-assessment included in this book, which immediately follows this introduction. The self-assessment tool will help you evaluate your knowledge base against the requirements for a Solaris 9 Network Administrator under both ideal and real circumstances.

Based on what you learn from the self-assessment exercise, you might decide to begin your studies with some classroom training or by reading one of the network administration guides available from Sun and third-party vendors. I also strongly recommend that you install, configure, and play around with Solaris 9 and other software on which you'll be tested. You need at least two Sun workstations because many networking aspects need to be tested, and nothing beats hands-on experience and familiarity when it comes to understanding the questions you are likely to encounter on a certification test. Book learning is essential, but hands-on experience is the best teacher of all!

The Sun Certified Network Administrator for Solaris 9 Certification

The certification program currently includes one exam, the *Sun Certified Network Administrator for the Solaris 9 Operating Environment (Exam 310-044)* exam. The exam covers local area networks, the TCP/IP Model, Address Resolution Protocol (ARP) and Reverse Address Resolution Protocol (RARP), basic Internet Protocol version 4 (IPv4) configuration, Routing with IPv4, Multipathing with IPv4, Internet Protocol version 6 (IPv6), the Transport layer, Domain Name System (DNS), Dynamic Host Configuration Protocol (DHCP), and Network Time Protocol (NTP).

To become a certified network administrator, you must already be a Sun Certified System Administrator, having passed the exams for any of the Solaris releases, 2.5, 2.6, 7, 8, or 9. This is a prerequisite that must be satisfied before you can take the Solaris 9 network administrator exam. The exam itself consists of 64 questions, and you have 105 minutes to complete the exam. You must attain a pass mark of 70% to pass the exam.

The questions on the exam will be of the following types:

➤ Multiple choice, single answer (only a single answer is correct).

➤ Multiple choice, multiple answers (multiple answers are correct and you have to get them all to score the point).

➤ Multiple match (drag-and-drop style, where a number of terms are displayed along with a number of answers—you have to use the mouse to drag the correct answer box and drop it on the corresponding term).

➤ Free response (where you have to enter the required command on the keyboard in a space provided).

It is not uncommon for the entire network administrator certification process to take six months, and many individuals find that they must take the test more than once to pass it. The primary goal of the *Exam Cram 2* series is to make it possible, given proper study and preparation, to pass the exam on the first try.

Although certification is associated with a particular version of the Solaris Operating Environment, there is no requirement to recertify. After a Solaris version becomes obsolete, however, being certified on that version will have little value, so it would be in your best interest to work on the certification for the next version of Solaris. Also, unfortunately there is no upgrade exam for the Network Administrator certification, unlike the Sun Certified System Administrator certification, where a single upgrade exam can be taken to become certified on the next Solaris version.

In the past, Sun has used the certification requirements and test objectives from the previous version as a starting point for the next version. So after you've been certified on a version of Solaris, you should be very familiar with most of the test objectives for certification in the next version of Solaris. Only about 15–20% of objectives seem to have changed between Solaris 8 and Solaris 9, the majority of those in the IPv6 section and the DHCP section.

The best place to keep tabs on Sun's certification program is on the Sun Web site. The current URL for Sun's Network Administrator program is `http://training.sun.com/US/certification/solaris/netadmin.html`. Sun's certification Web site changes frequently, so if this URL fails to work, then try using the Search tool on Sun's main Web site, `http://www.sun.com`, using keywords such as "certification" or "network administrator" as the search string. This will help you to find the latest and most accurate information about the company's certification programs.

Taking a Certification Exam

Each test you take costs $150.00 (£100 in the U.K.), whether you pass or fail. If you fail, the next attempt will also cost the same amount. In the United States and the U.K., tests are administered by Thomson Prometric.

The first thing you have to do is purchase an examination voucher from Sun Educational Services. In the U.S., you can contact Sun Education Services at 1-800-422-8020 and in the U.K. you can contact them at 01276-416520. This requires that you use a credit card. The voucher can be used for up to one year from the date of purchase.

Next, contact Thomson Prometric to register for the exam. In the U.S., their telephone number is 1-800-795-3926, and in the U.K. it is 0800-592873. You can also use the Thomson Web site at `http://www.2test.com`.

To schedule an exam, call at least one day in advance. To cancel or reschedule an exam, you must call at least one day before the scheduled test time; otherwise you might still be charged the full fee. When calling Thomson Prometric, please have the following information ready for the telesales staff member who handles your call:

➤ Your Thomson Prometric number, if you have previously taken exams with Thomson.

➤ Your name, organization, mailing address, and social security number.

➤ The name of the exam you want to take.

➤ The number of the Sun voucher you purchased (this information might not be required because the Thomson Prometric staff member may already have it).

An appointment confirmation will be sent to you by mail if you register more than five days before an exam, or will be sent by fax if there are fewer than five days before the exam. A Candidate Agreement letter, which you must sign to take the examination, will also be provided.

On the day of the test, try to arrive at the testing center at least 15 minutes before the scheduled time. You must supply two forms of identification, one of which must be a photo ID.

All Sun exams are closed book. You are not permitted to take anything with you into the testing area, although you will be provided with a pen and some blank paper (which you must leave behind when you've finished). I recommend that you review the most critical information about the test you're taking just before the test. (*Exam Cram 2* books provide a brief reference—The Cram Sheet, located inside the front of this book—that lists the essential information from the book in distilled form.) You will have some time to compose yourself and either mentally review this critical information or write some important facts down on the paper. There is a sample orientation test that you can do before taking your first exam; it's worth doing if this is the first time you've been to a Thomson Prometric testing center as it familiarizes you with the layout and functions that will be available to you during the test. The sample orientation test is not part of the actual exam—your time doesn't start until you click on the option to start the exam itself.

After you are in the test center, sitting at the computer, relax and stay calm. You cannot do any more reading now, so take a deep breath and read the first question.

I cannot stress enough how important it is to read a question at least twice before selecting an answer. Even though Sun does not deliberately pose "trick" questions, you could rush in and answer the question because you've already seen an answer that appears to be good. This is probably the most common cause of exam failure: not reading the question properly. Make sure you understand how many answers are required for a question. In a multiple choice question with multiple answers, Sun normally states how many answers are required—the question often ends with a sentence that says, "Choose 2," for example. If you're not sure of the answer, then try to eliminate as many "definitely wrong" answers as you can, so that in the event of having to guess, you have reduced the odds significantly in your favor. There's no penalty for getting an answer wrong, or not attempting a question, so you should try to answer all the questions.

When you complete a Solaris 9 certification exam, the testing software tells you whether you've passed or failed. Results are broken down into several topical areas. Regardless of whether you pass or fail, I recommend that you keep the detailed report that the test administrator prints for you. You can use the report to help you prepare for a re-take (if necessary), and even if you pass, the report shows areas you may need to review to keep your skills fresh. If you do need to retake an exam, you have to call Thomson Prometric and schedule a new test date—of course this unfortunately means paying the fee again.

Tracking Certification Status

Sun maintains a database that indicates the exams you have passed and your corresponding test scores. The database is accessible via Sun's web site at `http://training.sun.com/US/certification/certmanager/index.html`. You use your Thomson Prometric ID to log in to certmanager, where you have to assign a password if this is the first time you've accessed this facility. Verify and update, if necessary, your personal information. You can then view your certification status. Official certification normally takes anywhere from four to six weeks (but is generally within 30 days), so don't expect to receive your certificate immediately. The exam results will normally be available in certmanager after about 4 working days, so you can view the status online much sooner. After you have completed certification, you will receive a package with a Welcome Kit that contains a number of elements:

➤ A Network Administrator for Solaris 9 certificate, suitable for framing

➤ A logo sheet, which includes camera-ready artwork for use on letterheads, business cards, and so on

➤ A Sun Certified Network Administrator lapel pin

Many people believe that the benefits of certification go well beyond the perks that Sun provides to newly anointed members of this elite group. More and more job listings require applicants to have a Solaris certification, and many individuals who complete the program can qualify for increases in pay and/or responsibility. As an official recognition of hard work and broad knowledge, Solaris certification is a badge of honor in many IT organizations.

How to Prepare for the Exam

At a minimum, preparing for Solaris 9 exams requires that you obtain and study the following materials:

➤ The Solaris 9 documentation in printed form, on CD-ROM as delivered with Solaris 9, or on the Web at http://docs.sun.com. You can also download the documentation CD-ROM from Sun's Web site.

➤ The exam test objectives and sample questions on the Sun certification Web page (http://training.sun.com/US/certification/solaris/netadmin.html).

➤ This *Exam Cram 2* book. It's the first and last thing you should read before taking the exam.

Also, you'll find any or all of the following materials useful in your quest for Solaris 9 network administration expertise:

➤ *Hands-on Experience*—Obtain a copy of Solaris 9 from Sun's Web site (http://www.sun.com). Ideally, you need at least two (networked) workstations to be able to replicate the network environment and make use of the functionality. As you work your way through the book, try the commands and utilities, and explore the details of each. Experience is the best way to learn and remember the details that you need to know to pass the exam. The Solaris 9 Operating Environment can be downloaded, free of charge, or obtained on CD-ROM, with you paying only the cost of media and shipping.

➤ *Classroom Training*—Sun offers classroom training, computer-based training, and online training that you will find useful to help you prepare for the exam. The course SA-399 is the specific course that is most relevant to this exam. The classes are quite expensive, although they do offer a condensed form of learning to help you reinforce your Solaris knowledge. The exam is closely related to the classroom training provided by Sun, so it is an advantage to take the classes to get the Solaris-specific (and classroom-specific) terminology under your belt.

➤ *Other Publications*—In this book, you'll find direct references to other publications and resources that will provide you with further information on the subjects taught here. Each chapter ends with a "Need to Know More?" section, providing pointers to more complete resources.

In addition, don't forget the Cram Sheet at the front of the book. It is designed to capture the most important material that you should memorize right before you take the test.

Take at least one practice exam. Each chapter in this book ends with a number of exam-type questions that are designed to review what you've just studied. This book also includes two full practice exams (and answers) which should be taken as if you are taking the real test. Give yourself 105 minutes and be honest: Don't look up the answers until after you complete the test— the only person you'll be fooling is yourself!

Sun also provides a practice exam that can be purchased from them. This is a worthwhile expense if you want even more exposure to the type of questions that are going to be asked in the real test.

About This Book

Each topical *Exam Cram 2* chapter follows a regular structure, along with graphical cues about important or useful information. Here's the structure of a typical chapter:

➤ *Opening Hotlists*—Each chapter begins with a list of terms and concepts that you must learn and understand before you can be fully conversant with the chapter's subject matter. The section "Techniques You'll Need to Master" is very closely related to the formal objectives provided by Sun for that topic. The hotlists are followed by an introductory section to set the stage for the rest of the chapter.

➤ *Topical Coverage*—After the opening hotlists, each chapter covers a series of topics related to the chapter's subject title. Throughout this section, I will highlight topics or concepts that are likely to appear in the exam. A special Exam Alert layout is used, like this:

This is what an Exam Alert looks like. Normally it stresses concepts, terms, software, or activities that are likely to relate to one or more certification test questions. Anything found in Exam Alert format is worthy of greater attention on your part.

Even though the book is structured to the exam, these flagged items are often of particular importance.

➤ *Notes and Tips*—Throughout each chapter additional information is provided that, although not directly related to the exam itself, is still useful and will aid your preparation. A sample note is shown here:

 A note contains some additional information that is separate from the main content, but is still useful.

A tip might tell you another way of accomplishing something in a more efficient or time-saving manner. An example of a tip is shown here:

 You can also enter multiple commands on the same line by using the semicolon (;) character as a command separator—for example, to flush the routing table and add a new default route that uses host **ultra10** as the gateway, enter the following on a single line:

```
# route flush; route add default ultra10
```

➤ *Practice Questions*—A section at the end of each chapter presents a series of mock questions and explanations of the answers.

➤ *Further Reading*—Each chapter ends with a section titled "Need to Know More?" This section provides direct pointers to resources offering more detail on the subjects that have been covered in the chapter.

How to Use this Book

The topics in this book have been structured so that your knowledge builds progressively as you go through each chapter. For this reason, it is better to read the book from front to back; some topics in later chapters may make more sense after you've read earlier chapters.

Aside from being a test preparation book, this book is also useful if you are brushing up on your Solaris networking skills as it provides a condensed volume of information. It is excellent as a quick reference to some of the most important aspects of the Solaris Operating Environment.

Enjoy the book, and good luck on the exam!

Self-Assessment

This *Exam Cram 2* series includes a Self-Assessment to help you evaluate your readiness to tackle the Sun Certified Network Administrator for Solaris 9 certification. It should also help you understand what you need to know to master the topic of this book—namely, Exam 310-044, "Sun Certified Network Administrator for the Solaris 9 Operating Environment." Before you take this Self-Assessment, let's talk about the concerns you may face when pursuing Solaris 9 Network Administrator certification, and what an ideal candidate might look like.

Solaris 9 Network Administrators in the Real World

In the next section, I describe an ideal Solaris 9 Network Administrator candidate, knowing full well that only a few actual candidates meet this ideal. In fact, my description of that ideal candidate might seem downright scary. But take heart because although the requirements to obtain a Solaris 9 Network Administrator certification may seem pretty formidable, they are by no means impossible to meet. However, you should be keenly aware that it does take time, requires some expense, and consumes a substantial effort.

You can get all the real-world motivation you need from knowing that many others have gone before you. You can follow in their footsteps. If you're willing to tackle the process seriously and do what it takes to obtain the necessary experience and knowledge, you can take—and pass—the certification test. In fact, the *Exam Crams* and the companion *Exam Preps* are designed to make it as easy as possible for you to prepare for this exam.

The same, of course, is true for other Solaris certifications, including

➤ Solaris 9 System Administrator, which concentrates on the system administration aspects and consists of two exams: *Sun Certified System Administrator for the Solaris 9 Operating Environment Part I (CX-310-014)*

and *Sun Certified System Administrator for the Solaris 9 Operating Environment Part II (CX-310-015)*.

➤ Solaris 8 System Administrator, which is similar to the Solaris 9 exams, but concentrates on the previous version of Solaris. This, again, consists of two exams: *Sun Certified System Administrator for the Solaris 8 Operating Environment Part I (CX-310-011)* and *Sun Certified System Administrator for the Solaris 8 Operating Environment Part II (CX-310-012)*.

➤ Solaris 8 Network Administrator, which concentrates on the networking aspects of the Solaris 8 Operating Environment and, like the Solaris 9 certification, consists of a single exam: *Sun Certified Network Administrator for the Solaris 8 Operating Environment (CX-310-043)*.

The Ideal Solaris 9 Network Administrator Candidate

Just to give you some idea of what an ideal Solaris 9 Network Administrator candidate is like, here are some relevant statistics about the background and experience such an individual might have. Don't worry if you don't meet these qualifications (or, indeed, if you don't even come close), because this world is far from ideal, and where you fall short is simply where you'll have more work to do. The ideal candidate will have

➤ Sun Certified System Administrator status at one of the release levels (2.5, 2.6, 7, 8, or 9). This is a prerequisite for being able to take the Solaris 9 Network Administrator exam.

➤ Academic or professional training in Unix Operating Systems and more specifically the AT&T System V Release 4 (SVR4) Unix Operating System, on which Solaris is based.

➤ Three or more years of professional system administration experience with a thorough understanding of Solaris installation and configuration, as well as system administration duties.

➤ Three or more years of professional experience working in a networked environment, preferably in a Solaris environment, including troubleshooting various network problems and using the Solaris-provided network utilities, such as `ifconfig`, `snoop`, and `netstat`.

I believe that well under half of all certification candidates meet these requirements; most probably meet less than half. (At least when they begin the certification process candidates generally don't meet these ideal standards.) It's worth reminding you that to take the Solaris 9 Network Administrator Exam you *must* be a Sun Certified System Administrator—if you're not, you will not be allowed to take the exam. But, because all those who already have their network administrator certification have survived this ordeal, you can survive it, too—especially if you heed what this self-assessment can tell you about what you already know and what you need to learn.

Put Yourself to the Test

The following series of questions and observations is designed to help you determine how much work you'll face in pursuing Solaris certification and what kinds of resources you may consult on your quest. Be absolutely honest in your answers, or you'll end up wasting money on exams you're not ready to take. There are no right or wrong answers, only steps along the path to certification. Only you can decide where you really belong in the broad spectrum of aspiring candidates.

Two things should be clear from the outset, however:

➤ Even a modest background in computer science will be helpful.

➤ Hands-on experience with the Solaris Operating System and technologies is an essential ingredient to certification success.

Educational Background

1. Are you a Sun Certified System Administrator? [Yes or No]

   If yes, proceed to question 3; if no, proceed to question 2.

2. Do you intend to become a certified System Administrator? [Yes or No]

   If yes, you will have to study for exams *Sun Certified System Administrator for the Solaris 9 Operating Environment Part I (CX-310-014)* and *Sun Certified System Administrator for the Solaris 9 Operating Environment Part II (CX-310-015)*. There is an *Exam Cram 2* book available for these exams and I strongly recommend using it to gain this certification. If you are not a certified System Administrator, then you will not be able to take the Solaris 9 Network Administrator exam because it is a prerequisite that the candidate already be a Sun Certified System Administrator.

3. Have you taken any Solaris networking classes? [Yes or No]

   If yes, then you will already have a good understanding of the underlying technologies and concepts. This book will enhance your knowledge by providing updates for the Solaris 9 Network Administrator exam. If you have not taken a course, then you should consider additional reading in this area—a number of books are available, including Sun documentation at http://docs.sun.com. See the "Need to Know More?" section at the end of each chapter for further reading recommendations.

4. Have you read material on Unix networking? [Yes or No]

If your answer is yes, then studying with this book should be enough formal study to enable you to take—and pass—the Solaris 9 Network Administrator exam. If your answer is no, then follow closely the recommended reading section at the end of each chapter to broaden your knowledge. Increasing your background knowledge will be of great help in preparing you for this exam.

Hands-on Experience

Practical experience is one of the most important factors in achieving success on the Solaris exam. If I leave you with only one realization after taking this self-assessment, it should be that there is no substitute for time spent practicing and using the networking facilities and commands in Solaris that you'll be tested on repeatedly and in depth.

5. Have you installed and configured Solaris 9 networking facilities and advanced functionality, such as DHCP, DNS, and IPv6? [Yes or No]

If your answer is yes, then make sure that you understand the basic networking concepts covered in Exam 310-044.

 You can download objectives, practice questions, and other information about Sun exams from Sun's certification Web site pages at **http://training.sun.com/US/ certification/solaris/netadmin.html**.

If your answer is no, then you should obtain a copy of Solaris 9 and practice using the networking facilities, learning how they work and how they are configured and used.

 You can download the Solaris 9 Operating System (SPARC edition), free of charge, from **www.sun.com**. The Intel (x86) version can be downloaded at a cost of $20.00.

Before you even think about taking a Solaris exam, make sure you've spent enough time with Solaris 9 to understand how the networking functions work and are configured. Also, study how to troubleshoot the software when things go wrong. This will help you in the exam—as well as in real life.

Testing Your Exam Readiness

Whether you attend a formal class on a specific topic to get ready for an exam or use written materials to study on your own, some preparation for the Solaris certification exam is essential. At $150.00 U.S. (£100 U.K.) a try, pass or fail, you want to do everything you can to pass on your first attempt. That's where studying comes in.

I have included in this book several practice exam questions for each chapter, as well as two sample tests, so if you don't score well on the chapter questions, you can study more and then tackle the sample tests at the end of the book. The score needed to pass the exam is 70%. But if you don't earn a score of at least 75% on the sample tests included in this book in Chapters 14 and 16, I recommend that you investigate other practice test resources available via the Web—locate these using your favorite search engine.

For a given subject, consider taking a class if you've tackled self-study materials, taken the test, and failed anyway. If you can afford the privilege, the opportunity to interact with an instructor and fellow students can make all the difference in the world. For information about Sun classes, visit the Sun Training Web site at `http://training.sun.com/US/catalog/courses`.

If you can't afford to take a class, visit the Sun Training Web site anyway, because it includes free sample questions. Even if you can't afford to spend money, you should still invest in some low-cost practice exams from commercial vendors, because they can help you assess your readiness to pass a test better than any other tool. Check with `www.unixcert.net` for other available resources.

6. Have you taken a practice exam on your chosen test subject? [Yes or No]

If you answered yes—and you scored 75% or better—you are probably ready to tackle the real thing. If your score isn't above this crucial threshold, keep at it until you break that barrier. If you answered no, obtain all the free and low-budget practice tests you can find (or afford) and get to work. Keep at it until you can comfortably break the passing threshold.

When it comes to assessing your test readiness, there is no better way than to take a good-quality practice exam and pass with a score of 75% or better. When preparing myself, I always aim higher (80%), to allow for some extra contingency.

Assessing Your Readiness for Exam 310-044

In addition to the general exam-readiness information in the previous section, other resources are available to help you prepare for the exam. Two good sites are www.solariscentral.org and www.solarisguide.com. The tek-tips forum at www.tek-tips.com has a forum relating to Sun certification and contains other people's useful comments about the Sun certification exams. Also, it is well worth consulting the comp newsgroups—comp.unix.solaris and comp.sys.sun.admin—available via news services or via Google Groups. These are excellent places to ask questions about topics you are having trouble understanding and get good answers, or simply to observe the questions that others ask. The Sun Blueprints program at www.sun.com/solutions/blueprints provides many in-depth articles on various Solaris topics as well.

One last note: I can't stress enough the importance of hands-on experience in the context of exams. As you review the material for the exam, you'll realize that hands-on experience with Solaris 9 commands, tools, and utilities is invaluable.

Onward, Through the Fog!

After you've assessed your readiness, undertaken the right background studies, obtained the hands-on experience that will help you understand the products and technologies at work, and reviewed the many sources of information to help you prepare for the test, you'll be ready to take a round of practice tests. When your scores come back high enough to get you through the exam, you're ready to go for the real thing. The Introduction of this book includes information about obtaining vouchers and scheduling the exam. If you follow my assessment regime, you'll not only know what you need to study, but when you're ready to make a test date at Prometric. Good luck!

Local Area Networks

Terms you'll need to understand:

✓ Local area network
✓ Network topology
✓ Hubs
✓ Switches
✓ Bridges
✓ Routers
✓ Network media
✓ CSMA/CD
✓ Ethernet frames
✓ Ethernet addresses
✓ Collision rates

Concepts you'll need to master:

✓ Describe the features and functions of LAN components.
✓ Describe network topologies, media, and network devices.
✓ Describe ethernet concepts and major ethernet elements.
✓ Describe the CSMA/CD access method.
✓ Be familiar with the components of an ethernet frame.
✓ Troubleshoot ethernet interfaces using **ifconfig**, **snoop**, **netstat**, and **ndd**.

The first part of this chapter is a stepping stone to the rest of the book. It introduces some of the fundamental building blocks of a local area network (LAN) and the hardware used in creating one. The second part of this chapter concentrates on Ethernet, the most prevalent network protocol in use today, ending with sections on gathering network statistics and troubleshooting problems that might be encountered on an ethernet network.

 The exam often contains a few questions that require you to match a number of networking elements with their associated descriptions, so knowledge of the terms introduced here, and in the Glossary, is an easy way to gain an extra point, but you have to get them ALL right to get the point.

Network Topologies

The *topology* of a network refers to how the physical layout is organized—that is, how the nodes on the network are physically wired together. Some topologies are cheaper to implement than others; some require more maintenance; and some have single points of failure, making them less reliable and robust. When designing a network, it is important to consider how big the network is going to be, the levels of traffic, and whether any failover requirements exist. Each of these aspects influences the decision of which topology to use. The following sections describe some of the more common topologies.

Bus Topology

In a *bus* topology, hosts are connected to a single cable—also known as a *backbone*—that runs through an area. Each end of the bus is terminated to avoid data signals being reflected back along the network. This type of configuration makes maintenance difficult because the network cabling must be disconnected to add a new connection. The bus itself is also a single point of failure—a fault on the bus renders the whole network unusable—but it is a cheap option and easy to install for smaller networks. The bus topology is normally used in broadcast networks, allowing only one host to transmit at a time. Figure 1.1 shows an example of a typical bus configuration.

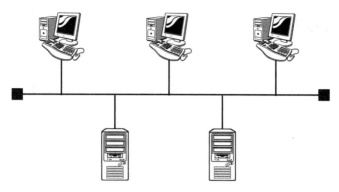

Figure 1.1   A bus configuration.

Star Topology

The *star* topology is the most common topology, mainly because it is cheap to install and easy to maintain. The hosts are connected to a central *hub*, which enables new hosts to be added without the need to interrupt the network's functionality. The number of hosts, or nodes, that can be used in a star network is limited by the number of connections on the central hub, although multiple hubs can be connected together to form larger networks. As with the bus configuration, a single point of failure, the hub itself, does exist. Figure 1.2 shows an example of a simple star network.

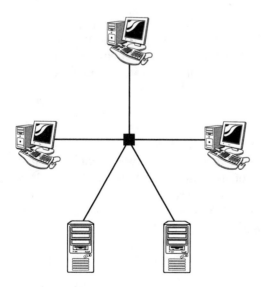

Figure 1.2   A star configuration.

Ring Topology

The *ring* network is a configuration in which the hosts are connected in a loop. Each host is directly connected to its two adjacent hosts, one on either side. This topology offers slightly better resilience than bus or star topologies because a single failure results only in a degradation of the network; it takes two cable breaks, in separate segments, before any hosts become disconnected from the network. Figure 1.3 shows an example of a simple ring configuration.

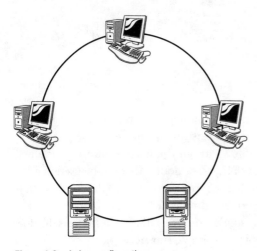

Figure 1.3 A ring configuration.

Two rings can also be used to provide added resilience. The Fiber Distributed Data Interface (FDDI) is the most common example of this, in which the second ring continues to function if the primary ring fails.

Mixed Topologies

Networks commonly use more than one topology because it is more practical and cost effective; this is called a *mixed* topology. For example, a department might use a bus configuration as its main backbone but have multiple star networks connecting the hosts in each section. In some colleges and universities, dual-ring networks, such as FDDI, are used as the backbone. Figure 1.4 shows how a mixed configuration may be used.

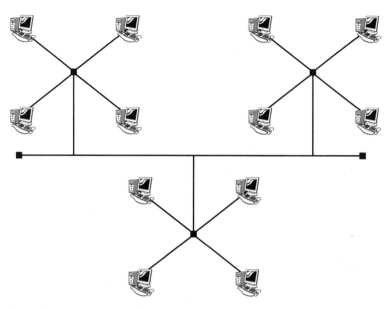

Figure 1.4   An example of a mixed configuration.

Virtual LAN Topologies

Virtual local area networks (VLANs) have become more popular, but they require the use of an intelligent central switch or hub. *VLANs* are similar in functionality to having multiple star networks, but in this case, they all use the same physical switch as the central hub. A VLAN is created by assigning specific ports on the central hub to separate networks. The hosts on each VLAN communicate with each other as if they were on the same physical network segment. An advantage of the VLAN concept is that the network traffic on one VLAN is separate from the network traffic on another VLAN, making more efficient use of the available bandwidth. A further advantage is that hosts can be moved between VLANs without requiring any hardware configuration. Of course, the central switch, or hub, remains a single point of failure. Figure 1.5 demonstrates how an intelligent hub can be used to create two separate VLANs, (the hosts are shaded and labeled to show to which network they belong).

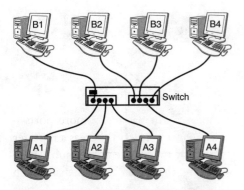

Figure 1.5 An example of a VLAN configuration.

Network Devices

Assembling the necessary hardware is the first step in setting up every network. This differs depending on the size and complexity of the network, but this section provides some fundamental descriptions of the more common network devices.

Network Adapters

The *network adapter* is usually a card installed into a server or workstation to enable the host to connect to the network. Some computer systems come with an *integrated* network adapter, which means it is built on to the main system board. Different network adapters are available depending on the type of network and the type of connection media. For example, ethernet and token-ring networks require different network adapters, as do twisted-pair and fiber-optic cable media. The different types of cable media are summarized in a later section. Every network adapter, whether in a Solaris workstation or a PC, is supplied with a unique 48-bit address, known as the *media access control (MAC) address*, which is described in the section "Ethernet" later in this chapter.

Repeaters

A *repeater* is used in computer networks to extend the length of a segment of the network. Cable media has defined maximum lengths that the cable can be. When longer distances are used, the electrical signals passed down the cable become distorted because of electrical noise and resistance from the cable itself, causing errors to appear on the network. The repeater acts as a booster for the electrical signal so that hosts situated farther away can still receive good-quality signals. In an ethernet network, you can connect a maximum of four repeaters, enabling five segments to appear as a single cable.

Hubs

A *hub*, or *shared hub*, is similar to a repeater but has many more ports—indeed, it is sometimes referred to as a *multiport repeater*. Whereas a repeater merely extends the network segment with only two connectors, a hub is used in a star topology network to connect a number of hosts. When the hub receives a signal, it is regenerated to all the other ports on the hub. Larger LANs normally use multiple hubs connected to a central backbone (see Figure 1.4 earlier in this chapter for an example of a mixed configuration using a backbone and several star networks). Collision rates can be higher using hubs because each signal is repeated to each port, which creates a greater amount of network traffic.

Switches

A *switch* can be thought of as an intelligent hub. It is a multiport device, similar to a hub, used as part of a star network. The main difference is that signals are not repeated to each port; instead, a signal is repeated only on the destination port, based on the MAC address of the destination host. This greatly reduces the amount of network traffic that is generated and enables multiple data paths to be established and used simultaneously without the high collision rates of a hub. If a broadcast data packet is received, it is replicated on all the ports of the switch. The switch is also a central part of VLAN networks, where ports can be configured to belong to separate virtual networks. Previously, this would have been achieved only through the use of a separate hub for each network. Figure 1.6 shows the before-and-after view of the advantages of using an intelligent switch in this way.

Bridges

A *bridge* is a device that connects a LAN to another LAN that uses the same protocol, such as ethernet. It can have multiple ports, with each port connected to a separate LAN. It determines whether to forward a packet based on the MAC address. When a data packet is received, the bridge consults a dynamically maintained forwarding table of MAC addresses and forwards the packet to the network with the host containing the address. If the destination MAC address is not known, the packet is forwarded to all networks connected to its ports. If a MAC address is not in the forwarding table, it is automatically added.

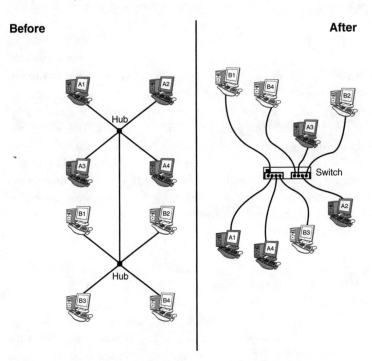

Figure 1.6   An example showing the advantages of an intelligent switch.

Routers

A *router* is a device—but can also be software—that determines part of the route a packet needs to take to reach its destination. A router is connected to a minimum of two networks and is used to determine which direction a packet takes, based on either static route definitions or dynamic information obtained from the network itself. Today, routers also act as security devices, where specified traffic can be either allowed through the router or blocked, depending on the security policy that is implemented. Routers are also frequently used as firewalls to protect company networks from unauthorized intruders on the Internet. The router determines whether to forward a data packet based on the IP address, unlike the bridge, which uses the MAC address.

Gateways

A *gateway* is often described as being synonymous with a *router*, but this is not entirely accurate. Similar to a router, the gateway connects networks together, but unlike a router, it can connect networks of different types. Networks connected by a router use a common protocol, whereas networks connected by a gateway can use different protocols. It is this capability that has led to gateways being called *protocol converters*.

 Be sure you understand the differences between a bridge, router, and gateway. You might be asked to differentiate between them.

Network Media

The *media* used in a network configuration refers to the medium used to convey packets of data between hosts on the network. The most common form of network media today is cable, which is covered in the next section. Wireless networks are also beginning to increase in popularity, but these are not discussed in this book because they are not relevant to the Sun Certified Network Administrator Exam for Solaris 9. The Institute of Electrical and Electronics Engineers (IEEE, pronounced *eye triple E*) is a professional body responsible for the majority of network media standards.

Network Cables

Cables used in a network configuration carry electrical or light signals to enable a host to communicate with another host. There are three major cable types in use today: coaxial, twisted-pair, and fiber-optic.

Coaxial

This type of cable was the mainstay of earlier ethernet networks before the introduction of twisted-pair and fiber-optic cables. *Coaxial* cable uses a central core wire that is insulated and wrapped into a conductive cladding. All this is then wrapped into an outer plastic coating. Coaxial cable is still used in environments with electromagnetic interference because it is well-insulated. The two types of coaxial cable are thick and thin. *Thick* cable is used for distances up to 500 meters, and *thin* is used for distances up to 185 meters. Coaxial cable uses a special connector at each end of the cable, called a *terminator*. Terminators possess the same resistance as the cable itself and effectively absorb the signals, preventing them from reflecting back along the cable.

Twisted-Pair

Twisted-pair is the most commonly used cable for LANs and consists of four pairs of twisted wire, all wrapped into a plastic insulator. The two types of twisted pair cabling are shielded twisted-pair (STP) and unshielded twisted-pair (UTP). An *STP* cable has a metallic shield surrounding the four pairs of wires, providing much better resistance to electromagnetic interference. STP is also more expensive, so it is used only in environments in which electromagnetic noise levels are high. A *UTP* cable has no such shield.

Fiber-Optic

Unlike coaxial and twisted-pair cables, *fiber-optic* signals are sent as light waves. These have a much higher capacity because greater bandwidth is available. Fiber-optic networks can also span larger geographical areas compared to the other cables. The two main modes of fiber-optic are *single mode fiber (SMF)*, in which only one signal can be sent along the cable at a time, and *multimode fiber (MMF)*, in which multiple signals can be sent along the cable simultaneously at different angles of reflection. Fiber-optic cables are popularly used as backbones in larger campus networks, with FDDI being the most common.

IEEE Ethernet Standards

The IEEE has developed and maintained a number of media standards for use with its 802.3 (ethernet) network type. Which one you use for your network depends on the following factors:

➤ The physical distance the network has to cover

➤ Security requirements of the media itself

➤ The cost of the media and of installing it

➤ Whether the media is supported by current technologies

The following sections describe the various IEEE media standards along with their properties, capacities, and distances where appropriate.

10BASE Types

The 10BASE family of media types has a maximum capacity of 10Mbps and uses baseband signaling. The properties of each is described in the following:

➤ *10BASE-2*—Thin coaxial cable that was the most popular, and cheapest, implementation prior to the introduction of twisted-pair. 10BASE-2 networks have a distance limit of 185 meters. The *2* in the designation is rounded up to 200 meters.

➤ *10BASE-5*—A thick (half inch) coaxial cable was the first media type to be used in the ethernet standard of 1980. This cable was quite inflexible, although still cheap to install given that it provided electrical shielding, too. It was frequently used as backbone cabling with a maximum distance of 500 meters.

➤ *10BASE-T*—The most widely used cabling for desktop connections, this was the first twisted-pair specification introduced in 1990. Hubs and switches are used to interconnect network segments, unlike the coaxial cable connections, which could be connected together directly using BNC connectors. Two pairs of twisted wires are used, one for receiving signals and one for sending over a distance of approximately 100 meters.

100BASE Types

The 100BASE family of media types has a maximum capacity of 100Mbps and uses baseband signaling. The properties of each are as follows:

➤ *100BASE-TX*—Twisted-pair cabling using two pairs of wires. It enables the use of both STP and UTP but can be implemented only on CAT-5 cabling. The maximum distance is approximately 100 meters.

➤ *100BASE-T4*—Twisted-pair cabling using four pairs of wires. Although CAT-5 cabling is normally used, it enables the use of both CAT-3 and CAT-4 UTP cabling: one pair for receiving, one pair for sending, and two bidirectional pairs. The maximum distance is approximately 100 meters.

➤ *100BASE-FX*—Fiber-optic cable consisting of two multimode fibers. The optional full-duplex mode enables a maximum distance of 2000 meters for a network segment. Fiber is inherently more secure because the signal cannot be tapped easily; it is also nonconductive, making it immune to hazards such as lightning.

1000BASE Types

The 1000BASE family of media types has a maximum capacity of 1000Mbps and uses baseband signaling. The properties of each is described in the following:

➤ *1000BASE-T*—IEEE Standard 802.3ab, a subset of the 802.3 Ethernet standard, was introduced in 1999. This standard is Gigabit Ethernet over four pairs of UTP CAT-5 cabling. Sun's implementation of 1000BASE-T supports distances of up to 100 meters.

➤ *1000BASE-X*—IEEE Standard 802.3z, a subset of the 802.3 Ethernet standard, was standardized in 1998. This standard provides Gigabit Ethernet over single- and multimode fiber-optic cable, as well as one using copper wire. This standard refers to three implementation types— namely 1000BASE-SX, 1000BASE-LX and 1000BASE-CX, which are described next.

➤ *1000BASE-SX*—This standard uses short wavelength lasers to send data on fiber-optic cable. Sun's implementation of this standard supports distances of 300 meters (using MMF 62.5-micron fiber) and 550 meters (using MMF 50-micron fiber).

➤ *1000BASE-LX*—This standard uses long wavelength lasers to send data on fiber-optic cable. Sun's implementation of this standard supports distances of 550 meters (using MMF 62.5- and 50-micron fiber) and 3,000 meters (using SMF 9-micron fiber).

➤ *1000BASE-CX*—This standard uses copper cables to connect short distances up to 25 meters. It is primarily used in computer rooms, specifically within wiring cabinets to connect networking equipment in close proximity.

Network Access Methods

This section describes the two most commonly used network access methods: *carrier sense multiple access with collision detection (CSMA/CD)* and *token ring*. Also briefly mentioned here is a middle-ground method called *token bus*.

CSMA/CD

Carrier sense multiple access with collision detection is the most commonly used access method in ethernet networks and is described in the IEEE 802.3 Ethernet standard. Since ethernet relies on broadcasts, any of the hosts connected to the network can transmit at any time, but the CSMA part listens to the network to see whether anyone else is transmitting. If the network is empty, the host starts sending its data; if it's busy, it waits for a random time before trying again. Having started sending, the CD part of the protocol detects whether any other host starts sending. If it detects activity, a collision is said to have occurred and both hosts stop sending, wait a random time, and then try again. The random time is based on time slots, which are usually set to 512-bit times, which is 51.2 microseconds (the time it would take to send 512 bits). The number of time slots increases exponentially if further collisions occur, thereby reducing the chances of another collision. If a host fails to send a data packet 10 times, the number of time slots to wait is fixed at 1,023. If it fails 16 times, it gives up and reports a failure. The algorithm used to determine how long a host waits before trying to retransmit is called *binary exponential backoff*.

CSMA/CD-based networks perform very well on lightly loaded networks, but they suffer higher collision rates when the network is heavily used. This leads to more retransmissions of data and, hence, worse performance.

Token-Ring

The token-ring access method, described in the IEEE 802.5 standard, is used mainly in IBM environments in which a token travels around the network in a predetermined order. If a host has data to send, it inserts its data onto the network when it has the token. Token-ring networks perform very well when the network is heavily used because there are no collisions and only one host sends data at a time. The disadvantage of using token-ring networks is that performance is not very good when the network is lightly loaded because each host has to wait for the token to reach it.

Token Bus

The token bus access method, described in the IEEE 802.4 standard, uses a bus topology, but also implements a token passing system that is similar to the token-ring access method. One main difference, however, is that because a broadcast medium is being used, all packets are received by all hosts. The token bus method also supports four classes of priority, enabling a host to send its highest-priority data first. As with token-ring networks, each host can send only a finite amount of data before relinquishing the token to the next host.

Ethernet

Ethernet was originally implemented by Xerox in the early 1970s. Because it was successful, DEC, Intel, and Xerox collectively defined a standard for 10Mb ethernet in 1978. This formed the basis for the IEEE 802.3 definition, which was specified in 1985. The following are three major elements of an ethernet network:

➤ *Packets*—Also called *frames*, these are the units of data that are sent across the network.

➤ *Hardware*—The cables, connectors, and computer circuitry that actually transfers the data between hosts on an ethernet network.

➤ *CSMA/CD*—The network access method that controls the flow of frames across the network.

The two types of ethernet in use today are the original DEC, Intel, and Xerox standard, (also called DIX, named after the initial letters from each company and known as Ethernet II) and the IEEE 802.3 ethernet. Some differences exist between the two, primarily in the composition of the frames, which are discussed in the next section.

Ethernet Frames

An ethernet *frame* is the basic unit of data transfer in ethernet networks. It contains a destination address, the sender (or *source*) address, other control information, and the actual data itself.

Ethernet Addresses

Hardware vendors providing network components use assigned starting ranges and globally unique MAC or hardware addresses (discussed below) to guarantee a component can be individually addressed, both within the local machine and on the network.

The ethernet address is a 48-bit address typically displayed in hexadecimal as 12 numbers in groups of two called *octets* separated by colons. An example of an ethernet address is 08:00:20:b3:41:53. Here, you can see that the third octet is 20 because it comprises 8 bits of the address. Ethernet addresses are assigned in two portions, each consisting of 24 bits, or three octets. The first three octets are the company identifier (CID), which is assigned and administered by the IEEE, and the second is a unique vendor-supplied identifier (VID). Sun Microsystems uses the CID 08:00:20 for most of its systems, the exceptions being 00:00:be for Sun E10K and Sun Fire E15K systems and 00:03:ba for SunBlade systems. A non-Sun example is 3Com, which uses 00:10:4b as its CID. Figure 1.7 summarizes how an ethernet address is assigned.

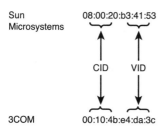

Figure 1.7 Components of an ethernet address.

Two forms of addressing can be used with the IEEE ethernet specification. The default is host-based addressing, in which the ethernet address is obtained from the hardware itself, and the other option is port-based addressing, in which a locally assigned ethernet address is specified instead of the hardware address. This latter method is described later in this chapter, in the section "Assigning a Port-Based Ethernet Address."

 On the exam, you could be asked to identify the CID or VID of an ethernet address or how many bits make up each portion. Make sure you are familiar with these values.

Ethernet uses three types of addresses:

➤ *Unicast*—A system sends a message to another single system, using the unique ethernet address to identify the recipient.

➤ *Multicast*—A system sends a message to a subset of systems on the network. When using a multicast address, the first three octets identify whether the address is a multicast address and the last three octets identify the actual multicast group.

➤ *Broadcast*—A system sends a message to all systems on the network. A reserved ethernet address of ff:ff:ff:ff:ff:ff is used as the broadcast address in which all 48 bits are set to 1.

Ethernet Frame Composition

An Ethernet II frame comprises a number of fields containing the necessary information to transmit and receive data. Figure 1.8 shows a graphical representation of an Ethernet II frame.

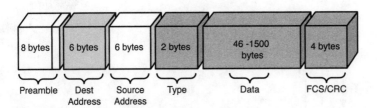

Figure 1.8 The fields of an Ethernet II frame.

Each of the fields comprising an Ethernet II frame is described here:

➤ *Preamble*—This field consists of 8 bytes, the first 7 bytes of which contain a long sequence of alternating 1 and 0 bits. It is used for synchronization and tells the destination host that a frame is starting. The final byte of the preamble is called the *start frame delimiter* and signifies the actual start of the ethernet frame. This bit sequence is 10101011. Together, these two items make up the preamble of any ethernet frame.

➤ *Destination address*—The ethernet address of the host being sent the message. This would normally just be a host's ethernet address, but it could also be a broadcast address intended for every host on the network, or a multicast address intended for a specific group of hosts. The ethernet address is 48 bits long (6 bytes).

➤ *Source address*—The ethernet address of the sending host. This ethernet address is also 48 bits long (6 bytes).

➤ *Type*—This field describes the kind of data contained within the data field. Examples are IP, ARP, RARP, and IPv6.

➤ *Data*—The actual data being transmitted.

➤ *FCS/CRC*—This is the checksum that is used to ensure the message arrived without corruption. The frame check sequence (FCS) or cyclic redundancy check (CRC) value is calculated before the message is transmitted. The receiving host recalculates the value, and if they match, the transmission has been successful. If they don't, the frame is in error and is discarded.

Ethernet II frames differ from IEEE 802.3 frames primarily in the fourth field. In Ethernet II, this field is a type field, identifying the type of data being carried in the data field. In IEEE 802.3 frames, however, this field is a length field, specifying the length in bytes of the data field. Because networks might be carrying both Ethernet II and IEEE 802.3 frames, the frame format can be easily identified by the value of this fourth field. In Ethernet II frames, the value of this field is always greater than 1536, whereas in IEEE 802.3 frames, the length must be less than 1500. The Ethernet II frame format is typically used in a TCP/IP environment.

Maximum Transfer Units

An Ethernet II frame can be a maximum of 1518 bytes long, but the maximum transfer unit (MTU) is 1500 bytes because the MTU refers to the maximum size of the data field that can be transmitted in a single ethernet frame. An ethernet frame that is fully populated is broken down as follows:

➤ 6 bytes for the destination address

➤ 6 bytes for the source address

➤ 2 bytes for the type of frame

➤ 1500 bytes for the data itself

➤ 4 bytes for the error checking CRC

Conversely, an Ethernet II frame has a minimum size of 64 bytes. This is broken down as follows:

➤ 6 bytes for the destination address

➤ 6 bytes for the source address

➤ 2 bytes for the type of frame

➤ 46 bytes for the data itself

➤ 4 bytes for the error checking CRC

If an ethernet frame contains a data field with less than 46 bytes of data, padding is added until it is equal to the specified minimum.

 The minimum and maximum sizes do not include the preamble field. This field is used only for synchronization and does not form part of the actual frame.

As you have just seen, the maximum size of an ethernet frame is 1518 bytes, of which 1500 bytes can be data. If the data to be transmitted exceeds the MTU, it is automatically fragmented, meaning it is split up into 1500-byte pieces to fit into an ethernet frame. For example, 3050 bytes of data would be split into three separate ethernet frames for physical transmission across the network. The first two frames would each contain 1500 bytes of data, and the last one would contain the remaining 50 bytes of data. Each fragment contains all the headers that would be expected in an ethernet frame and is a self-contained unit.

 The MTU for a physical ethernet interface is 1500 bytes. A loopback device is a pseudo-device that allows a host to send frames to itself and is identified by the interface name **lo0**. The MTU for loopback devices is 8232 bytes.

Frame Errors

When sending ethernet frames across a network, errors can occur due to various causes, ranging from faulty network cards to electrical interference on the network itself. Table 1.1 lists some of the more common error conditions encountered on ethernet networks and offers a description of possible causes.

Table 1.1	Ethernet Frame Error Conditions
Error	**Description/Cause**
Bad CRC	Each ethernet frame contains a CRC—a checksum that can be calculated to ensure the frame has been received correctly. If the CRC value calculated by the receiving host does not match the value in the FCS/CRC field of the ethernet frame, the frame has been corrupted in some way during transmission and is discarded by the receiving host. The cause of this could be electrical interference on the network or a faulty network device.
Jabber	An ethernet frame is received that is longer than the MTU. It is normally due to a faulty network card, where the card is continually detecting a collision on the network and sending a jamming signal. This kind of error can bring a network to a virtual standstill, so the offending card should be removed from the network at the earliest opportunity.
Runt	An ethernet frame is received that is less than the required minimum of 64 bytes. These are often caused by collisions on the network or bad wiring.
Long frame	An ethernet frame is received that is greater than the MTU of 1518 bytes and less than 6000 bytes. This error is usually caused by faulty hardware on the system that sent the frame.
Giant frame	An ethernet frame is received that is greater than 6000 bytes long. This error is normally caused by faulty hardware on the system that sent the frame.

Assigning a Port-Based Ethernet Address

Earlier in this chapter, I mentioned that host-based addressing is the default method used for obtaining the ethernet address. This is where the address is obtained from the hardware itself. In cases in which obtaining the address from the hardware is impossible or you are creating a multihomed host containing several physical interfaces (using a Quad Fast ethernet card, for example), port-based addressing is necessary. Therefore, a locally assigned, unique ethernet address has to be provided for the device so it can participate in network communication.

To assign the ethernet address locally, you need to inspect, and modify if necessary, one of the EEPROM values, namely `local-mac-address?`.

The default value of this variable is `false`, meaning that port-based addressing is disabled. Verify this by logging in as root and using the `eeprom` or `prtconf` command as follows:

```
# eeprom local-mac-address?
local-mac-address?=false
```

or

```
# prtconf -pv ¦ grep local-mac-address?
        Local-mac-address?  'false'
```

The value of this variable needs to be modified to `true`. Do this as follows:

```
# eeprom local-mac-address?=true
```

 You can also use the Openboot PROM commands to view and set the same variable. With the system at the **ok** prompt, enter the **printenv** command to see all variables. The value can also be changed if you use the **set** command.

You can assign a locally defined ethernet address to an interface using the `ifconfig` command with the `ether` switch. The seventh bit of the ethernet address denotes whether the ethernet address is globally or locally assigned. If the bit is not set (0), the address is global; if it is set (1), the address is local. This changes the CID of a Sun ethernet address from `08:00:20` to `0a:00:20`. The VID part of the ethernet address should be assigned locally, ensuring that it is unique on the local network. Some use the existing VID, whereas others start a sequence of their own, such as `00:00:01` and so on. The following example shows the commands to set (and verify) the `hme0` interface to a locally assigned ethernet address.

The current configuration shows the `hme0` interface with a globally assigned ethernet address:

```
# ifconfig hme0
hme0: flags=1000843<UP,BROADCAST,RUNNING,MULTICAST,IPv4> mtu 1500 index 2
        inet 192.168.1.28 netmask ffffff00 broadcast 192.168.1.255
        ether 8:0:20:b3:41:53
```

To set the ethernet address to `0a:00:20:00:00:01`, enter the following command:

```
# ifconfig hme0 ether 0a:00:20:00:00:01
```

If you now rerun the `ifconfig` command, the new address will be displayed, as such:

```
# ifconfig hme0
hme0: flags=1000843<UP,BROADCAST,RUNNING,MULTICAST,IPv4> mtu 1500 index 2
        inet 192.168.1.28 netmask ffffff00 broadcast 192.168.1.255
        ether a:0:20:0:0:1
```

 This command changes the ethernet address only until the next reboot. If you want to make the change permanent, the **ifconfig** command, with the correct parameters, must be added to the startup script **/etc/rc2.d/S72inetsvc**.

 If you run the **ifconfig** command as a nonprivileged user (not root), the ethernet address will not be displayed.

Ethernet Interface Statistics

Various statistics about ethernet interfaces can be displayed to show which ethernet interfaces are installed on the local system, the number of packets or frames being sent or received, and whether any errors are being encountered. The following sections describe each of these.

Displaying Installed Ethernet Interfaces

Use the `ifconfig -a` command to display all ethernet interfaces that are present on the local system. This includes physical and pseudo interfaces, such as the loopback device. Remember that, if you run this command as a non-root user, the ethernet addresses will not be displayed. The following example shows the result of running `ifconfig -a` as root on a system with one physical interface installed, namely `hme0`:

```
#ifconfig -a
lo0: flags=1000849<UP,LOOPBACK,RUNNING,MULTICAST,IPv4> mtu 8232 index 1
      inet 127.0.0.1 netmask ff000000
hme0: flags=1000843<UP,BROADCAST,RUNNING,MULTICAST,IPv4> mtu 1500 index 2
      inet 192.168.1.28 netmask ffffff00 broadcast 192.168.1.255
      ether 8:0:20:b3:41:53
```

 You might often be asked for alternative ways of finding an ethernet address. The commands **netstat -p** and **arp -a** also display details of ethernet addresses. The local system's ethernet address can also be found by using the **dmesg** command and looking in the **/var/adm/messages** file, both of which contain messages from the most recent system reboot.

Collision Rates

A *collision* is said to have occurred when more than one host on a network tries to send a packet at the same time.

The netstat -i command shows the current level of usage for all ethernet interfaces on the local system. To determine the collision rate, apply the following formula:

([number of collisions] × 100) / total number of output packets

The following example shows the result of running netsat -i:

```
# netstat -i
Name  Mtu   Net/Dest    Address     Ipkts   Ierrs Opkts   Oerrs Collis Queue
lo0   8232  loopback    localhost   10156   0     10156   0     0      0
hme0  1500  ultra10     ultra10     184835  0     209364  0     21840  0
```

Applying the formula, you would calculate the collision rate as follows (the affected fields appear as bold text in the previous code):

(21840 × 100) / 209364 = 10.43

The result of 10.43 means that 1 in 10 packets being sent across the network is resulting in a collision. For an ethernet network running at 10Mbps, the collision rate should not be higher than 5%, and it should not be higher than 10% for one running at 100Mbps. The numbers in the previous equation were taken from a network running at 10Mbps, indicating that a performance problem is being caused either by faulty or poor network cabling or by the network having too many hosts connected to the segment.

 Remember from earlier in this chapter that a switch forwards packets only to the port on which the host is connected, unlike a hub, which forwards packets to all the connected ports. Implementing a switch instead of a hub on busy networks with high collision rates can drastically improve the performance of the network by reducing the amount of network traffic and hence reducing the collision rate.

Input/Output Errors

In the previous section, the `netstat -i` command was used to show the level of usage of ethernet interfaces on the network. This command is also used to detect input and output errors. Collisions, as you have seen, are a network-related problem, whereas input and output errors are specific to the local system and the cause could be one of the following:

➤ A faulty network interface card

➤ A faulty port on a hub or switch

➤ A faulty network connection

➤ A duplicate IP address, meaning another host on the network is using the same IP address as the local host (although you would normally see a message to this effect in the console window or the `/var/adm/messages` file)

➤ A software fault (you might have one of these problems, which produces precisely the same symptoms as a hardware fault, but requires an operating system patch to cure it)

Troubleshooting Ethernet Problems

Solaris provides a number of network utilities that can be used to troubleshoot an ethernet interface. This section describes the utilities `ifconfig`, `ping`, `netstat`, `snoop`, and `ndd`. When used together, they can diagnose the majority of network-related problems.

ifconfig

As root, use the `ifconfig -a` command to verify the status of all installed ethernet interfaces, as shown in the following:

```
#ifconfig -a
lo0: flags=1000849<UP,LOOPBACK,RUNNING,MULTICAST,IPv4> mtu 8232 index 1
    inet 127.0.0.1 netmask ff000000
hme0: flags=1000843<UP,BROADCAST,RUNNING,MULTICAST,IPv4> mtu 1500 index 2
    inet 192.168.1.28 netmask ffffff00 broadcast 192.168.1.255
    ether 8:0:20:b3:41:53
```

As shown in the preceding code, you can use the `flags=` line to verify that the ethernet interface is up and running and that the `netmask` is correct for the specific interface IP address. Problems such as this can often be encountered when an ethernet interface has been manually configured incorrectly.

ping

The ping command (ping stands for Packet Internet Groper), although relatively basic, is an extremely useful utility for checking the reachability of a host on the network. If the alive response is received, the ethernet interface is responding and you can quickly check that the host can be contacted across the network. When network problems occur, you can also send a continuous ping to an unreachable host so that you know when the network becomes available again.

netstat

You have already seen the netstat -i command used to display the current usage for the ethernet interfaces installed, but you can also use the netstat -s command to display network statistics for each of the network protocols in use. The output from this command can be several pages, but it shows useful information relating to parameters and errors. The following code shows the result after running this command (the output has been truncated).

```
RAWIP
     rawipInDatagrams    =     0     rawipInErrors      =     0
...
UDP
     udpInDatagrams    = 14443     udpInErrors        =     0
     udpOutDatagrams   = 14446     udpOutErrors       =     0
TCP    tcpRtoAlgorithm    =    4     tcpRtoMin          =   400
     tcpRtoMax         = 60000     tcpMaxConn         =    -1
     tcpActiveOpens    =    30     tcpPassiveOpens    =    33
...
IPv4    ipForwarding       =    2     ipDefaultTTL       =   255
     ipInReceives      = 93136     ipInHdrErrors      =     0
     ipInAddrErrors    =     0     ipInCksumErrs      =     0
     ipForwDatagrams   =     0     ipForwProhibits    =     0
IPv6    ipv6Forwarding     =    2     ipv6DefaultHopLimit =  255
...
ICMPv4    icmpInMsgs       =    56     icmpInErrors       =     0
     icmpInCksumErrs   =     0     icmpInUnknowns     =     0
     icmpInDestUnreachs =    3     icmpInTimeExcds    =     0
     icmpInParmProbs   =     0     icmpInSrcQuenchs   =     0
     icmpInRedirects   =     0     icmpInBadRedirects =     0
     icmpInEchos       =    53     icmpInEchoReps     =     0
...
ICMPv6    icmp6InMsgs      =     0     icmp6InErrors      =     0
...
     icmp6InOverflows  =     0
IGMP:
          50 messages received
...
```

snoop

The snoop command is run by the root user and is arguably the best network diagnostic program available in the Solaris operating environment. It is used to capture network packets and either display them on the screen or write them to a file for further analysis. You can use snoop to monitor all network traffic that passes the local ethernet interface or to monitor selected hosts and protocols. The amount of detail captured can also be tailored because snoop provides three levels of detail: *summary*, *summary verbose*, and *verbose*.

The following examples demonstrate the type of information that can be collected, using three levels of detail (basic summary, summary verbose and verbose), from a simple ping command from host puma: IP address 192.168.1.28, to host lion: IP address 192.168.1.19.

The basic summary level of information is obtained using the default option, as shown here:

```
# snoop -d hme0
1  0.00000  puma -> lion   ICMP Echo request (ID: 725 Sequence number: 0)
2  0.00031  lion -> puma   ICMP Echo reply (ID: 725 Sequence number: 0)
```

The summary verbose option of snoop uses the -V switch as follows and provides more information for exactly the same ping operation (from host puma to host lion):

```
# snoop -V -d hme0
1 0.00000    puma -> lion   ETHER Type=0800 (IP), size = 98 bytes
1 0.00000    puma -> lion   IP  D=192.168.1.19 S=192.168.1.28 LEN=84,
  ➥ID=43864, TOS=0x0, TTL=255
1 0.00000    puma -> lion   ICMP Echo request (ID: 725 Sequence number: 0)
2 0.00031    lion -> puma   ETHER Type=0800 (IP), size = 98 bytes
2 0.00031    lion -> puma   IP  D=192.168.1.28 S=192.168.1.19 LEN=84,
  ➥ID=7736, TOS=0x0, TTL=128
2 0.00031    lion -> puma   ICMP Echo reply (ID: 725 Sequence number: 0)
```

The verbose option of snoop uses the -v switch and provides the most detailed information. Again, the same ping command is used:

```
# snoop -v -d hme0
ETHER:  ----- Ether Header -----
ETHER:
ETHER:  Packet 1 arrived at 15:32:40.70
ETHER:  Packet size = 98 bytes
ETHER:  Destination = 0:b0:d0:e7:9f:fd, Computer Products International
ETHER:  Source      = 8:0:20:b3:41:53, Sun
ETHER:  Ethertype = 0800 (IP)
ETHER:
IP:   ----- IP Header -----
IP:
IP:   Version = 4
IP:   Header length = 20 bytes
IP:   Type of service = 0x00
IP:         xxx. .... = 0 (precedence)
IP:         ...0 .... = normal delay
IP:         .... 0... = normal throughput
IP:         .... .0.. = normal reliability
IP:         .... ..0. = not ECN capable transport
IP:         .... ...0 = no ECN congestion experienced
```

```
IP:    Total length = 84 bytes
IP:    Identification = 43864
IP:    Flags = 0x4
IP:          .1.. .... = do not fragment
IP:          ..0. .... = last fragment
IP:    Fragment offset = 0 bytes
IP:    Time to live = 255 seconds/hops
IP:    Protocol = 1 (ICMP)
IP:    Header checksum = 1b22
IP:    Source address = 192.168.1.28, puma
IP:    Destination address = 192.168.1.19, lion
IP:    No options
IP:
ICMP:  ----- ICMP Header -----
ICMP:
ICMP:  Type = 8 (Echo request)
ICMP:  Code = 0 (ID: 725 Sequence number: 0)
ICMP:  Checksum = 592d
ICMP:


ETHER:  ----- Ether Header -----
ETHER:
ETHER:  Packet 2 arrived at 15:32:40.70
ETHER:  Packet size = 98 bytes
ETHER:  Destination = 8:0:20:b3:41:53, Sun
ETHER:  Source      = 0:b0:d0:e7:9f:fd, Computer Products International
ETHER:  Ethertype = 0800 (IP)
ETHER:
IP:    ----- IP Header -----
IP:
IP:    Version = 4
IP:    Header length = 20 bytes
IP:    Type of service = 0x00
IP:          xxx. .... = 0 (precedence)
IP:          ...0 .... = normal delay
IP:          .... 0... = normal throughput
IP:          .... .0.. = normal reliability
IP:          .... ..0. = not ECN capable transport
IP:          .... ...0 = no ECN congestion experienced
IP:    Total length = 84 bytes
IP:    Identification = 7736
IP:    Flags = 0x4
IP:          .1.. .... = do not fragment
IP:          ..0. .... = last fragment
IP:    Fragment offset = 0 bytes
IP:    Time to live = 128 seconds/hops
IP:    Protocol = 1 (ICMP)
IP:    Header checksum = 2743
IP:    Source address = 192.168.1.19, lion
IP:    Destination address = 192.168.1.28, puma
IP:    No options
IP:
ICMP:  ----- ICMP Header -----
ICMP:
ICMP:  Type = 0 (Echo reply)
ICMP:  Code = 0 (ID: 725 Sequence number: 0)
ICMP:  Checksum = 612d
ICMP:
```

You can see that, depending on which level of detail is required, you can either obtain simple, higher-level information, or detailed information about all protocols that were used to complete the operation (in this case, a single `ping` command).

 snoop can generate a lot of output and will, by default, continue to capture packets until you either press Ctrl+C (^C) or run out of disk space. Alternatively, you can use the **-c** *<maxcount>* option on the command line to specify that **snoop** should quit after capturing *<maxcount>* packets. You should be familiar with the various options of **snoop**. Consult the online manual page for further information.

It is not always convenient or manageable to display the packet capture results to the screen. Instead, you can save the results to a file for offline analysis. To do this, use the `-o` *<filename>* option of `snoop`. The saved file will not be human readable, but you can load it back into `snoop` later using the `-i` *<filename>* option as shown here:

```
# snoop -d hme0 -o /tmp/file.out
```

Then, to read the contents of the saved output file, use the following command:

```
# snoop -i /tmp/file.out
```

If you do want to save the information to a text file that can be read like any other file, simply redirect the output as follows:

```
# snoop -v -d hme0 >> /tmp/snooptmp
```

ndd

The `ndd` utility is used to inspect, and modify if necessary, the network driver parameters. Many of the network protocols are implemented as drivers. The main ones we are concerned about in this book, however, are `arp`, `tcp`, `udp`, `ip` (`ipv6`), `icmp` (`icmpv6`), and `hme/le/qfe` (depending on the type of ethernet interface installed).

 Any changes you make to driver parameters using **ndd** on the command line are valid only until the next reboot. If you want to make the changes permanent, the specific **ndd** commands must be included in a system startup script, such as **/etc/rc2.d/S69inet**, or one of your own customized scripts in the **/etc/rc2.d** directory.

The `?` option to `ndd` displays all the parameters for a given driver, although it is typically preceded by a \ character to escape the `?` from the shell. Otherwise it might be interpreted as a special shell character. As an example, consider the `hme` driver as shown here:

```
# ndd /dev/hme \?
?                             (read only)
transceiver_inuse             (read only)
link_status                   (read only)
link_speed                    (read only)
link_mode                     (read only)
ipg1                          (read and write)
ipg2                          (read and write)
use_int_xcvr                  (read and write)
pace_size                     (read and write)
adv_autoneg_cap               (read and write)
adv_100T4_cap                 (read and write)
adv_100fdx_cap                (read and write)
adv_100hdx_cap                (read and write)
adv_10fdx_cap                 (read and write)
adv_10hdx_cap                 (read and write)
autoneg_cap                   (read only)
100T4_cap                     (read only)
100fdx_cap                    (read only)
100hdx_cap                    (read only)
10fdx_cap                     (read only)
10hdx_cap                     (read only)
lp_autoneg_cap                (read only)
lp_100T4_cap                  (read only)
lp_100fdx_cap                 (read only)
lp_100hdx_cap                 (read only)
lp_10fdx_cap                  (read only)
lp_10hdx_cap                  (read only)
instance                      (read and write)
lance_mode                    (read and write)
ipg0                          (read and write)
```

Notice that each parameter listed also contains permission information, such as whether you can only inspect the value or change it as well. The link_speed parameter is frequently the cause of problems, particularly with older network interfaces. Newer interfaces can autosense whether the network is running at 10Mbps or 100Mbps, for example, and set this parameter automatically. Older interface cards, however, might be hardwired to 10Mbps, so a problem occurs when you connect it to a 100Mbps network. The following example shows how to inspect two values that provide useful information: link_speed and autoneg_cap. The first shows a value of 0 because it is running at 10Mbps (the value would be 1 if it was running at 100Mbps). The second identifies whether the interface can automatically negotiate the link speed, meaning it can set itself to whatever the network is running at. In this case, note that the value of 1 indicates that this interface can set the value depending on the network:

```
# ndd /dev/hme link_speed
0
# ndd /dev/hme autoneg_cap
1
```

Sun Microsystems does not generally advise customers to set these parameters manually because Solaris 9 is already optimized for most situations. Using **ndd** on the command line is useful for testing problem resolution and should be made permanent only when it has been verified that a change has been successful. Make sure you always have a backup of any system startup script that you modify.

Another useful example is the system startup script /etc/rc2.d/S69inet (which is a hard link to /etc/init.d/inetinit), in which the ndd command is used to either enable or disable the forwarding of IP requests, depending on whether the host is a router. The relevant fragment of this script is shown here to demonstrate the use of ndd in a script (setting the parameter to 1 enables forwarding, whereas 0 disables it). I have highlighted, in bold, the two lines that set the forwarding parameter:

```
...
    if [ ! -f /etc/notrouter -a $numdhcp -eq 0 -a \
       \( $numifs -gt 2 -o $numptptifs -gt 0 -o -f /etc/gateways \) ]; then
            #
            # Machine is an IPv4 router: turn on ip_forwarding, run
            # in.routed, and advertise ourselves as a router using router
            # discovery.
            #
            echo 'Machine is an IPv4 router.'
            /usr/sbin/ndd -set /dev/ip ip_forwarding 1

            [ -f /usr/sbin/in.routed ] && /usr/sbin/in.routed -s
            [ -f /usr/sbin/in.rdisc ] && /usr/sbin/in.rdisc -r
    else
            #
            # Machine is an IPv4 host: if router discovery finds a router
            # then we rely on router discovery. If there are no routers
            # advertising themselves through router discovery
            # run in.routed in quiet mode.  In both cases, turn off
            # ip_forwarding.
            /usr/sbin/ndd -set /dev/ip ip_forwarding 0
            if [ -f /usr/sbin/in.rdisc ] && /usr/sbin/in.rdisc -s; then
                    echo 'Starting IPv4 router discovery.'
            elif [   -f /usr/sbin/in.routed ]; then
                    /usr/sbin/in.routed -q
                    echo 'Starting IPv4 routing daemon.'
            fi
    fi
...
```

Exam Prep Questions

Question 1

Your network is configured with a central hub that has cables coming from it to each host on the network. Which type of network topology is being described?

- ○ A. Ring
- ○ B. Bus
- ○ C. Star
- ○ D. VLAN

Answer C is correct because a star network is configured with a central hub that has cables coming from it to each host on the network. Answer A is incorrect because this topology consists of hosts connected to each other in a loop, with each host connecting to its adjacent neighbors. Answer B is incorrect because this topology has a single spur, with hosts connected at regular intervals. Answer D is incorrect because this topology normally represents multiple networks using a single, central intelligent switch. It comprises multiple star networks.

Question 2

A host that provides network resources to other hosts on the network is known as which of the following?

- ○ A. Client
- ○ B. Server
- ○ C. Router
- ○ D. Bridge

Answer B is correct. A server provides network resources to other hosts on the network. Answer A is incorrect because this type of host uses the resources provided by a server. Answer C is incorrect because this device is used to connect networks together and forwards packets based on IP address. Answer D is incorrect because this device is used to connect networks together and forwards packets based on the MAC address.

Question 3

Your network is classified as a 10BASE-T network. What is the network media and speed of the network?

○ A. Coaxial cable running at 10Mbps

○ B. Twisted-pair cable running at 10Mbps

○ C. Twisted-pair cable running at 100Mbps

○ D. Fiber-optic cable running at 10Mbps

The correct answer is B because 10BASE-T refers to a twisted pair cable running at 10Mbps. Answer A is incorrect because the classification would be 10BASE-2 or 10BASE-5. Answer C is incorrect because this would be a 100BASE specification. Answer D is incorrect because fiber-optic cable runs at a minimum of 100Mbps.

Question 4

Which of the following gigabit network classifications are implemented using fiber-optic cable? Choose 2.

❑ A. 1000BASE-T

❑ B. 1000BASE-X

❑ C. 1000BASE-SX

❑ D. 1000BASE-LX

❑ E. 1000BASE-CX

Answers C and D are correct because fiber-optic cable is used to implement both 1000BASE-SX and 1000BASE-LX. Answer A is incorrect because this type of network is implemented using Cat-5 twisted-pair cable. Answer B is incorrect because 1000BASE-X refers to three implementations and one of them is 1000BASE-CX, which uses copper cabling. Answer E is incorrect because this type of network is implemented using standard copper cable.

Question 5

> You have a star topology network using a central hub and have noticed that the number of collisions is very high. Which device would you install to reduce the number of collisions?
>
> O A. Bridge
> O B. Hub
> O C. Switch
> O D. Repeater

Answer C is correct. A switch only forwards packets to the port containing the destination host, and would reduce the network traffic, which in turn, would reduce the number of collisions. Answer A is incorrect because this device is used to connect LANs together and forwards packets based on the destination MAC address. Answer B is incorrect because this device would be the cause of the high collision rate, due to the fact that it forwards packets to all ports instead of just the port containing the host with the destination address. Answer D is incorrect because this device is used to connect network segments by simply boosting the signal.

Question 6

> In an Ethernet II frame, what is the preamble field used for?
>
> O A. To determine the type of data being sent
> O B. To provide synchronization between the sender and the receiver
> O C. To provide error checking
> O D. To detect collisions

Answer B is correct. The preamble field provides synchronization between the sender and the receiver. Answer A is incorrect because the type field contains this information. Answer C is incorrect because the CRC field contains this information. Answer D is incorrect because this is carried out by the network access method (CSMA/CD).

Question 7

What are the two parts of an ethernet address called? Choose 2.

❑ A. PID

❑ B. CID

❑ C. BID

❑ D. VID

❑ E. SID

Answers B and D are correct. The CID is the company identifier, an assigned portion of the ethernet address. The VID is the vendor-specified identifier and is administered by the vendor, who assigns a unique value to this portion of the ethernet address. Answers A, C, and E are invalid because they have no relevance to ethernet addresses.

Question 8

Which command is used to capture packets on the network?

○ A. **ping**

○ B. **netstat**

○ C. **snoop**

○ D. **ndd**

Answer C is correct. The snoop command is used to capture packets on the network. Answer A is incorrect because the ping command is used to test the reachability of another host. Answer B is incorrect because the netstat command provides network statistics. Answer D is incorrect because the ndd command is used to inspect and modify network driver parameters.

Question 9

What is the MTU for a physical ethernet interface?

○ A. 1500 bytes

○ B. 1518 bytes

○ C. 46 bytes

○ D. 64 bytes

Answer A is correct. The maximum transfer unit (MTU) for a physical ethernet interface is 1500 bytes. This is the largest amount of data that can be sent in a single Ethernet II frame. Answer B is incorrect because this value is the maximum size of the ethernet frame, including headers. Answer C is incorrect because this value is the minimum size the data field can be. Answer D is incorrect because this value is the minimum size of an ethernet frame, including headers.

Question 10

Which of the following statements describe an ethernet address? Choose 2.

❑ A. A 48-bit address, displayed in hexadecimal, separated by colons (:).

❑ B. A 32-bit address, displayed in decimal, separated by dots (.).

❑ C. The address is made up of a company identifier and a vendor identifier.

❑ D. The address is made up of a network address and a host address.

Answers A and C are correct. An ethernet address is a 48-bit address displayed in hexadecimal and separated by colons. The ethernet address is made up of a company identifier (CID) and a vendor identifier (VID). Answers B and D are incorrect because they describe IP addresses.

Need to Know More?

 Comer, Douglas. *Internetworking with TCP/IP: Principles, Protocols and Architecture*. Prentice Hall, 2000.

 Sun Microsystems. *Solaris 9 System Administrator Collection: Solaris Tunable Parameters Reference Manual*. Available in printed form, on the Web at docs.sun.com, and from the online documentation provided with the Solaris 9 operating system.

 Sun Microsystems. *System Reference Manual, Section 1M—System Administration Commands*. Available in printed form, on the Web at docs.sun.com, and from the online documentation provided with the Solaris 9 operating system.

The TCP/IP Model

. . . .

Terms you'll need to understand:

✓ Application Layer

✓ Encapsulation

✓ Hardware Layer

✓ Internet Layer

✓ ISO/OSI Reference Model

✓ Layered Model

✓ Network Interface Layer

✓ Network Protocol

✓ TCP/IP

✓ Transport Layer

Concepts you'll need to master:

✓ Describe the advantages of using a layered network model.

✓ Describe the functions of the Network Interface, Internet, Transport, and Application layers of the TCP/IP model.

✓ Describe basic peer-to-peer communication and related TCP/IP protocols.

Chapter 1, "Local Area Networks," introduced some fundamental networking concepts you need to understand to progress through the rest of this book. This chapter builds on the previous one and describes the TCP/IP network model, which is the most commonly used family of protocols across the Internet. The TCP/IP model is a layered model. In this chapter, you'll see how the layers fit together to provide a complete network communication service as well as the protocols that are used in each layer of the model.

 The ISO/OSI 7 Layer Reference Model is not discussed in any detail in this book as it is not specifically required for the Solaris 9 Network Administrator exam. It is assumed, however, that the reader possesses a basic familiarity with this model, for comparison purposes only. This chapter contains a small section outlining the differences between the two models, and the "Need to Know More" section at the end of this chapter identifies a reference for additional reading about the ISO/OSI Reference model.

The TCP/IP Protocol Stack

The TCP/IP model is an example of a protocol stack, that is, a number of protocols that work together in a well-defined hierarchy, to provide communications between devices on a network, and is the mechanism used by the Solaris operating environment. You saw in the previous chapter that a protocol is a set of rules that govern how data communication takes place. A protocol stack, such as this, is hierarchical in that the overall structure is the model itself. The structure contains a number of layers, each carrying out a separate function, and each function is subjected to certain rules about how the function is executed—the protocol.

A protocol stack has the following properties:

➤ Each layer exists to carry out a specific function.

➤ Each layer is present on both the sending host and the receiving host.

➤ Each layer communicates with its opposite number (peer) on another host, following well-defined procedures.

➤ Each layer on a host is independent of the other layers on the same host; the relationship is with its peer layer on another host—the application layer on host A is a peer of the application layer on host B, for example.

So, for communication to take place between two hosts, there are a number of sequential steps that must be followed; think of these steps as the layers.

There are several advantages in using a layered model:

➤ The format of the data, how the data is actually transmitted, the transport mechanism used, and the actual route taken by the data are broken down into several functions (layers), thereby simplifying the issue of communicating across a network.

➤ Standards exist, allowing a common approach to be taken by hardware and software suppliers.

➤ Modifications can be made to one of the layers without affecting the whole model because each layer is independent of the other layers.

➤ The modular structure of the layers makes resolution of problems easier because a problem will point to a specific layer or function.

Consider this simple example:

When you write a letter to someone (this is the application), you are interested only in the letter getting there in one piece and what the response is (the Transport layer). You don't have any interest in which specific route the delivery takes (the Internet layer), or in which postman delivers the letter (the Network Interface layer)—that is the responsibility of the postal service or courier (the Application layer).

The Layers of the TCP/IP Model

The TCP/IP model was developed by the U.S. Department of Defense (DoD) in the late 1970s. A number of standards have been defined for this model and are listed in Request For Comments (RFC) documents. These documents describe the architecture and use of the various protocols and layers. The RFCs are listed and can be retrieved on the Web at http://www.ietf.org/rfc.html. For example, RFCs 0760 and 0761 describe the DoD standard Internet Protocol (IP) and standard Transmission Control Protocol (TCP), respectively.

The TCP/IP model is described as a four-layer model that functions on a common hardware platform. The four layers are Application, Transport, Internet, and Network Interface. This model has also been commonly described as a five-layer model, which treats the hardware layer as a separate layer. This discrepancy arises as a result of interpretation, depending on whether the Physical layer is treated as part of the Network Interface layer or not.

Sun describes the TCP/IP model as a four-layer model on a common hardware platform. However, in the exam objectives for the Solaris 8 Network Administrator exam, Sun wrote "Identify the purpose of each layer in the TCP/IP five layer model." You should read any question relating to the number of layers very carefully. For example, if you are asked to list the 4 layers of the TCP/IP model, then the answer would be "Application," "Transport," "Internet," and "Network Interface." If you are asked to list the 5 layers of the TCP/IP model, then include "Hardware" in your choice of answers.

This book treats the TCP/IP model as a four-layer model because the published Sun Microsystems objective for this exam mentions only four layers—the inference is that the Hardware layer is integrated into the Network Interface layer. Figure 2.1 shows the hierarchical nature of the TCP/IP model layers as well as each layer's position in the hierarchy.

| Application Layer |
| Transport Layer |
| Internet Layer |
| Network Interface Layer |
| Hardware Layer |

Figure 2.1   The TCP/IP model layer hierarchy.

Network Interface Layer

As you can see from Figure 2.1, the Network Interface layer is the lowest in the TCP/IP hierarchy and provides the communication service to the Internet layer. The Network Interface layer prepares data packets received from the Internet layer into suitably sized packets for transmission across the physical network. Also, it receives packets from its peer layer on another host and passes them upward to the Internet layer. Addressing at this layer is based on the MAC address. Specifically, this layer does the following:

➤ Handles the transmission of data across the physical network.

➤ Assembles data for transmission into Ethernet frames. (Ethernet frames are discussed in Chapter 1.)

➤ Detects errors through the use of the Cyclic Redundancy Check (CRC) field in the Ethernet frame.

Internet Layer

The Internet layer resides above the Network Interface layer, is responsible for the routing of data to the destination host, and tries to ensure that the most efficient route is taken. IP addresses are used at this layer, unlike the Network Interface layer, where MAC addresses are used. This layer uses a routing table to find the next host on the network that is on the route to the destination. This might be the actual destination node, or the nearest gateway. Data packets at this layer are called *IP packets*. Chapter 4, "Fundamental IPv4," and Chapter 7, "Basic IPv6," discuss the IP protocol and addressing in more detail.

Transport Layer

The Transport layer is responsible for the end-to-end delivery of the data through the use of

➤ Sequencing of packets so that receipt of all packets can be verified.

➤ Acknowledgements so that the sending host can verify that each packet has arrived at its destination.

➤ Flow control so that network congestion can be handled effectively.

The Transport layer is located above the Internet layer and provides a more reliable service. The Network Interface layer, for example, might encounter a CRC error, indicating that a data packet was corrupted—this layer would flag the error, but wouldn't request a retransmission of the failed packet; the Transport layer would handle this. This layer is discussed in more detail in Chapter 9, "TCP and UDP."

Application Layer

The Application layer is the top layer of the TCP/IP model and interacts with the running processes that make use of network communications. Examples of network communication processes are Telnet, File Transfer Protocol (FTP), Dynamic Host Configuration Protocol (DHCP), Domain Name System (DNS), Network File System (NFS), email, and of course, the Web browser.

Specifically, this layer does the following:

➤ *Handles the data format*—For example, when a Unix system is communicating with an IBM system, the Unix system encodes in ASCII (American Standard Code for Information Interchange), whereas IBM uses EBCDIC (Extended Binary Coded Decimal Interchange Code). This layer handles the data conversion.

➤ *Manages application connections (sessions)*—This layer handles how applications interoperate between the two connecting hosts, an example being when an NFS client connects to the NFS server to mount a file system, using Remote Procedure Calls (RPC), or when a user accesses a page on a Web server when using a Web browser.

➤ *Handles how the end user wants the data presented*—In addition to handling the formatting of data, this layer also handles how data is displayed, such as in the formatting of email messages.

Peer-to-Peer Communication

As discussed previously, an advantage of a layered model is that it breaks the process down into manageable units—the layers. Each layer actually communicates with its peer layer on another host, so the Application layer on a host sends a message to the Application layer on another host; the fact that the message passes through the Transport, Internet, and Network Interface layers on the local host (and the same layers on the other host) is transparent to the user. The Internet layer, for example, where the IP addresses are added, talks to only the Internet layer on another host. The following section describes the process of encapsulation, which is what enables the corresponding layers to interpret the messages received.

Encapsulation

Each layer in the TCP/IP model communicates with its peer layer on another host. To do this, each layer must add some control information that will be understood by the receiving host, so that the message is dealt with correctly. This process of adding header information at each layer is known as *encapsulation*. Figure 2.2 describes what happens when a running application needs to send data to a remote host.

As you can see from Figure 2.2, the running application has some data. The Application layer adds its own header information and passes the message to the Transport layer. This layer treats the entire message received as data (or its payload), because it doesn't differentiate (nor does it need to) between the application data and the Application layer header. The Transport layer adds such control information as sequencing and passes the message to the Internet layer, where the IP header is added, containing such items as the source and destination IP addresses. This process goes on until the Network Interface layer breaks the information down into manageable packets (Ethernet frames) for transmission across the network.

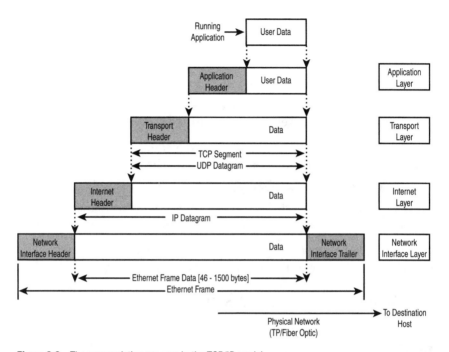

Figure 2.2   The encapsulation process in the TCP/IP model.

When the Ethernet frames reach the remote host, the reverse of the encapsulation process occurs, known as *decapsulation*. Here, header information is removed by the relevant layer and passed to the next highest layer, starting with the Network Interface layer. Eventually the data reaches the application running on the remote host, as the user intended.

 Data encapsulation occurs as data moves *down* the TCP/IP protocol stack on the sending host, and decapsulation occurs as data moves *up* the stack at the receiving end. It is important to remember which process occurs at which host and in which direction the data flows.

The Protocols of the TCP/IP Model

Each layer of the TCP/IP model adheres to a different set of rules for communication. These are the protocols that are used at each of the layers to ensure that peer-to-peer communication occurs correctly between hosts. This section lists the protocols that are in operation for each of the layers.

Network Interface Layer Protocols

Protocols of the Network Interface layer also include those of the Hardware layer because the Hardware layer is seen as being incorporated into the Network Interface layer. The following protocols operate at the Network Interface layer:

➤ *IEEE 802.3 Ethernet including CSMA/CD*—The standard network access method used in Ethernet networks.

➤ *IEEE 802.4 Token Bus*—A network access method used in a bus topology, which also utilizes a token passing mechanism.

➤ *IEEE 802.5 Token Ring*—A network access method used primarily in a ring topology, which utilizes a token passing mechanism.

➤ *Serial Line Internet Protocol (SLIP)*—A protocol used for serial communication between two machines that have been configured to talk to each other, such as a dialup connection to an Internet service provider (ISP).

➤ *Point-to-Point Protocol (PPP)*—A protocol used for serial communication, such as a dialup connection to an ISP. PPP is preferred over SLIP because it can share a line with other users and provides error detection—facilities not provided with SLIP.

Internet Layer Protocols

Protocols in use at the Internet layer include the following:

➤ *Address Resolution Protocol (ARP)*—A protocol used to map a 32-bit IP address to a 48-bit Ethernet address.

➤ *Reverse Address Resolution Protocol (RARP)*—A protocol used to map a 48-bit Ethernet address to a 32-bit IP address.

➤ *Internet Protocol (IP)*—A protocol that handles connectionless delivery of datagrams across the network.

➤ *Internet Control Message Protocol (ICMP)*—An integral part of IP that is used to send error and control messages to other hosts on the network.

➤ *Various Internet Security protocols (IPSEC)*—A collection of protocols that provides additional security to data traveling across networks.

Each of the protocols listed here are discussed in more detail in Chapters 3 and 4.

ARP and RARP are protocols that actually operate between the Network Interface layer and the Internet layer, but are generally described as Internet layer protocols.

Transport Layer Protocols

The Transport layer includes the following two protocols:

➤ *Transmission Control Protocol (TCP)*—A connection-oriented, stateful, and reliable protocol used to exchange data between hosts on a network.

➤ *User Datagram Protocol (UDP)*—A connectionless, stateless, and unreliable protocol used to exchange data between hosts on a network—the reliability is provided by the network itself or the application.

 TCP and UDP are discussed in more detail in Chapter 9.

Application Layer Protocols

A number of protocols are in use at the Application layer, some of which are listed here:

➤ *Telnet*—Terminal communication between two hosts on a network.

➤ *FTP*—The File Transfer Protocol, used for copying files between two hosts on a network.

➤ *SMTP*—Simple Mail Transfer Protocol, used for email transfer.

➤ *POP3*—Post Office Protocol version 3, used to allow the remote retrieval of email, from the Internet for example.

➤ *DNS*—Domain Name System, used to resolve addresses to hostnames. DNS is discussed in Chapter 10, "Domain Name System (DNS)."

➤ *DHCP*—Dynamic Host Configuration Protocol, used to assign IP addresses to hosts automatically. DHCP is discussed in Chapter 11, "Basic DHCP."

➤ *HTTP*—Hypertext Transfer Protocol, used to access data via a Web browser.

Comparison of the TCP/IP Model and the ISO/OSI Reference Model

The ISO/OSI reference model is a seven-layer model (which includes the Physical layer), whereas the TCP/IP model is a five-layer model (if you include the Hardware layer).

> The Hardware layer has been included in this discussion for comparison purposes because the ISO/OSI Reference model has always been described as a seven-layer model, one layer of which is the Physical layer, and corresponds directly with the Hardware layer of the TCP/IP model.

Figure 2.3 shows how the layers differ between the two models. Note that the Application layer in the TCP/IP model carries out the same function as three of the layers in the ISO/OSI Reference model—the Application, Presentation, and Session layers.

TCP/IP Model	ISO/OSI Model
	Application Layer
Application Layer	Presentation Layer
	Session Layer
Transport Layer	Transport Layer
Internet Layer	Network Layer
Network Interface Layer	Data Link Layer
Hardware Layer	Physical Layer

Figure 2.3   TCP/IP model and ISO/OSI reference model layers.

Exam Prep Questions

Question 1

> Which of the following are features of a layered model? Choose 3.
>
> ❑ A. Each layer performs many functions.
>
> ❑ B. Each layer performs one specific function.
>
> ❑ C. Each layer is independent from the other layers.
>
> ❑ D. Each layer relies on the other layers for information.
>
> ❑ E. Each layer is present on both the sending and receiving hosts.
>
> ❑ F. Each layer does not need to be present on both the sending and receiving hosts because another layer will assume the responsibility if the layer does not exist.

Answers B, C, and E are correct. Each layer in a layered model has a specific purpose, is independent from the other layers, and is present on both the sending and receiving hosts. Answer A is incorrect because each layer in the TCP/IP model performs a specific function, not multiple functions. Answer D is incorrect because each layer is independent of the other layers in the protocol stack. Answer F is incorrect because each layer does exist on both the sending and receiving hosts.

Question 2

> Which of the following are advantages of using a layered model? Choose 2
>
> ❑ A. Problem resolution is more difficult with a layered model.
>
> ❑ B. Problem resolution is made easier because the problem is modularized to a specific layer and can be traced to a particular protocol, such as IP.
>
> ❑ C. Changes can be made to a layer without affecting the other layers.
>
> ❑ D. Changes to one layer require changes to other layers.
>
> ❑ E. The layered model is more complex because it creates many smaller functions.

Answers B and C are correct. A layered model offers the advantages of making problem resolution easier because of the modular nature of the model and, because the layers are independent of each other, changes can be made to one layer without affecting the other layers. Answer A is incorrect because breaking the model down into a number of layers makes problem resolution easier. Answer D is incorrect because each layer is independent of the other layers, so that changes made to one layer do not affect the other layers. Answer E is incorrect because the modular approach to the layered model simplifies the issue of network communication.

Question 3

Which layer in the TCP/IP model handles sequencing of messages and ensures end-to-end delivery?

○ A. Application layer

○ B. Internet layer

○ C. Network Interface layer

○ D. Transport layer

Answer D is correct. The Transport layer handles the sequencing of messages and ensures end-to-end delivery. Answer A is incorrect because this layer interacts with the running application. Answer B is incorrect because this layer is responsible for the routing of data to the destination host. Answer C is incorrect because this layer provides the communication service across the network.

Question 4

Which layer in the TCP/IP model uses the MAC address as its basis for addressing purposes?

○ A. Application Layer

○ B. Internet Layer

○ C. Network Interface Layer

○ D. Transport Layer

Answer C is correct. The Network Interface layer uses the MAC address as its basis for addressing purposes. Answer A is incorrect because this layer does not use addressing. Answer B is incorrect because this layer uses IP addressing. Answer D is incorrect because this layer does not use addressing; it only specifies the port to use.

Question 5

At which layer in the TCP/IP model would you find the Telnet protocol being used?

○ A. Application layer

○ B. Internet layer

○ C. Transport layer

○ D. Network Interface layer

Answer A is correct. The Telnet protocol would be found in the Application layer of the TCP/IP model because this layer consists of applications that are run by users. Answer B is incorrect because this layer does not contain user applications; it handles the delivery and addressing of data. Answer C is incorrect because this layer does not contain user applications; it handles the end-to-end communication between hosts on a network. Answer D is incorrect because this layer does not contain user applications; it handles the physical transfer of data across the network.

Question 6

At which layer in the TCP/IP model would you find the IP protocol being used?

○ A. Application layer

○ B. Internet layer

○ C. Transport layer

○ D. Network Interface layer

Answer B is correct. The IP protocol would be found in the Internet layer of the TCP/IP model because this layer handles the delivery and addressing of data, which includes the IP and ICMP protocols. Answer A is incorrect because this layer contains user applications and does not use the IP protocol. Answer C is incorrect because this layer handles the end-to-end communication between hosts on a network and does not use the IP protocol. Answer D is incorrect because this layer handles the physical transfer of data across the network and does not use the IP protocol.

Need to Know More?

 Douglas Comer, *Internetworking with TCP/IP: Principles, Protocols, and Architecture*, (Prentice Hall, 2000).

 Sun Microsystems, Solaris 9 System Administrator Collection. *System Administration Guide: IP Services*. Available in printed form, on the Web at http://docs.sun.com, and from the online documentation provided with the Solaris 9 operating system.

ARP and RARP

Terms you'll need to understand:

✓ Address Resolution Protocol (ARP)
✓ ARP Cache
✓ Ethernet Address
✓ **/etc/ethers** file
✓ **/etc/inet/hosts** file
✓ **/tftpboot** directory
✓ **in.rarpd**
✓ Reverse Address Resolution Protocol (RARP)

Concepts you'll need to master:

✓ Describe the function and management of ARP.
✓ Describe the function and management of RARP.

This chapter introduces two protocols that operate between the Network Interface layer and the Internet layer of the TCP/IP model—ARP and RARP. These protocols are used to provide address resolution between ethernet and IP addresses. This chapter explores what these protocols are and how they work, as well as the files they reference.

Address Resolution Protocol (ARP)

ARP is used to map a 32-bit IP address to a 48-bit ethernet address. As you saw in Chapter 1, "Local Area Networks," an ethernet frame contains the sending and receiving ethernet addresses. If two systems need to communicate across a network, these ethernet addresses are needed; otherwise the ethernet frame will not be delivered to the correct recipient, very much like what would happen if you sent a letter to someone but left the address blank.

ARP uses the broadcast mechanism to try to find a host's ethernet address. The only information that ARP possesses, at this point, is the IP address (say 192.168.0.1), so it basically sends a request to all stations on the local network, asking, "Who has the IP address 192.168.0.1?" The receiving station that has been assigned the relevant IP address responds with its own ethernet address.

The following fragment of output from the snoop command shows a remote host that is booting. Initially, it doesn't respond, but when its network interface has been initialized, it answers with its ethernet address. The items of interest are in bold:

```
ETHER:  ----- Ether Header -----
ETHER:
ETHER:  Packet 1 arrived at 10:54:40.99
ETHER:  Packet size = 42 bytes
ETHER:  Destination = ff:ff:ff:ff:ff:ff, (broadcast)
ETHER:  Source      = 8:0:20:b3:41:1b, Sun
ETHER:  Ethertype = 0806 (ARP)
ETHER:
ARP:   ----- ARP/RARP Frame -----
ARP:
ARP:   Hardware type = 1
ARP:   Protocol type = 0800 (IP)
ARP:   Length of hardware address = 6 bytes
ARP:   Length of protocol address = 4 bytes
ARP:   Opcode 1 (ARP Request)
ARP:   Sender's hardware address = 8:0:20:b3:41:1b
ARP:   Sender's protocol address = 192.168.0.28, ultra10
ARP:   Target hardware address = ?
ARP:   Target protocol address = 192.168.0.21, systema
ARP:
...
ETHER:  ----- Ether Header -----
ETHER:
```

```
ETHER:   Packet 28 arrived at 10:55:10.80
ETHER:   Packet size = 42 bytes
ETHER:   Destination = 8:0:20:8e:48:de, Sun
ETHER:   Source      = 8:0:20:b3:41:1b, Sun
ETHER:   Ethertype = 0806 (ARP)
ETHER:
ARP:   ----- ARP/RARP Frame -----
ARP:
ARP:   Hardware type = 1
ARP:   Protocol type = 0800 (IP)
ARP:   Length of hardware address = 6 bytes
ARP:   Length of protocol address = 4 bytes
ARP:   Opcode 2 (ARP Reply)
ARP:   Sender's hardware address = 8:0:20:b3:41:1b
ARP:   Sender's protocol address = 192.168.0.28, ultra10
ARP:   Target hardware address = 8:0:20:8e:48:de
ARP:   Target protocol address = 192.168.0.21, systema
ARP:
```

Notice that in the first packet, the ethernet destination address is ff:ff:ff:ff:ff:ff, which is the ethernet broadcast address, but several packets later, the destination is the system's ethernet address because it has responded to the request.

Also, it is interesting to note that in the first packet, the ARP: Target hardware address is set to ?, indicating that it is unknown, but several packets later, this value has been set to the remote system's ethernet address as it has been provided in the response.

ARP Cache

ARP stores its responses in a cache, so that the information is available if it is required again. The cache stores this information for only up to 20 minutes by default, as can be seen by inspecting the contents of the ip_ire_arp_interval variable, using the ndd command as shown in the following:

```
# ndd /dev/ip ip_ire_arp_interval
1200000
```

The value 1200000 is in microseconds and equates to 20 minutes.

There are two types of ARP messages:

➤ *Solicited*—A solicited ARP message means that a specific ethernet address was asked for by a host.

➤ *Unsolicited*—An unsolicited ARP message is information stored about a host that issued an ARP request.

The value of 20 minutes in the previous command relates only to solicited ARP entries in the cache; unsolicited ARP entries are held for only 5 minutes.

The arp command is used to manage entries in the ARP cache. To display the entries in the ARP cache, use the -a option, which shows the following output:

```
ultra10# arp -a

Net to Media Table: IPv4
Device   IP Address                Mask         Flags   Phys Addr
------   -------------------    ---------------  -----   ----------------
hme0     systema                255.255.255.255          08:00:20:8e:48:de
hme0     dell14                 255.255.255.255          00:b0:d0:e7:9f:f2
hme0     ultra10                255.255.255.255  SP      08:00:20:b3:41:1b
hme0     224.0.0.0              240.0.0.0        SM      01:00:5e:00:00:00
```

The flags entry in the preceding output can consist of a number of values. These are described in the following list:

➤ *S*—A static entry that is not subject to the limit specified in the ip_ire_arp_interval variable. Static entries persist until the next reboot.

➤ *P*—A published entry that is advertised to other systems.

➤ *M*—A mapped entry indicating that this is a multicast entry.

➤ *U*—An unresolved or incomplete entry.

The previous code shows that the ARP entry for the local system is a static entry and is published to other hosts. The multicast entry (224.0.0.0) is also static and contains the M flag.

Table 3.1 shows all the options for the arp command.

Table 3.1	Options of the arp command	
Option	**Format**	**Description**
-a	**arp -a** or **arp *hostname***	Displays all entries, or a single entry.
-d	**arp -d *hostname***	Deletes a single entry from the ARP cache.
-f <*file*>	**arp -f *file***	Adds multiple entries to the cache. Entries must be in the following form: ***Hostname Eth_addr [pub]***

(continued)

Table 3.1	Options of the **arp** command *(continued)*	
Option	Format	Description
-s	**arp -s** *hostname Eth_addr* *[pub temp trail]*	Adds a static entry to the ARP cache. The **pub** option publishes the entry to other systems, the **temp** option specifies a temporary entry, and the **trail** option allows trailer encapsulations to be sent to the host.

When **arp -a** is used to display the entries in the ARP cache, hostnames are normally resolved where possible. If you do not want hostnames to be resolved, so that only the IP address is displayed, add the **-n** option. For example, **arp -an**.

Reverse Address Resolution Protocol (RARP)

RARP provides the opposite service to ARP in that it is used when only the ethernet address is known and the IP address is needed.

RARP requests are most commonly sent by diskless clients and JumpStart clients during bootup. A *diskless client* contains no local storage and knows only its own ethernet address. A *JumpStart* client contains local storage, but uses the ethernet address to locate the JumpStart boot server (to start a remote installation of the Solaris operating environment). The client uses the RARP protocol to broadcast this ethernet address and asks for the corresponding IP address.

The following fragment of output from the snoop command shows a client that is booting. The client issues a RARP request to attempt and find its IP address. The server that is listening for RARP requests responds. The items of interest are in bold:

```
...
ETHER:  ----- Ether Header -----
ETHER:
ETHER:  Packet 5 arrived at 14:35:1.14
ETHER:  Packet size = 64 bytes
ETHER:  Destination = ff:ff:ff:ff:ff:ff, (broadcast)
ETHER:  Source      = 8:0:20:8e:48:de, Sun
ETHER:  Ethertype = 8035 (RARP)
```

```
ETHER:
ARP:   ----- ARP/RARP Frame -----
ARP:
ARP:   Hardware type = 1
ARP:   Protocol type = 0800 (IP)
ARP:   Length of hardware address = 6 bytes
ARP:   Length of protocol address = 4 bytes
ARP:   Opcode 3 (REVARP Request)
ARP:   Sender's hardware address = 8:0:20:8e:48:de
ARP:   Sender's protocol address = 255.255.255.255, BROADCAST
ARP:   Target hardware address = 8:0:20:8e:48:de
ARP:   Target protocol address = ?
ARP:

ETHER:   ----- Ether Header -----
ETHER:
ETHER:   Packet 6 arrived at 14:35:1.18
ETHER:   Packet size = 42 bytes
ETHER:   Destination = 8:0:20:8e:48:de, Sun
ETHER:   Source      = 8:0:20:b3:41:1b, Sun
ETHER:   Ethertype = 8035 (RARP)
ETHER:
ARP:   ----- ARP/RARP Frame -----
ARP:
ARP:   Hardware type = 1
ARP:   Protocol type = 0800 (IP)
ARP:   Length of hardware address = 6 bytes
ARP:   Length of protocol address = 4 bytes
ARP:   Opcode 4 (REVARP Reply)
ARP:   Sender's hardware address = 8:0:20:b3:41:1b
ARP:   Sender's protocol address = 192.168.0.28, ultra10
ARP:   Target hardware address = 8:0:20:8e:48:de
ARP:   Target protocol address = 192.168.0.21, systema
ARP:
...
```

Notice that in the first packet, the type is REVARP request and the ethernet destination address is ff:ff:ff:ff:ff:ff, which is the ethernet broadcast address. Also, the ARP: Target protocol address is set to ? because the IP address is unknown at this point.

Also in the first packet, the receiving boot server knows which ethernet address to respond to because the sender's hardware address is the same as the Target hardware address—8:0:20:8e:48:de.

The second packet shows the type is REVARP reply and the ARP: Target protocol address is now set to the IP address of the client (192.168.0.21). This is the server responding to the client with its IP address.

The in.rarpd daemon

The daemon that listens on a server for incoming RARP requests is in.rarpd. The daemon is started at boot time by the script /etc/rc3.d/S16boot.server. The script starts the daemon only if the directory /tftpboot exists.

The **in.rarpd** daemon is started by the **/etc/rc3.d/S16boot.server** script. Prior to Solaris 9, **in.rarpd** was started by a different script, namely, **/etc/rc3.d/S15nfs. server**. Make sure you are not tricked by this if it appears in a question on the exam.

When an incoming RARP request is received from a client, the server process refers to two files to satisfy the request. The first is /etc/ethers, which contains the ethernet address and the corresponding hostname. The second file is /etc/inet/hosts, which contains the hostname and the corresponding IP address. Because it references both of these files, in.rarpd is capable of resolving the IP address from the ethernet address provided by the client. It is the IP address that is returned to the client.

 The file **/etc/hosts** is a symbolic link to **/etc/inet/hosts**. The link has been retained for compatibility with Berkeley Software Distribution (BSD) versions of Unix. You should be aware that this link exists.

If you encounter problems with a client that is failing to locate its IP address, you can use the snoop command to monitor RARP packets and you can also run in.rarpd with the -d option to obtain additional debug messages. The following output from running in.rarpd -d, shows the messages that are displayed when the server does not know the ethernet address:

```
/usr/sbin/in.rarpd:[1]  device hme0 ethernetaddress 8:0:20:b3:41:53
in.rarpd:[1]  device hme0 address 192.168.0.28
in.rarpd:[1]  device hme0 subnet mask 255.255.255.0
in.rarpd:[3]  starting rarp service on device hme0 address 8:0:20:b3:41:1b
in.rarpd:[3]  RARP_REQUEST for 8:0:20:8e:48:de
in.rarpd:[3]  could not map hardware address to IP address
in.rarpd:[3]  RARP_REQUEST for 8:0:20:8e:48:de
in.rarpd:[3]  could not map hardware address to IP address
in.rarpd:[3]  RARP_REQUEST for 8:0:20:8e:48:de
in.rarpd:[3]  could not map hardware address to IP address
```

This code shows what happens on the server. The client, however, receives a different message—the following is displayed repeatedly because it is not receiving a response from the server:

```
Timeout waiting for ARP/RARP packet
```

The error is normally due to one of the following:

➤ The ethernet address for the client has been entered incorrectly in /etc/ethers.

➤ The ethernet address entry for the client does not exist in /etc/ethers.

➤ The IP address or hostname entry for the client has been entered incorrectly in /etc/inet/hosts.

➤ The IP address or hostname entry for the client does not exist in /etc/inet/hosts.

➤ The in.rarpd daemon is not running on the server.

You can also gain useful information from the debug option of in.rarpd because it can be used to eliminate some of the potential causes of problems. The following output shows the messages that are displayed when a JumpStart client successfully obtains its IP address:

```
ultra10# in.rarpd -d

in.rarpd:[1]   device hme0 ethernetaddress 8:0:20:b3:41:1b
in.rarpd:[1]   device hme0 address 192.168.0.28
in.rarpd:[1]   device hme0 subnet mask 255.255.255.0
in.rarpd:[3]   starting rarp service on device hme0 address 8:0:20:b3:41:1b
in.rarpd:[3]   RARP_REQUEST for 8:0:20:8e:48:de
in.rarpd:[3]   trying physical netnum 192.168.0.0 mask ffffff00
in.rarpd:[3]   good lookup, maps to 192.168.0.21
in.rarpd:[3]   immediate reply sent
in.rarpd:[3]   RARP_REQUEST for 8:0:20:8e:48:de
in.rarpd:[3]   trying physical netnum 192.168.0.0 mask ffffff00
in.rarpd:[3]   good lookup, maps to 192.168.0.21
in.rarpd:[3]   immediate reply sent
```

The previous code shows that a RARP request has been received (RARP REQUEST for 8:0:20:8e:48:de) and executes a successful search for the ethernet address (good lookup, maps to 192.168.0.21). It then returns the requested information (the IP address) to the client (immediate reply sent).

Exam Prep Questions

Question 1

Which of the following is the ethernet broadcast address used in ARP and RARP requests?

○ A. **255.255.255.255**

○ B. **08:00:20:11:aa:01**

○ C. **ff:ff:ff:ff:ff:ff**

○ D. **224.0.0.0**

Answer C is correct. ff:ff:ff:ff:ff:ff is the ethernet broadcast address used in ARP and RARP requests. Answer A is incorrect because this represents a netmask. Answer B is incorrect because this is an example of a specific ethernet address that would identify a single interface. Answer D is incorrect because this represents an IP address used for multicast messages.

Question 2

Which of the following describes the function of ARP?

○ A. It is used to map a 32-bit IP address to a 48-bit ethernet address.

○ B. It is used to map a 48-bit ethernet address to a 32-bit IP address.

○ C. It is used to map a 32-bit ethernet address to a 48-bit IP address.

○ D. It is used to map a 48-bit IP address to a 32-bit ethernet address.

Answer A is correct. ARP maps a 32-bit IP address to a 48-bit ethernet address. Answer B is incorrect because this describes the function of RARP, not ARP. Answers C and D are incorrect because an ethernet address is 48 bits long and an IP address is 32 bits long. These answers identify the incorrect lengths.

Question 3

Which of the following describes the function of RARP?

○ A. It is used to map a 32-bit IP address to a 48-bit ethernet address.

○ B. It is used to map a 48-bit ethernet address to a 32-bit IP address.

○ C. It is used to map a 32-bit ethernet address to a 48-bit IP address.

○ D. It is used to map a 48-bit IP address to a 32-bit ethernet address.

Answer B is correct. RARP maps a 48-bit ethernet address to a 32-bit IP address. Answer A is incorrect because this describes the function of ARP, not RARP. Answers C and D are incorrect because an ethernet address is 48 bits long and an IP address is 32 bits long. These answers identify the wrong lengths.

Question 4

Which of the following configuration files are consulted by the RARP daemon? Choose 2.

❏ A. /etc/inet/netmasks

❏ B. /etc/inet/hosts

❏ C. /etc/ethers

❏ D. /etc/inetd.conf

❏ E. /etc/bootparams

Answers B and C are correct. /etc/inet/hosts and /etc/ethers are the configuration files consulted by the RARP daemon. Answer A is incorrect because /etc/inet/netmasks is used to associate IPv4 network masks with IPv4 network numbers. Answer D is incorrect because /etc/inetd.conf is the configuration file for the inetd daemon, which is the Internet services daemon. Answer E is incorrect because /etc/bootparams contains client boot information.

Question 5

In the Solaris 9 operating environment, **in.rarpd** is started at boot time by which startup script?

- ○ A. /etc/rc3.d/S15nfs.server
- ○ B. /etc/rc3.d/S16boot.server
- ○ C. /etc/rc2.d/S73nfs.client
- ○ D. /etc/rc2.d/S69inet

Answer B is correct. /etc/rc3.d/S16boot.server is the startup script. Answer A is incorrect because this script was used to start in.rarpd prior to Solaris 9. Answer C is incorrect because this script is used to startup the NFS client functionality. Answer D is incorrect because this script carries out the second phase of TCP/IP configuration during the system startup process.

Question 6

Which option of the **in.rarpd** command enables you to obtain additional debug messages?

- ○ A. -a
- ○ B. -d
- ○ C. -s
- ○ D. -f

Answer B is correct. -d is the debug option. Answer A is incorrect because this option is used by default to start in.rarpd on all ethernet interfaces. Answer C is incorrect because the -s option is not valid for in.rarpd—it is an option for the arp command to add an ARP entry to the cache. Answer D is incorrect because -f is not valid for in.rarpd—it is an option for the arp command to add multiple entries from a file to the ARP cache.

Question 7

You are trying to boot a custom JumpStart client, but get the following message repeatedly on the console when the boot process starts:

```
Timeout waiting for ARP/RARP packet
```

What could be the possible cause? Choose 2.

❑ A. The **in.rarpd** daemon is not running on the server that is expected to reply to the RARP request.

❑ B. The **inetd** daemon is not running on the server that is expected to reply to the RARP request.

❑ C. The client's ethernet address has been entered incorrectly or is not present in **/etc/ethers** on the server.

❑ D. The client's ethernet address is not present in the ARP cache.

Answers A and C are correct because the two causes could be that the in.rarpd daemon is not running on the server that is expected to reply to the RARP request, or the client's Ethernet address has been entered incorrectly or is not present in /etc/ethers on the server. Answer B is incorrect because this daemon does not have any effect on RARP requests. Answer D is incorrect because the ARP cache stores responses from ARP requests and does not affect RARP requests.

Need to Know More?

 Douglas Comer, *Internetworking with TCP/IP: Principles, Protocols and Architecture* (Prentice Hall, 2000).

 Sun Microsystems, *System Reference Manual*, Section 1M—"System Administration Commands." Available in printed form, on the Web at `http://docs.sun.com`, and from the online documentation provided with the Solaris 9 operating system.

 Sun Microsystems, *Solaris 9 System Administrator Collection—System Administration Guide*, "IP Services." Available in printed form, on the Web at `http://docs.sun.com`, and from the online documentation provided with the Solaris 9 operating system.

Fundamental IPv4

Terms you'll need to understand:

✓ IP Address Classes
✓ Broadcast Address
✓ */etc/hostname.<interface>* File
✓ **/etc/inet/hosts** File
✓ **/etc/inet/netmasks** File
✓ **/etc/nodename** File
✓ Internet Control Message Protocol (ICMP)
✓ Internet Protocol (IP)
✓ Multicast Address
✓ Subnetworks
✓ Unicast Address
✓ Variable Length Subnet Mask (VLSM)

Concepts you'll need to master:

✓ Describe the purpose, features, and functionality of Internet layer protocols, IP datagrams, IP address types, subnetting, and VLSM, and interface configuration files as used in an IP configuration.
✓ Explain how to configure and unconfigure logical interfaces in IP.

The Internet Protocol (IP) is delivered with the Solaris 9 release as part of the operating system kernel and operates at the Internet layer of the TCP/IP model. This chapter concentrates on the fundamental aspects of IP, including the address structure, subnetworking, and how to configure and troubleshoot network interfaces.

 Since the emergence of IPv6, there has been a tendency to describe the existing IP functionality as IPv4. You should be aware that IP, on its own, without a version descriptor, refers to IPv4.

The Internet Layer Protocols

IP consists of the following protocols:

➤ *IP*—The Internet Protocol which has two main functions:

> ➤ The delivery of datagrams across the network. The delivery mechanism is connectionless because there is no direct connection made between the sender and the receiver.

> ➤ The splitting up of application data into smaller units, based on the maximum transfer unit (MTU) of the network interface, to fit into an Ethernet II frame. This is known as *fragmentation*. IP also handles the reassembly of these fragments, after they have been transmitted across the network, in ethernet frames.

➤ *IGMP*—The Internet Group Management Protocol, which enables a computer to advertise its multicast group membership to routers on the network.

➤ *ICMP*—The Internet Control Message Protocol, an integral part of IP that is used to send error and control messages to other hosts on the network. ICMP communicates using IP and is often used as an invaluable means of diagnosing network problems.

Some of the more common ICMP messages include:

> ➤ *Echo request*—The request sent by the ping command.

> ➤ *Echo reply*—The reply from a ping command.

> ➤ *Destination unreachable*—No route to the specified destination host (or port) can be found.

> ➤ *Network unreachable*—No route to the specified network can be found.

> ➤ *Redirect*—The specified route cannot find the destination, but another route already knows how to get to the destination.

> ➤ *Time Exceeded*—A response has not been received within a specified time.

IP Addresses

IPv4 addresses are logical and are assigned by the network administrator, unlike ethernet addresses, which are physical addresses relating to a network component. An IPv4 address is 32 bits long, consisting of four octets, each of eight bits. IPv4 addresses are represented in decimal, using what is called *dot notation*; that is, each octet is separated by a dot (.). An example of an IPv4 address is 192.168.28.25.

An IPv4 address is used to identify a host on the network, through a combination of network number and host number within the network number. The preceding example represents host number 25 on network 192.168.28, but as you'll see in the following subsections, the portion of the IP address assigned to the network varies according to its class.

IPv4 uses three types of addresses: unicast, multicast, and broadcast.

Unicast IPv4 Addresses

An IPv4 unicast address is used for one-to-one communication, that is, when a single host communicates with another single host. There are three classes of IPv4 unicast address—class A, B, and C—which are assigned depending on the size of your network and the number of hosts that need to be addressed:

> ➤ *Class A*—Used for the largest networks, it permits 16,777,214 addressable hosts. In a class A network, the first eight bits of the IPv4 address define the network portion, and the first (leftmost) bit is always 0 (binary). This produces 128 possible class A networks (1–127), although the 127.0.0.0 network cannot be used because this contains the reserved loopback address (127.0.0.1). The remaining 21 bits are used to identify the hosts. An example of a class A IPv4 address is 47.20.16.8 (the network is 47 and the host is 20.16.8).

> ➤ *Class B*—Used for large- and medium-sized networks, it permits 65,534 addressable hosts. In a class B network, the first sixteen bits of the IPv4 address define the network portion, and the first two (leftmost) of these

bits are always 10 (binary). This produces 16,384 class B networks (128–191). The remaining sixteen bits are used to identify the hosts. An example of a class B IPv4 address is 145.212.8.15 (the network is 145.212 and the host is 8.15).

➤ *Class C*—Used for smaller networks, it permits 254 addressable hosts. In a class C network, the first 24 bits of the IPv4 address define the network portion, and the first three (leftmost) of these bits are always 110 (binary). This produces 2,097,152 class C networks (192–223). The remaining 8 bits are used to identify the hosts. An example of a class C IPv4 address is 215.156.18.185 (the network is 215.156.18 and the host is 185).

The IANA (Internet Assigned Numbers Authority) reserved a range of IPv4 addresses in each class for private networks that will not be connected to the Internet. These networks have no routing established and can be used by private individuals or companies for their local networks. The ranges of private IPv4 addresses are defined in RFC 1918. The reserved addresses are

➤ *Class A*—10.0.0.0–10.255.255.255

➤ *Class B*—172.16.0.0–172.31.255.255

➤ *Class C*—192.168.0.0–192.168.255.255

Figure 4.1 shows the three classes of IPv4 unicast addresses in binary format, along with the relevant ranges applicable to each class.

For each IPv4 network address that is assigned, without respect to its class, both the first and last host addresses are reserved and cannot be used as operational IPv4 addresses because they represent the network itself (the first address) and the broadcast address (the last address). For example, if you are assigned the network **192.168.28**, then the address **192.168.28.0** is the network itself and **192.168.28.255** is the default broadcast address. This is why a class C network address, for example, permits only 254 addressable hosts, instead of the 256 that you might expect from eight bits.

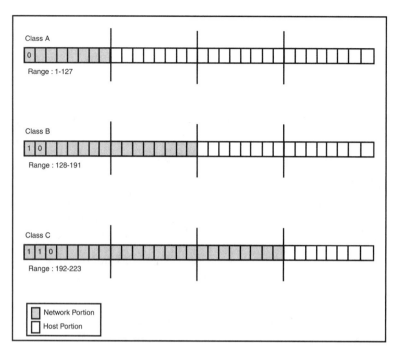

Figure 4.1 IPv4 unicast class types.

Multicast IPv4 Addresses

A multicast address is one where data is transmitted from a single host to a number of specific hosts at the same time, and it is referred to as a class D IPv4 address. This differs from the unicast address, where data is sent to a single host, in that it applies to a group of hosts that are associated with the multicast address—that is, they belong to the same multicast group. A multicast address might be used for example, to distribute an online newsletter to a list of subscribed hosts, or to update mobile address books. An IPv4 multicast address is 32 bits long, like all other IPv4 addresses, but the first (leftmost) four bits are always 1110 (binary), making the first octet in the range 224–239. The remaining 21 bits make up the multicast address for a specific group. The most common multicast address used by Solaris 9 is 224.0.0.1, which references a multicast group comprising all hosts on this subnet. The three octets (0.0.1) are mapped to the lower three octets of the ethernet multicast address for the network interface, so if your ethernet address is 08:00:20:4b:1e:52, the ethernet multicast address will be 08:00:20:00:00:01.

There is a class E IPv4 address type where the first octet is **240** or above. This address class is currently reserved and cannot be assigned for normal use on a Solaris system.

Broadcast IPv4 Addresses

A broadcast address is one in which data is transmitted to all systems on the LAN at the same time, using a reserved host address for each network. In binary, the host address is all 1s; in decimal it is 255. The default broadcast addresses for each unicast IPv4 address type are as follows:

➤ *Class A*—The leftmost octet identifies the network address, for example 10. The default broadcast address for this network is 10.255.255.255.

➤ *Class B*—The leftmost two octets identify the network address, for example 172.16. The default broadcast address for this network is 172.16.255.255.

➤ *Class C*—The leftmost three octets identify the network address, for example 192.168.1. The default broadcast address for this network is 192.168.1.255.

The broadcast address 255.255.255.255 is a special kind of broadcast address because it refers to all hosts on all networks, not just the hosts on your own particular network. Using this address is not recommended because you can flood the network with excessive, unwanted traffic, especially if a host is connected to the Internet.

Subnetworks and Network Masks

A network address can be subdivided into a number of smaller networks, called subnetworks. The reasons that an organization might want to do this include the following:

➤ To provide additional security by limiting access to a particular subnetwork of hosts

➤ To make better, more effective use of the assigned IPv4 address range

➤ To divide administrative domains into smaller logical units

➤ To reduce the network traffic by isolating subnetworks

➤ To associate a subnetwork with a specific organizational department, based on geographical location, or function within the organization

The **/etc/inet/netmasks** File

For any given IPv4 address, or range of addresses, it is necessary to be able to calculate the network portion of the address. The file `/etc/inet/netmasks` exists for this purpose, to associate IPv4 address masks with IPv4 network numbers. The entries in this file are permanent and persist across system reboots.

 Entries in **/etc/inet/netmasks** are normally in decimal dot notation. Even though you can specify the network mask in hexadecimal (for example **ffffff00**) by using the **ifconfig** command, you must prefix hexadecimal addresses with **0x** when making permanent entries in this file. You might be asked about the format of entries in the **/etc/inet/netmasks** file.

Each IPv4 unicast address class has a default network mask associated with it. They are as follows:

➤ *Class A*—Default network mask is `255.0.0.0`.

➤ *Class B*—Default network mask is `255.255.0.0`.

➤ *Class C*—Default network mask is `255.255.255.0`.

A network mask entry is 32 bits long—the same as an IPv4 address. If you convert the network mask to binary, you will see that it consists of a number of contiguous `1`s (`255` in decimal is equal to `11111111` in binary) followed by a number of contiguous `0`s. It is the `1`s portion of the mask that determines the network part of the IPv4 address. You'll see that for a class C IPv4 address, the default network mask is `255.255.255.0`, indicating that the first 24 bits of the mask are `1`s and the last 8 bits are `0`s.

 You can assign a network mask that does not consist of contiguous **1**s, such as **255.255.254.128** (**11111111 11111111 11111110 10000000** in binary), but this is not normally done because it increases the complexity of administering the network address space.

The format of entries in the `/etc/inet/netmasks` file is:

```
<network number>    <network mask>
```

The host portion of the address is entered as `0` and the separator character can be spaces or tabs, so for a system with an IPv4 address of `172.16.24.56` (class B), the entry is as follows:

```
172.16.0.0    255.255.0.0
```

The file **/etc/netmasks** is a symbolic link to **/etc/inet/netmasks** and is included for Berkeley Software Distribution (BSD) compatibility. The actual file is **/etc/inet/netmasks**; be aware of this because it is a frequent exam question.

The /etc/inet/netmasks file is referenced when the system boots up to establish network masks for the network interfaces installed in the system. At the single user level, the startup script /etc/rcS.d/S30network.sh first references this file, and later on at run level 2, the startup script /etc/rc2.d/S72inetsvc recalculates the network mask in case a naming service is running.

Subnetting a Network

So far, you've seen the default network masks that are assigned to the relevant classes of IPv4 addresses. Sometimes it is necessary to divide your network into a number of smaller networks. You can do so by specifying your own network mask to create a number of smaller networks with fewer hosts on each one.

As an example, take the class C network 192.168.28: The default network mask is 255.255.255.0. Suppose you want to split this network into 16 smaller networks, each comprising 14 useable hosts (because the first address is the network itself and the last address is the broadcast address). The network mask to use to do this is 255.255.255.240. What you're effectively doing is allocating some of the host address space to the network address. Table 4.1 shows how this network address would break down into its separate subnetworks, as well as the useable host addresses that each subnetwork creates.

Table 4.1 Dividing a Class C Network Address

Network Address	Addressable Hosts Range	Broadcast Address	Network Mask
192.168.28.0	192.168.28.1–192.168.28.14	192.168.28.15	255.255.255.240
192.168.28.16	192.168.28.17–192.168.28.30	192.168.28.31	255.255.255.240
192.168.28.32	192.168.28.33–192.168.28.46	192.168.28.47	255.255.255.240
192.168.28.48	192.168.28.49–192.168.28.62	192.168.28.63	255.255.255.240
192.168.28.64	192.168.28.65–192.168.28.78	192.168.28.79	255.255.255.240

(continued)

Table 4.1	Dividing a Class C Network Address *(continued)*		
Network Address	**Addressable Hosts Range**	**Broadcast Address**	**Network Mask**
192.168.28.80	192.168.28.81–192.168.28.94	192.168.28.95	255.255.255.240
192.168.28.96	192.168.28.97–192.168.28.110	192.168.28.111	255.255.255.240
192.168.28.112	192.168.28.113–192.168.28.126	192.168.28.127	255.255.255.240
192.168.28.128	192.168.28.129–192.168.28.142	192.168.28.143	255.255.255.240
192.168.28.144	192.168.28.145–192.168.28.158	192.168.28.159	255.255.255.240
192.168.28.160	192.168.28.161–192.168.28.174	192.168.28.175	255.255.255.240
192.168.28.176	192.168.28.177–192.168.28.190	192.168.28.191	255.255.255.240
192.168.28.192	192.168.28.193–192.168.28.206	192.168.28.207	255.255.255.240
192.168.28.208	192.168.28.209–192.168.28.222	192.168.28.223	255.255.255.240
192.168.28.224	192.168.28.225–192.168.28.238	192.168.28.239	255.255.255.240
192.168.28.240	192.168.28.241–192.168.28.254	192.168.28.255	255.255.255.240

Note that the network address (the first address) does not end in 0, except for the first subnetwork, and that the broadcast address is different for each subnetwork.

Each of the subnetworks created must also have its own entry in the /etc/inet/netmasks file so that the correct assignments are made when the system initiates the network interface at boot time. The /etc/inet/netmasks file now looks like this:

```
# cat /etc/inet/netmasks
#
# The netmasks file associates Internet Protocol (IP) address
# masks with IP network numbers.
#
#       network-number  netmask
#
# The term network-number refers to a number obtained from the Internet
➡ Network
```

```
# Information Center.
#
# Both the network-number and the netmasks are specified in
# "decimal dot" notation, e.g:
#
#                   128.32.0.0 255.255.255.0
#
192.168.28.0      255.255.255.240
192.168.28.16     255.255.255.240
192.168.28.32     255.255.255.240
192.168.28.48     255.255.255.240
192.168.28.64     255.255.255.240
192.168.28.80     255.255.255.240
192.168.28.96     255.255.255.240
192.168.28.112    255.255.255.240
192.168.28.128    255.255.255.240
192.168.28.144    255.255.255.240
192.168.28.160    255.255.255.240
192.168.28.176    255.255.255.240
192.168.28.192    255.255.255.240
192.168.28.208    255.255.255.240
192.168.28.224    255.255.255.240
192.168.28.240    255.255.255.240
```

The action of subnetting has actually reduced the number of useable host addresses you have to 224 (from 254 when it was a single network), but you now have sixteen separate subnetworks.

Variable Length Subnet Mask (VLSM)

The previous section showed how a network can be divided into a number of smaller networks, but they were all the same size. Now you'll see how to divide a network into a number of smaller networks, but each will be a different size and, consequently, have a different network mask. You can divide a single network this way by using a number of network masks, known as variable length subnet masks (VLSM).

Although you might wonder why anyone would want to do this, it could make much better use of the available IPv4 addresses.

As an example, imagine a company with a large accounting department (for example, 125 people), a medium-sized HR department, and a medium-sized administration marketing department (for example, 60 in each). With your class C network (192.168.28.0), you can divide this network into three smaller networks, one with 126 addressable hosts and two further networks with 62 addressable hosts in each. Table 4.2 shows how this network address would break down into the three separate subnetworks, as well as the useable host addresses that each subnetwork creates.

Table 4.2 Using VLSM to Divide a Class C Network Address			
Network Address	Addressable Hosts Range	Broadcast Address	Network Mask
192.168.28.0	192.168.28.1–192.168.28.126	192.168.28.127	255.255.255.128
192.168.28.128	192.168.28.129–192.168.28.190	192.168.28.191	255.255.255.192
192.168.28.192	192.168.28.193–192.168.28.254	192.168.28.255	255.255.255.192

Each of the subnetworks created must also have its own entry in the /etc/inet/netmasks file so that the correct assignments are made when the system initiates the network interface at boot time. The /etc/inet/netmasks file now looks like this:

```
# cat /etc/inet/netmasks
#
# The netmasks file associates Internet Protocol (IP) address
# masks with IP network numbers.
#
#       network-number   netmask
#
# The term network-number refers to a number obtained from the Internet
➥ Network
# Information Center.
#
# Both the network-number and the netmasks are specified in
# "decimal dot" notation, e.g:
#
#               128.32.0.0 255.255.255.0
#
192.168.28.0       255.255.255.128
192.168.28.128     255.255.255.192
192.168.28.192     255.255.255.192
```

IP Datagrams

Just as the Ethernet frame is the basic unit of transfer at the Network Interface layer of the TCP/IP model (discussed in Chapter 1, "Local Area Networks"), the IP datagram is the basic unit of transfer at the Internet layer. Figure 4.2 shows the structure of an IPv4 datagram header.

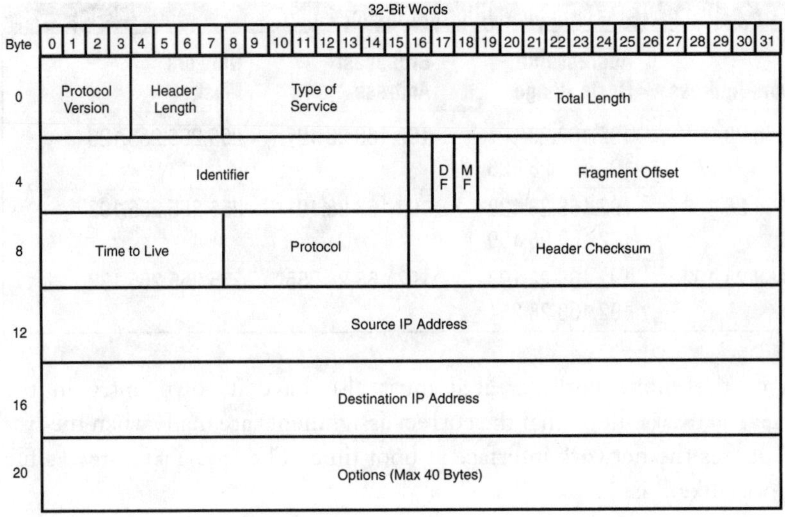

Figure 4.2 IPv4 datagram header format.

The fields are as follows:

➤ *Protocol version*—The IP version number, currently 4.

➤ *Header length*—The length (in 32-bit words) of the IPv4 datagram header. The header length is always a minimum of 5 words (20 bytes), but because of the field's 4-bit length, there is a maximum of 15 words (60 bytes).

➤ *Type of service*—This field consists of a 3-bit precedence field, which is ignored, a 4-bit service field, and an unused bit. The service bits indicate the quality of service, with four possible values:

➤ 1000—Minimize delay

➤ 0100—Maximize throughput

➤ 0010—Maximize reliability

➤ 0001—Minimize monetary cost

Not all implementations support this field, but some have additional information in the routing table to indicate delay, throughput, reliability, and monetary cost.

➤ *Total length*—The total length of the datagram, including the data (in bytes). The header length is already known from the header length field, so the data length can be known by calculating total length–header length. The maximum total length of an IPv4 datagram is 65,535 bytes.

➤ *Identifier*—This field is a 16-bit identification field. If a datagram is fragmented into a number of frames, then the same identifier is used so that the fragments can be correctly reassembled at the destination.

➤ *Flags*—This 3-bit field consists of an unused bit and two flag fields, DF and MF. The DF bit (Do not Fragment), if set, is an instruction to routers not to fragment the data, normally because the destination is not able to reassemble the pieces. The MF bit (More Fragments) is set when there are more fragments to follow. Only the last fragment will see this bit set to 0.

➤ *Fragment offset*—This 13-bit field identifies the location of the fragment in the IPv4 datagram.

➤ *Time to live*—The maximum number of routers through which the datagram can pass. Each router decrements the value by one until it reaches zero, when it is discarded. TCP sets this value by default to 64, whereas UDP sets it to 255. You can see the current values by using the ndd command as shown here:

➤ The TCP value:

```
#ndd /dev/tcp tcp_ipv4_ttl
64
```

➤ The UDP value:

```
#ndd /dev/udp udp_ipv4_ttl
255
```

➤ *Protocol*—This field identifies the Transport layer protocol to which the datagram should be delivered. A value of 6 indicates TCP, whereas a value of 17 indicates UDP. These values are listed in the protocols file—`/etc/inet/protocols`.

➤ *Header checksum*—This field verifies the integrity of the datagram header to ensure it has not become corrupted. Note that the checksum applies to only the header and does not include the data.

➤ *Source IP address*—The IPv4 address of the system sending the datagram.

➤ *Destination IP address*—The IPv4 address of the final destination system that will receive the datagram.

➤ *Options*—This field contains optional information and may not always be present. This field can contain five options and will always end on a 32-bit boundary, using padding if necessary:

   ➤ *Security*—Specifies the datagram's security level.

   ➤ *Strict source routing*—Specifies the entire path to be followed.

➤ *Loose source routing*—Specifies a list of routers that must not be missed.

➤ *Record route*—Specifies that each router must append its own IP address.

➤ *Timestamp*—Specifies that each router must append its own IP address and also append a timestamp.

An IPv4 datagram consists of a header and some data. The data portion of the datagram can consist of a TCP segment, a UDP datagram, an ICMP message, or an IGMP message.

Interface Configuration

System and network administrators regularly use three main network interface configuration files. The use of configuration files enables changes, or additions, to persist across reboots so that the network interfaces are automatically configured when the system goes through the boot process. These files are

➤ /etc/hostname.<*interface*>

➤ /etc/inet/hosts

➤ /etc/nodename

/etc/hostname.<*interface*>

The Solaris installation program configures the primary network interface for you. It does this by creating the necessary /etc/hostname.<*interface*> file. For example, if your system has an hme0 primary interface, the file /etc/hostname.hme0 is created and populated with either the hostname or IPv4 address that is associated with the interface. When the system reboots, the startup script, /etc/rcS.d/S30network.sh, configures and enables the interface.

/etc/inet/hosts

The /etc/inet/hosts file provides IPv4 address-to-hostname mapping, so that you don't have to always specify a host by its IPv4 address. It allows normal names to be assigned, such as ultra10 or server1. This file also allows aliases and comments, permitting a system to have several names.

The file **/etc/hosts** is a symbolic link to **/etc/inet/hosts** and is included for BSD compatibility. The actual file is **/etc/inet/hosts**, so be aware of this because it is a frequent exam question.

The following is a typical /etc/inet/hosts file:

```
# cat /etc/hosts
#
# Internet host table
#
localhost
192.168.28.11    test1
192.168.28.19    inetpc
192.168.28.25    winpc
192.168.28.28    ultra10 ultra10.mobile-ventures.net        loghost
192.168.28.127   sparc5 nismaster
209.67.50.203    www.mobile-ventures.net
```

The /etc/inet/hosts file is referenced when the system boots and configures the network interfaces.

/etc/nodename

This file contains a single entry—the hostname of the system—and is used to identify the authoritative name by which applications and remote systems will know this system. This name is called the *canonical name*—canonical because it is the ultimate authority (derived from canonical law in the church) that is to be believed.

Configuring a Network Interface

During the Solaris 9 installation program, only the primary network interface is configured, so any other network interfaces must be configured manually. For example, if you have a system with a primary interface, hme0, and a second interface, hme1, then you will have to configure hme1. The following instructions will achieve this:

1. Edit the file /etc/inet/hosts and assign an IPv4 address and hostname for this interface. To use the IPv4 address 192.168.28.79 and the hostname testnet, add the following entry to the file:

   ```
   192.168.28.79    testnet
   ```

   Save the file and exit the editor.

2. Edit the file /etc/hostname.hme1 and insert the hostname of the system you just entered. In this case the file contains the single entry, testnet.

3. Reboot the system and the network interface is automatically configured.

The configuration is permanent and persists across subsequent reboots of
the system.

Sometimes, such as when a company reorganizes, it becomes necessary to
change a system's hostname. There are two ways of achieving this:

➤ Run the sys-unconfig command, which will reset the system to its "as-
manufactured" state and shut down. When you start the system again,
you have to re-enter the configuration information that was entered
when the Solaris operating system was installed. You can assign a new
hostname at this point. You should note that this command does not
affect the file systems and data held on disks; only the system identification is affected.

➤ Modify the following six files to reflect the new hostname, and then
reboot the system:

  ➤ /etc/inet/hosts

  ➤ /etc/nodename

  ➤ /etc/hostname.<*interface*> files, such as /etc/hostname.hme0

  ➤ /etc/net/ticlts/hosts—This file is referenced by the Transport
  Layer Interface (TLI).

  ➤ /etc/net/ticots/hosts—This file is referenced by the Transport
  Layer Interface (TLI).

  ➤ /etc/net/ticotsord/hosts—This file is referenced by the Transport
  Layer Interface (TLI) .

Logical Interfaces

Logical interfaces, also known as virtual interfaces, enable you to assign more
than one IPv4 address to a single network interface, and each IPv4 address
can be of a different unicast class. It is a very simple way to make a single system appear as many systems. You might want to use logical interfaces when

➤ A Web server requires multiple URLs to appear to have multiple Web
resources

➤ An application server runs multiple applications, where each application
requires a dedicated IP address or hostname

➤ You are running a high-availability failover mechanism where a logical interface can act as a failover for another network interface

Each logical interface that is configured is assigned its own unique IPv4 address and a unique hostname, and appears as if it is a completely separate network interface.

The main advantages of using logical interfaces are

➤ *Cost*—There is no need to purchase additional network cards.

➤ *Administration*—With everything on a single system, rather than multiple systems, the administration overhead is reduced.

➤ *Appearance*—Your department appears to be much larger than it really is.

The disadvantages are

➤ *Network load*—Even though the appearance of multiple interfaces might look good, logical interfaces are actually tied to a specific physical network interface, so the network traffic could increase, creating potential network problems.

➤ *Startup overhead*—When a system boots, each interface, including logical interfaces, is configured and enabled, so if a number of logical interfaces are operational, the boot time will increase significantly.

Configuring a Logical Interface

A logical interface is configured using the same command (`ifconfig`) that is used to configure a physical network interface. For example, in a system with a physical interface `hme0`, the first logical interface is named `hme0:1`, the second `hme0:2`, and so on.

To view the current network interface configuration, enter the `ifconfig -a` command as shown here:

```
#ifconfig -a
lo0: flags=1000849<UP,LOOPBACK,RUNNING,MULTICAST,IPv4> mtu 8232 index 1
        inet 127.0.0.1 netmask ff000000
hme0: flags=1000843<UP,BROADCAST,RUNNING,MULTICAST,IPv4> mtu 1500 index 2
        inet 192.168.28.28 netmask ffffff00 broadcast 192.168.28.255
        ether 8:0:20:b3:41:13
```

To create a logical interface `hme0:1`, with an IPv4 address of `192.168.28.128`, use the following command:

```
#ifconfig hme0:1 plumb 192.168.28.128 up
```

Now, view the current network interface configuration again to see the newly created logical interface:

```
#ifconfig -a
lo0: flags=1000849<UP,LOOPBACK,RUNNING,MULTICAST,IPv4> mtu 8232 index 1
        inet 127.0.0.1 netmask ff000000
hme0: flags=1000843<UP,BROADCAST,RUNNING,MULTICAST,IPv4> mtu 1500 index 2
        inet 192.168.28.28 netmask ffffff00 broadcast 192.168.28.255
        ether 8:0:20:b3:41:13
hme0:1: flags=1000843<UP,BROADCAST,RUNNING,MULTICAST,IPv4> mtu 1500 index 2
        inet 192.168.28.128 netmask ffffff00 broadcast 192.168.28.255
```

At this point, you can add an entry to /etc/inet/hosts for the new IPv4 address and reference this as if it were a separate system.

Note that a logical interface contains the same index number as the physical interface when you use the **ifconfig -a** command to view it because it is physically tied to the physical interface.

Alternatively, rather than having to remember the next logical interface number, you can use the addif option of ifconfig to select the next number for you. The following command creates an additional logical interface, which is named hme0:2, with an IPv4 address of 192.168.28.29:

```
#ifconfig hme0 addif 192.168.28.29 up
Created new logical interface hme0:2
```

View the current network interface configuration to see the second logical interface:

```
#ifconfig -a
lo0: flags=1000849<UP,LOOPBACK,RUNNING,MULTICAST,IPv4> mtu 8232 index 1
        inet 127.0.0.1 netmask ff000000
hme0: flags=1000843<UP,BROADCAST,RUNNING,MULTICAST,IPv4> mtu 1500 index 2
        inet 192.168.28.28 netmask ffffff00 broadcast 192.168.28.255
        ether 8:0:20:b3:41:13
hme0:1: flags=1000843<UP,BROADCAST,RUNNING,MULTICAST,IPv4> mtu 1500 index 2
        inet 192.168.28.128 netmask ffffff00 broadcast 192.168.28.255
hme0:2: flags=1000843<UP,BROADCAST,RUNNING,MULTICAST,IPv4> mtu 1500 index 2
        inet 192.168.28.29 netmask ffffff00 broadcast 192.168.28.255
```

When you use **ifconfig -a** to view the network interface configuration, only the physical interface displays an associated ethernet address. Logical interfaces do not have their own ethernet address because they are tied to the physical interface.

Removing a Logical Interface

A logical interface is removed in the same way a physical interface is removed: by using the ifconfig command.

To remove the `hme0:2` interface, created in the previous subsection, enter the following command:

```
#ifconfig hme0:2 down unplumb
```

The **down** option must come before the **unplumb** option to ensure the logical interface is first disabled, then unconfigured. Exam questions frequently offer several alternative syntax options; make sure you get the right one.

Alternatively, if you know the IPv4 address of the logical interface you want to remove, you can use that instead. The following command removes the logical interface that was created in the previous subsection, with an IPv4 address of `192.168.28.128`:

```
#ifconfig hme0 removeif 192.168.28.128
```

Troubleshooting IPv4

You can use various commands to troubleshoot IPv4 to diagnose a problem; the most common ones are `ifconfig`, `ping`, and `traceroute`. These commands are each discussed briefly below.

ifconfig

Use the `ifconfig -a` command to view the current network interface configuration. The output from the command includes all physical and logical interfaces that are configured as shown here, where there are two logical interfaces:

```
#ifconfig -a
lo0: flags=1000849<UP,LOOPBACK,RUNNING,MULTICAST,IPv4> mtu 8232 index 1
        inet 127.0.0.1 netmask ff000000
hme0: flags=1000843<UP,BROADCAST,RUNNING,MULTICAST,IPv4> mtu 1500 index 2
        inet 192.168.28.28 netmask ffffff00 broadcast 192.168.28.255
        ether 8:0:20:b3:41:13
hme0:1: flags=1000843<UP,BROADCAST,RUNNING,MULTICAST,IPv4> mtu 1500 index 2
        inet 192.168.28.128 netmask ffffff00 broadcast 192.168.28.255
hme0:2: flags=1000843<UP,BROADCAST,RUNNING,MULTICAST,IPv4> mtu 1500 index 2
        inet 192.168.28.29 netmask ffffff00 broadcast 192.168.28.255
```

This output shows the status of each interface, in the `flags=` section. You can also verify that you are using the correct IPv4 address for each interface.

ping

Use the ping command to verify that you can contact the network interface and that it is responding to network requests. The following example contacts the logical interface hme0:2:

```
#ping 192.168.28.29
192.168.28.29 is alive
```

traceroute

The traceroute command is extremely useful when you're trying to establish why you cannot contact a remote host; it identifies the path taken to reach a remote host. The following example traces the route, across the Internet, to the Web site www.example.com. It lists all the routers that are used to establish contact:

```
#traceroute www.example.com
Tracing route to www.example.com [192.0.34.166]

over a maximum of 30 hops:

    1     9 ms    10 ms     8 ms   10.25.0.1
    2    11 ms     9 ms     9 ms   gsr01-st.blueyonder.co.uk [62.30.65.1]
    3    13 ms    12 ms    14 ms   172.18.6.69
    4    27 ms    14 ms    13 ms   tele1-azt-pos.telewest.net [194.117.136.2]
    5    13 ms    12 ms    14 ms   pos50402hsd-gsr2-linx.cableinet.net
➡[194.117.154.190]
    6    14 ms    14 ms    12 ms   166.63.222.37
    7   104 ms   103 ms   105 ms   dcr1-loopback.Washington.cw.net
➡[206.24.226.99]
    8   106 ms   105 ms   108 ms   bpr1-so-0-0-0.VirginiaEquinix.cw.net
➡[208.173.52.113]
    9   105 ms   105 ms   106 ms   bpr2-ae0.VirginiaEquinix.cw.net
➡[208.173.50.253]
   10   105 ms   106 ms   106 ms   208.173.50.146
   11   137 ms   100 ms    95 ms   p16-1-0-0.r21.asbnva01.us.bb.verio.net
➡[129.250.5.21]
   12   108 ms   107 ms   106 ms   p16-5-0-0.r01.mclnva02.us.bb.verio.net
➡[129.250.2.180]
   13   108 ms   105 ms   108 ms   p16-7-0-0.r02.mclnva02.us.bb.verio. net
➡[129.250.5.10]
   14   166 ms   166 ms   184 ms   p16-0-1-2.r20.plalca01.us.bb.verio.net
➡[129.250.2.192]
   15   169 ms   168 ms   169 ms   p64-0-0-0.r20.snjsca04.us.bb.verio.net
➡[129.250.2.71]
   16   169 ms   167 ms   171 ms   xe-0-2-0.r21.snjsca04.us.bb.verio.net
➡[129.250.2.73]
   17   180 ms   214 ms   162 ms   p16-1-1-1.r21.lsanca01.us.bb.verio.net
➡[129.250.2.186]
   18   167 ms   182 ms   163 ms   ge-3-0-0.a02.lsanca02.us.ra.verio.net
➡[129.250.29.131]
   19   164 ms   166 ms   166 ms   ge-1-2.a01.lsanca02.us.ra.verio.net
➡[129.250.46.93]
   20   162 ms   165 ms   165 ms   ge-2-3-0.a02.lsanca02.us.ce.verio.net
➡[198.172.117.163]
```

```
21    164 ms    164 ms    165 ms    lngw2-isi-1-pos.ln.net [130.152.80.29]
22    164 ms    164 ms    164 ms    207.151.118.18
23    165 ms    166 ms    165 ms    www.example.com [192.0.34.166]
Trace complete.
```

The output shows a successful trace of the route between two hosts. When there are problems, or there is no route, traceroute displays a * character instead.

Exam Prep Questions

Question 1

What is the minimum length that an IP datagram header can be?

○ A. 20 bytes

○ B. 60 bytes

○ C. 20 words

○ D. 60 words

Answer A is correct because an IP datagram header must be at least 20 bytes long. Answer B is incorrect because this is the maximum length an IP datagram header can be. Answers C and D are incorrect because the minimum number of 32-bit words an IP datagram header can be is 5.

Question 2

You have a system with a physical network interface **hme0**. Which command creates a logical interface using the next available logical interface number and assigns an IPv4 address of **192.168.5.5**?

○ A. **ifconfig hme0:1 plumb 192.168.5.5 up**

○ B. **ifconfig hme0:1 addif 192.168.5.5 up**

○ C. **ifconfig addif 192.168.5.5 up**

○ D. **ifconfig hme0 addif 192.168.5.5 up**

Answer D is correct because the command `ifconfig hme0 addif 192.168.5.5 up` creates a logical interface using the next available logical interface number and the IPv4 address `192.168.5.5`. Answer A is incorrect because this command, although it will configure a logical interface, specifically states which logical interface to use. In this case, it could destroy and replace an existing logical interface. Answer B is incorrect because the syntax is wrong. In this answer, the `hme0:1` logical interface is being specified, as well as the `addif` option, which uses the next available logical interface number. Answer C is incorrect because the command is missing the physical interface `hme0` as the first argument.

Question 3

In an IP datagram header, what does the flag field **DF** mean?

- ○ A. Indicates that this datagram is a fragment.
- ○ B. Identifies the location of the fragment in the datagram.
- ○ C. Indicates that this datagram should not be fragmented.
- ○ D. Indicates that the flag is not used.

Answer C is correct because the use of the DF flag indicates that the IP datagram should not be fragmented. The main reason for this is that the destination is not capable of reassembling the fragments. Answer A is incorrect because this is the description of the MF flag. Answer B is incorrect because the location of a fragment in an IP datagram is identified by the fragment offset field. Answer D is incorrect because this flag field is used.

Question 4

This protocol is used at the Internet layer of the TCP/IP model to send control and error messages. Which protocol is being described?

- ○ A. IP
- ○ B. ICMP
- ○ C. TCP
- ○ D. UDP

Answer B is correct because the Internet Control Message Protocol (ICMP) sends control and error messages at the Internet layer of the TCP/IP model. Answer A is incorrect because IP is a protocol that handles connectionless delivery and fragmentation at the Internet layer of the TCP/IP model. Answers C and D are incorrect because TCP and UDP are Transport layer protocols.

Question 5

Which file contains the canonical hostname of a system?

- ○ A. **/etc/inet/hosts**
- ○ B. **/etc/inet/netmasks**
- ○ C. **/etc/hostname.hme0**
- ○ D. **/etc/nodename**

Answer D is correct because the file /etc/nodename contains a system's canonical hostname. Answer A is incorrect because /etc/inet/hosts is used to provide IPv4 address-to-hostname mapping. Answer B is incorrect because /etc/inet/netmasks is used to associate IPv4 network masks with IPv4 network numbers. Answer C is incorrect because /etc/hostname.hme0 is the configuration file used to configure a physical network interface named hme0.

Question 6

Which of the following are advantages of using logical interfaces? Choose 2.

❏ A. They are cheaper because there is no need to purchase additional network cards.

❏ B. Administration is easier because everything is done on a single system, rather than on multiple systems.

❏ C. They provide hardware resilience in case the physical interface fails.

❏ D. They enhance network performance by reducing network traffic.

Answers A and B are correct because the logical interfaces are cheaper. There is no need to purchase additional network cards, and the administration overhead is reduced because everything can be done on a single system, rather than on multiple systems. Answers C and D are incorrect because they are false; logical interfaces do not provide any hardware resilience because they are tied to the physical interface, and they can also increase the amount of network traffic because logical interfaces use the same physical interface.

Question 7

Which of the following are reserved private network ranges of IP addresses as defined in RFC 1918? Choose 2.

❏ A. 10.0.0.0–10.255.255.255

❏ B. 11.0.0.0–11.255.255.255

❏ C. 172.16.0.0–172.31.255.255

❏ D. 172.100.0.0–172.100.255.255

Answers A and C are correct because the IP address ranges that are reserved for private networks, and defined in RFC 1918, are 10.0.0.0–10.255.255.255, 172.16.0.0–172.31.255.255 and 192.168.0.0–192.168.255.255. Answers B and D are incorrect because they do not fall within the ranges defined in RFC 1918.

Question 8

Which of the following files must be edited to effect a manual change of the system hostname? Choose 3.

☐ A. **/etc/nodename**

☐ B. **/etc/inet/networks**

☐ C. **/etc/inet/netmasks**

☐ D. **/etc/system**

☐ E. **/etc/inet/hosts**

☐ F. **/etc/net/ticlts/hosts**

Answers A, E, and F are correct because /etc/nodename, /etc/inet/hosts, and /etc/net/ticlts/hosts are all files that must be edited to effect a manual change of the system hostname. Answer B is incorrect because /etc/inet/networks is used to provide network number–to–network name translation. Answer C is incorrect because /etc/inet/netmasks is used to identify the network masks for subnetting purposes. Answer D is incorrect because /etc/system is a file used for customizing the operation of the Solaris kernel.

Question 9

To which IP address class does the address **192.168.20.35** belong?

○ A. A

○ B. B

○ C. C

○ D. D

Answer C is correct because IP addresses in the range 192–223 are classified as class C IP addresses. Answer A is incorrect because class A network addresses must be in the range 0–127. Answer B is incorrect because class B network addresses must be in the range 128–191. Answer D is incorrect because class D network addresses are used for multicasting and must be in the range 224–239.

Question 10

Your system has an **hme** network interface named **hme0**. Which configuration
file needs to be edited to configure the interface?

○ A. **/etc/inet/netmasks**

○ B. **/etc/hostname.hme0**

○ C. **/etc/inet/networks**

○ D. **/etc/hostname.hme1**

Answer B is correct because the /etc/hostname.hme0 file needs to be edited to
configure an hme0 interface. Answer A is incorrect because /etc/inet/netmasks
is used to identify the network masks for subnetting purposes. Answer C is
incorrect because /etc/inet/networks is used to provide network
number–to–network name translation. Answer D is incorrect because
/etc/hostname.hme1 would be the configuration file to edit if you were configuring the second hme network interface, hme1.

Need to Know More?

 Comer, Douglas. *Internetworking with TCP/IP: Principles, Protocols and Architecture*. Prentice Hall, 2000.

 Sun Microsystems, *Solaris 9 System Administrator Collection—System Administration Guide: IP Services*. Available in printed form, on the Internet at http://docs.sun.com, and from the online documentation provided with the Solaris 9 operating system.

 Sun Microsystems, *System Reference Manual, Section 1M—System Administration Commands*. Available in printed form, on the Internet at http://docs.sun.com, and from the online documentation provided with the Solaris 9 operating system.

IP Multipathing

. . . .

Terms you'll need to understand:

✓ **/etc/default/mpathd** file
✓ **/etc/release** file
✓ Fat Network Pipe
✓ **if_mpadm** command
✓ **in.mpathd** daemon
✓ Internet Protocol MultiPathing (IPMP)
✓ Multicast Group
✓ Trunking
✓ Trunking Policies

Concepts you'll need to master:

✓ Explain the purpose, benefits, and limitations of multipathing.
✓ Explain how to configure multipathing by using configuration files and command-line parameters.
✓ Describe the purpose and limitations of trunking, and explain how the four supported trunking policies impact how trunking is implemented.

With the demand for greater bandwidth and higher availability increasing all the time, Sun provides two products that satisfy these demands: IP Multipathing (IPMP), which provides a failover detection and repair facility for network interfaces, and Sun Trunking, which provides increased bandwidth by allowing the aggregation of multiple network interfaces.

Configuring Multipathing

IP multipathing (IPMP) is delivered as part of the Solaris 9 operating environment and provides a failover mechanism for network interfaces, allowing an alternate network interface to dynamically assume the address of a failed interface and handle the network traffic until the failed interface is restored to operational status. IPMP also delivers increased throughput by balancing the load across the interfaces. IPMP has the following features:

➤ *Failure detection*—IPMP detects when a network interface has failed and switches the network access to an alternate network interface. This is called *failover*.

➤ *Repair detection*—In addition to detecting the failure of a network interface, IPMP also detects when a failed network interface has been repaired and is operational again. The network access is restored to the original network interface. This is called *failback*.

➤ *Load balancing*—IPMP provides load balancing of outbound traffic across multiple network interfaces to achieve a higher throughput rate, but network traffic must be going to multiple destinations.

A number of requirements need to be satisfied before IPMP can be used:

➤ You must be running Solaris 8, release 10/00 or later. Even though this book is based on Solaris 9, you might have other systems running earlier versions of the Solaris operating environment. Check the contents of the file /etc/release on your system to confirm the version and release that is installed.

➤ There must be more than one physical network interface installed to allow IPMP to function in a meaningful way. IPMP can be implemented on a system with a single network interface, but this would normally be done to gain extra status information, or to prepare the system for the addition of a second network interface.

➤ A test address must be configured for each network interface that uses IPMP. This address is not used for normal operations, but is used to probe the interface as part of the failure detection facility.

➤ Each interface participating in IPMP must be configured to be a member of the same multicast group.

➤ Each network interface present in the system must be configured with a unique ethernet address. This includes those interfaces that may not be part of the multipathing group.

The in.mpathd Daemon

The in.mpathd daemon process detects both interface failures and when failed interfaces have been repaired. It does this in two ways:

➤ It sends and receives ICMP echo messages (known as *probes*) via the IPMP logical interface to other hosts connected to the network. Five failed probes constitutes a failure and ten consecutive responses constitutes a repaired interface.

➤ It monitors the internal flag IFF_RUNNING on the interface. This flag is defined as part of IP and can be seen when running the ifconfig -a command.

If either of these two methods reports a failure, then the interface can be considered failed. Conversely, both methods have to report the interface as operational before it is marked as repaired.

When the in.mpathd daemon starts up, it reads default information from the file /etc/default/mpathd. This file contains three variables that are used to determine the standard behavior of the daemon. The standard /etc/default/mpathd file that is delivered with Solaris 9 is as follows:

```
#
#pragma ident   "@(#)mpathd.dfl 1.2     00/07/17 SMI"
#
# Time taken by mpathd to detect a NIC failure in ms. The minimum time
# that can be specified is 100 ms.
#
FAILURE_DETECTION_TIME=10000
#
# Failback is enabled by default. To disable failback turn off this option
#
FAILBACK=yes
#
# By default only interfaces configured as part of multipathing groups
# are tracked. Turn off this option to track all network interfaces
# on the system
#
TRACK_INTERFACES_ONLY_WITH_GROUPS=yes
```

The three variables in the above file are

➤ `FAILURE_DETECTION_TIME=10000`—This is the time in milliseconds (10 seconds) that it takes `in.mpathd` to detect an interface failure. It can be tuned as required, higher or lower, but the minimum is 100 milliseconds (0.1 seconds).

➤ `FAILBACK=yes`—This option is enabled by default and allows the automatic failback of a repaired interface. Change this value to "no" if you do not want automatic failback.

➤ `TRACK_INTERFACES_ONLY_WITH_GROUPS=yes`—This option is enabled by default and means that `in.mpathd` monitors only those interfaces that belong to a multicast group. You can change this value to `no` to monitor all network interfaces on the system, but the interfaces must all have unique ethernet addresses.

 The only method of detection to which the **FAILURE_DETECTION_TIME** variable in the **/etc/default/mpathd** file applies is the sending of ICMP messages; it doesn't apply to the monitoring of the **IFF_RUNNING** flag.

As part of the repair detection mechanism, `in.mpathd` continues to send ICMP echo requests to a failed network interface, so that it can determine if it becomes operational again.

A *group failure* is said to have occurred if it appears that all the interfaces in a multipath group fail at the same time, or if none of the hosts respond to the ICMP messages. In this instance, `in.mpathd` flushes its list of hosts to probe and tries to find new targets instead.

 The **in.mpathd** process determines the hosts to probe dynamically; you cannot configure them. Routers are chosen as targets for probing—if there are no routers, nonrouting hosts are arbitrarily chosen. You should ensure there is at least one other system on the network to allow probing to take place.

Using Configuration Files

Configuration files can be used to configure IPMP, which can then be activated on the next system reboot. The `/etc/hostname.<interface>` file needs to be edited for each network interface participating in IP multipathing. `/etc/inet/hosts` should also contain meaningful names so that the interfaces do not have to be referred to by IP addresses.

Each network interface must have a unique address, so if necessary, you will have to assign local addresses to each interface. This was described in

Chapter 1 "Local Area Networks" in the section, "Assigning a Port-Based Ethernet Address."

For this example, assume a system with two network interfaces, hme0 (hostname ultra10, IP address 192.168.28.28) and hme1 (hostname ultra10_1, IP address 192.168.28.30), and the multicast group is called ultra.

The first thing to do is to make note of the current configuration by using the ifconfig -a command as shown in the following example. Do this before making any changes in case you need to restore it.

```
# ifconfig -a
lo0: flags=1000849<UP,LOOPBACK,RUNNING,MULTICAST,IPv4> mtu 8232 index 1
        inet 127.0.0.1 netmask ff000000
hme0: flags=1000843<UP,BROADCAST,RUNNING,MULTICAST,IPv4> mtu 1500 index 2
        inet 192.168.28.28 netmask ffffff00 broadcast 192.168.28.255
        ether 8:0:20:b3:41:53
hme1: flags=1000843<UP,BROADCAST,RUNNING,MULTICAST,IPv4> mtu 1500 index 3
        inet 192.168.28.30 netmask ffffff00 broadcast 192.168.28.255
        ether 8:0:20:b1:40:55
```

To make life easier, add the IP addresses and hostname details to /etc/inet/hosts for each of the logical interfaces that will be used as test addresses. In this example, use ultra10_mp and 192.168.28.29 for hme0, and ultra10_1_mp and 192.168.28.31 for hme1.

To configure IPMP, you need to edit both of the interface configuration files, /etc/hostname.hme0 and /etc/hostname.hme1, so that they look like the following:

```
# cat /etc/hostname.hme0
ultra10 netmask + broadcast + group ultra up \
addif ultra10_mp deprecated netmask + broadcast + -failover up
#
# cat /etc/hostname.hme1
ultra10_1 netmask + broadcast + group ultra up \
addif ultra10_1_mp deprecated netmask + broadcast + -failover up
```

The **deprecated** option means that the interface should not be used for normal operations, and the **-failover** option means that this address is not to be used as a failover when a failed interface is detected. This is only a test address for **in.mpathd** to use for failure and repair detection.

Reboot the system and then run ifconfig -a again to verify that the configuration has been successful:

```
# ifconfig -a
lo0: flags=1000849<UP,LOOPBACK,RUNNING,MULTICAST,IPv4> mtu 8232 index 1
        inet 127.0.0.1 netmask ff000000
hme0: flags=1000843<UP,BROADCAST,RUNNING,MULTICAST,IPv4> mtu 1500 index 2
        inet 192.168.28.28 netmask ffffff00 broadcast 192.168.28.255
        groupname ultra
        ether 8:0:20:b3:41:53
```

```
hme0:1: flags=9040843<UP,BROADCAST,RUNNING,MULTICAST,DEPRECATED,IPv4,
➥NOFAILOVER> mtu 1500 index 2
        inet 192.168.28.29 netmask ffffff00 broadcast 192.168.28.255
hme1: flags=1000843<UP,BROADCAST,RUNNING,MULTICAST,IPv4> mtu 1500 index 3
        inet 192.168.28.30 netmask ffffff00 broadcast 192.168.28.255
        groupname ultra
        ether 8:0:20:b1:40:55
hme1:1: flags=9040843<UP,BROADCAST,RUNNING,MULTICAST,DEPRECATED,IPv4,
➥NOFAILOVER>  mtu 1500 index 3
        inet 192.168.28.31 netmask ffffff00 broadcast 192.168.28. 255
```

Using the Command Line

IPMP can also be configured via the command line, but you should note that, using this method, your changes exist only until the next reboot. To make permanent changes that are persistent across system reboots, edit the configuration files as in the preceding section.

Configuring IPMP from the command line is the same as using the configuration files, except that you don't edit the /etc/hostname.<*interface*> files.

To configure, for example, the hme0 interface, using the same details as in the preceding section, start by making the hme0 interface a member of the multicast group ultra, as follows:

```
# ifconfig hme0 group ultra
```

Now, configure the next logical interface to be the test address.

```
# ifconfig hme0 addif ultra10_mp deprecated netmask + broadcast + \
 -failover up
Created new logical interface hme0:1
Setting netmask of hme0:1 to 255.255.255.0
```

Again, verify the configuration has been successful by running the ifconfig -a command. The results should be identical to the output produced in the previous example.

Managing Multipathing

You can manage network interfaces that have been configured to use IPMP by using the command if_mpadm. There are only two options to this command:

➤ -d—To detach a network interface and place it in an offline state

➤ -r—To re-attach an interface that was previously offline or failed

Consider the scenario in the preceding section, where hme0 and hme1 were both configured to use IPMP.

If you detach the hme0 interface by using if_mpadm -d, which is currently using the IP address 192.168.28.28, the failover mechanism can be seen to work. The output shown here includes the ifconfig -a command to enable you to view the status after the interface has been detached:

```
# if_mpadm -d hme0
Apr 14 13:05:22 ultra10 in.mpathd[4668]: Successfully failed over from NIC
➥ hme0 to NIC hme1
#
# ifconfig -a
lo0: flags=1000849<UP,LOOPBACK,RUNNING,MULTICAST,IPv4> mtu 8232 index 1
        inet 127.0.0.1 netmask ff000000
hme0: flags=1000842<BROADCAST,RUNNING,MULTICAST,IPv4,NOFAILOVER,OFFLINE>
➥ mtu 1500 index 2
        inet 0.0.0.0 netmask ffffff00 broadcast 192.168.28.255
        groupname ultra
        ether 8:0:20:b3:41:53
hme0:1: flags=9040843<BROADCAST,RUNNING,MULTICAST,DEPRECATED,IPv4,
➥NOFAILOVER,OFFLINE>
➥mtu 1500 index 2
        inet 192.168.28.29 netmask ffffff00 broadcast 192.168.28.255
hme1: flags=1000843<UP,BROADCAST,RUNNING,MULTICAST,IPv4> mtu 1500 index 3
        inet 192.168.28.30 netmask ffffff00 broadcast 192.168.28.255
        groupname ultra
        ether 8:0:20:b1:40:55
hme1:1: flags=9040843<UP,BROADCAST,RUNNING,MULTICAST,DEPRECATED,IPv4,
➥NOFAILOVER>
➥ mtu 1500 index 3
        inet 192.168.28.31 netmask ffffff00 broadcast 192.168.28.255
hme1:2: flags=9040843<UP,BROADCAST,RUNNING,MULTICAST,IPv4> \
 mtu 1500 index 3
        inet 192.168.28.28 netmask ffffff00 broadcast 192.168.28.255
```

From the previous code, you can see that

➤ The detached interface hme0 is now showing a status of OFFLINE in the flags= section.

➤ The IP address for the detached hme0 has been set to 0.0.0.0.

➤ The IP address previously used by hme0 (192.168.28.28) has been assigned to a newly created logical interface on hme1.

➤ The logical interface hme1:2 is now taking the network traffic from the detached hme0 interface.

➤ The hme0:1 logical interface remains configured, because in.mpathd needs to be able to continue to probe for repair detection and uses this test address for this purpose.

The following message will be displayed if no interfaces are available for the failover:

Offline failed as there is no other functional interface available in the multipathing group for failing over the network access.

When you re-attach a network interface, using the `if_mpadm -r` command, the configuration performs a failback to the original interface.

Troubleshooting Multipathing

Error messages from IPMP can be found in the `/var/adm/messages` file and, if you're running CDE, the window in which the command was entered.

The following message indicates that IPMP was not set up correctly and that no test address is specified for `in.mpathd` to use for failure and repair detection:

```
Apr 14 14:29:48 ultra10 in.mpathd[354]: [ID 255185 daemon.error]
Failures cannot be detected on hme0 as no IFF_NOFAILOVER address \
is available
```

`in.mpathd` cannot perform any failure detection until a test address is configured for each interface that is to be used with IPMP.

When you have successfully configured a test address, the following message appears in the `/var/adm/messages` file:

```
Apr 14 14:31:08 ultra10 in.mpathd[354]: [ID 490503 daemon.error]
Failure detection restored on hme0 as an IFF_NOFAILOVER address \
is available
```

Always use the `ifconfig -a` command to verify the configuration. This command displays the current status of all network interfaces, including logical interfaces. You can also use this output to see that a failover (or failback) has occurred.

Sun Trunking

The Sun Trunking software is an unbundled product from Sun Microsystems—that is, it is not supplied with the Solaris 9 operating environment and must be purchased separately. Sun Trunking allows you to

➤ Aggregate up to two Sun Quad FastEthernet (qfe) cards (each having four 100Mbps network interfaces) to produce a fat network pipe running at 800Mbps, in full-duplex mode (concurrent bi-directional communication). If a specific network interface fails, then the remaining interfaces continue to operate, taking the additional load from the failed interface.

➤ Aggregate up to two Sun Gigabit Ethernet (ge) cards to produce a fat network pipe running at 2Gbps, in full-duplex mode, between a Sun server and a switch that is Sun Trunking–compatible. If one of the network interfaces fails, then the remaining interface continues to operate, taking the additional load from the failed interface.

Basically, Sun Trunking enables you to combine up to eight 100Mbps network interfaces to act as if you had installed a single 800Mbps network interface, or two Sun gigabit interfaces as if you had installed a single 2Gb network interface. Figure 5.1 shows a server with a traditional 100Mbps network interface connecting to a switch, serving a number of clients, and a server utilizing Sun Trunking connecting to a switch, serving a number of clients at a greatly increased throughput rate.

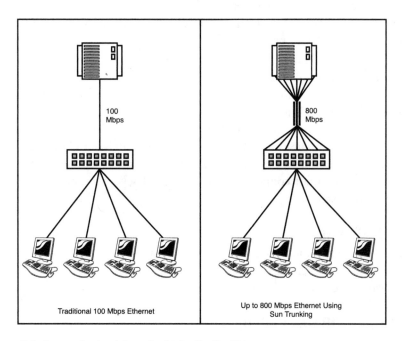

Figure 5.1   Increased network throughput using Sun Trunking.

 A restriction of Sun Trunking with a Quad Fast Ethernet (qfe) card is that the network interfaces cannot be used to boot from the network, to use JumpStart for example.

A further feature of Sun Trunking is that it supports load balancing across the physical interfaces that make up the trunk, or fat pipe. It distributes the network traffic, however, according to a trunking policy, an algorithm that determines the transmission path—a policy is selected by the system administrator when trunking is configured. Sun Trunking supports four trunking policies: MAC, Round robin, IP destination, and IP source/IP destination.

 Sun Trunking supports load balancing on outbound traffic only. There is no load balancing on inbound traffic.

MAC

This is the default policy used for Sun Trunking and the preferred one to use when the interfaces connect to a switch. Remember that the switch must be capable of supporting trunking. This policy uses the last three bits of both the source and destination ethernet addresses to ensure the data is evenly distributed across the available physical interfaces. This policy is the best to use when a large number of clients is being supported.

Round Robin

This policy uses each physical interface of the trunk, in turn, to evenly distribute the traffic. It is the preferred policy to use when a server is connected to another server (that is, not through a switch), which is also known as a *back-to-back* configuration. This policy is ideal for data warehousing, where large amounts of data are transferred between servers, and also for backup servers, where a fast connection is required to back up a number of servers to a central backup server.

IP Destination

This policy uses the four bytes of the destination IP address to determine which physical interface is used for transmission. It is the preferred policy to use when a server has multiple clients that are connected to the same router.

IP Source/IP Destination

This policy is the preferred policy to use if the system is part of a cluster—for example, where multiple logical (or virtual) interfaces are used for a physical interface. The policy uses the four bytes of both the source and destination IP addresses to determine which physical interface is used for transmission. If a failure occurs on a given interface, the logical IP address will failover to a physical interface on a different system in the cluster, providing much higher availability.

Exam Prep Questions

Question 1

How many Sun Quad Fast Ethernet cards can be aggregated to take full advantage of Sun Trunking?

◯ A. 2

◯ B. 4

◯ C. 6

◯ D. 8

Answer A is correct because up to two Sun Quad Fast Ethernet cards can be aggregated to produce a throughput of 800Mbps. Answers B, C, and D are incorrect because these are not valid Sun Trunking configurations.

Question 2

Which file does the **in.mpathd** daemon reference when it starts up?

◯ A. **/etc/default/ipmp.conf**

◯ B. **/etc/default/mpathd**

◯ C. **/etc/inet/mpathd**

◯ D. **/etc/inet/ipmp.conf**

Answer B is correct because the file that `in.mpathd` references on startup is `/etc/default/mpathd`. Answers A, C, and D are incorrect because these filenames do not exist.

Question 3

Which of the following are features of IPMP? Choose 2.

❑ A. Enables network interfaces to failover to an alternate interface

❑ B. Provides outbound load balancing of network traffic when multiple destinations are used

❑ C. Allows up to 8 full-duplex ports on two Sun Quad Fast Ethernet cards to obtain 800Mbps full-duplex throughput

❑ D. Links up to two full-duplex ports on a Sun Gigabit Ethernet Adapter to obtain 2Gbps full-duplex performance between a Sun server and a trunking-enabled switch

Answers A and B are correct because IPMP enables network interfaces to failover to alternate network interfaces, and it also provides outbound load balancing of network traffic when multiple destinations are used. Answers C and D are incorrect because these are features of Sun Trunking.

Question 4

Which of the following conditions would constitute a repaired network inter-face?

- ○ A. Ten consecutive ICMP responses are received from target hosts.
- ○ B. The **IFF_RUNNING** flag returns an operational status.
- ○ C. Five consecutive ICMP responses are received from target hosts.
- ○ D. Ten consecutive ICMP responses are received from target hosts and the **IFF_RUNNING** flag returns an operational status.

Answer D is correct because both of the conditions need to be satisfied to mark an interface as "repaired"—namely, that ten consecutive ICMP responses are received from target hosts and the IFF_RUNNING flag returns an operational status. Answer A is incorrect because although this is one of the conditions that needs to be met, it is insufficient on its own to mark an interface as "repaired." Answer B is incorrect for the same reason. Answer C is incorrect because it is not a condition that can mark an interface as "repaired."

Question 5

Which command creates a test address for the **hme0** interface, to use the IP address **192.168.28.55**, and uses the next available logical interface number?

- ○ A. **ifconfig hme0 addif 192.168.28.55 deprecated netmask + broadcast + -failover up**
- ○ B. **ifconfig hme0:2 192.168.28.55 deprecated netmask + broadcast + -failover up**
- ○ C. **ifconfig hme0 addif 192.168.28.55 netmask + broadcast + up**
- ○ D. **ifconfig hme0 addif 192.168.28.55 deprecated netmask + broadcast + failover up**

Answer A is correct because the command ifconfig hme0 addif 192.168.28.55 deprecated netmask + broadcast + -failover up creates a test address for hme0 that uses the next available logical interface number. Answer B is incorrect because even though this would create a valid test address for hme0, it would not use the next available logical interface number and could destroy and replace an existing logical network interface. Answer C is incorrect because this creates an operational logical interface, not a test address for in.mpathd to use. Answer D is incorrect because this would create a logical address to be used as a failover. The test address cannot be used as a failover.

Question 6

Which of the following are requirements of IPMP to be able to provide a Failover interface in the event of a failure? Choose 3.

❏ A. You must be running Solaris 9 or later.

❏ B. You must be running Solaris 8 10/00 or later.

❏ C. There must be more than one physical network interface installed.

❏ D. Each interface participating in IPMP must belong to the same multicast group.

❏ E. Each interface participating in IPMP must belong to a unique multicast group.

Answers B, C, and D are correct because IPMP requires that you must be running Solaris 8 10/00 or later, there must be more than one physical network interface installed, and each interface participating in IPMP must belong to the same multicast group. Answer A is incorrect because you do not need to be running Solaris 9 to use IPMP—you must be running Solaris 8 10/00 or later. Answer E is incorrect because each interface participating in IPMP must belong to the same multicast group, not a unique one.

Question 7

Which Trunking policy distributes the traffic evenly across the physical interfaces that make up the trunk by using each interface in turn?

○ A. MAC

○ B. Round Robin

○ C. IP Destination

○ D. IP Source / IP Destination

Answer B is correct because the round robin Trunking policy uses each physical interface in turn to evenly distribute the traffic. Answer A is incorrect because this Trunking policy uses the last three bits of the source and destination MAC address to determine the port to use. Answer C is incorrect because this Trunking policy uses the four bytes of the destination IP address to determine the path to take. Answer D is incorrect because this Trunking policy uses the four bytes of both the source and destination IP addresses to determine the path to take.

Question 8

Which option to the **ifconfig** command identifies an interface as a test address?

- ○ A. **deprecated**
- ○ B. **+failover**
- ○ C. **-failover**
- ○ D. **group**

Answer C is correct because the `-failover` option marks an interface as a test address that must not be used as a failover in the case of an interface failing. Answer A is incorrect because the `deprecated` option is used to prevent normal applications from using the interface. Answer B is incorrect because the `+failover` option identifies the interface as a failover address to be used in the event of an interface failing. Answer D is incorrect because the `group` option identifies a multicast group that is assigned to network interfaces participating in a multipathing environment.

Need to Know More?

 Sun Microsystems, *Solaris 9 System Administrator Collection—System Administration Guide*, "IP Services" (Chapters 26 thru 28). Available in printed form, on the Internet at http://docs.sun.com, and from the online documentation provided with the Solaris 9 operating system.

 Sun Microsystems, *System Reference Manual, Section 1M—"System Administration Commands."* Available in printed form, on the Internet at http://docs.sun.com, and from the online documentation provided with the Solaris 9 operating system.

 Sun Microsystems, *Sun Trunking Software Documentation Collection*, "Sun Trunking 1.2.1 Installation and User Guide." Available on the Internet at http://docs.sun.com for download.

 Sun Microsystems, "Sun Trunking 1.2 White Paper," available on the Web at www.sun.com/products/networking/whitepapers/SunTrunkWhPaper_fm.pdf.

6

IPv4 Routing

Terms you'll need to understand:

✓ Classless Interdomain Routing (CIDR)
✓ Default route
✓ Dynamic route
✓ Distance vector routing protocol
✓ IP forwarding
✓ Link-state routing protocol
✓ Router Discovery Protocol (RDISC)
✓ Router Information Protocol (RIP)
✓ Route table
✓ Static route

Concepts you'll need to master:

✓ Explain the purpose and usage of routing types (direct and indirect), routing schemes (static and dynamic), and routing protocol types (autonomous systems, interior routing protocols, and exterior routing protocols).
✓ Given a routing table example, describe table entries, identify the routing table search order, and associate a network name to a network number.
✓ Explain how to configure static and dynamic routing, and the configuration of routing at boot time.
✓ Describe the operation of CIDR.
✓ Given a routing scenario problem, troubleshoot the router configuration and/or network names and select a resolution.

Routing is fundamental to any TCP/IP network because it provides the facility to forward IP datagrams to hosts on a different network. When networks are connected together, there must be a mechanism to route data packets to the other networks. Routing accomplishes this. Routing occurs at the Internet layer of the TCP/IP model.

Routing Types

Solaris uses a memory-based table to store information on how to route packets to different destinations. There are two types of route—direct and indirect:

> ➤ *Direct*—A direct route exists when two (or more) hosts are connected to the same physical network and the two hosts can exchange information without any other device being involved. If you wrote a letter, for example, to your next door neighbor, you would simply deliver the letter to the house; there would be no need to involve the postal system.

> ➤ *Indirect*—An indirect route exists when two (or more) hosts are not connected to the same physical network. For communication to take place, an intermediate device is required that is connected to both the source and destination networks. If you wrote a letter, for example, to a friend in another state, you would use the postal system to deliver the letter because the postal system knows how to get the letter to the destination and can do so efficiently.

The routing table is populated with entries that determine how to forward packets to the destination. The entries can be either static or dynamic, as described here:

> ➤ *Static*—Static routes, as the name implies, are permanent entries in the routing table. These entries can only be removed manually. A number of static routes are added to the route table when a system boots; these are for networks that are directly connected to the installed network interfaces, the multicast address, and the loopback address. You can add other static routes to non-local networks by using the command line, but they do not persist across reboots of the system and have to be added again when the system comes back up. A disadvantage of static routes is that, because of the fixed nature of these routes, communication with the destination host or network can be lost by the failure of the device being used to route the packets.

> *Dynamic*—Dynamic routes, as the name implies, can change depending on information provided by processes such as in.routed and in.rdisc, both of which are discussed later in this chapter. The routing table is updated regularly with information about networks that can be reached—this information is received from other routers advertising known routes on the network. Dynamic routing has the advantage of providing resilience when more than one route exists between two destinations, because if one route becomes inaccessible, the other is used automatically. Using dynamic routing, routers advertise on the network about networks they know about. Other hosts on the network "listen" to these advertisements and update their own routing tables according to the latest information.

Types of Routing Protocol

When describing types of routing protocols, it is first necessary to understand the concept of an *autonomous system*. Autonomous systems are best defined as collections of routers and networks that come under a common administrative control. An autonomous system could comprise an organization, such as a university campus. It is also sometimes called a *routing domain* and is identified by a globally unique 16-bit number—assigned by the Internet Corporation for Assigned Names and Numbers (ICANN). The 16-bit number is often called an Autonomous System Number (ASN). There are two types of routing protocols: interior routing protocol and exterior routing protocol:

> *Interior routing protocol*—Interior routing protocols are used to route packets within an autonomous system, such as the departments of an organization. Two protocols, Routing Information Protocol (RIP) and Open Shortest Path First (OSPF), are the most common examples of IGPs, and have the following characteristics:

> > *Routing Information Protocol (RIP)*—RIP is a distance-vector protocol that uses the number of hops taken to calculate the path to the destination. Using RIP, the entire routing table is passed to the closest neighbor, by default every 30 seconds. The process continues until each node contains the same network information, making it much slower to propagate changes to the route configuration because the entire routing table is transmitted each time a change occurs. RIP works well in smaller networks, but for larger networks, it can greatly increase the network traffic and affect the network's performance.

➤ *Open Shortest Path First (OSPF)*—OSPF is a link-state protocol that maintains a complex knowledge of the network topology. Information concerning the state of the network is exchanged between routers by a link-state advertisement (LSA). OSPF uses other information in addition to hop counts to determine the best route to a destination. A major difference from RIP is that when changes occur, it is not the entire routing table that is sent to other hosts, but only the changed part. As soon as a change is detected, the LSA is triggered, which means that routing tables can be updated to reflect the change more quickly than they would with RIP.

➤ *Exterior routing protocol*—Exterior routing protocols are used to route packets between autonomous systems, such as between organizations or universities. The two main exterior routing protocols are Exterior Gateway Protocol (EGP) and Border Gateway Protocol (BGP):

➤ *Exterior Gateway Protocol (EGP)*—EGP is used to exchange routing table information in a network of autonomous systems. Each router polls its neighbor at regular intervals (approximately every five minutes) and the neighbor's response consists of its entire routing table, which is similar to what happens with RIP. The routing table contains known routers and the addresses that the routers know about. Also included is a cost metric so that the optimal available route can be used to exchange data. The latest version of EGP is EGP-2, although EGP has been largely replaced by the Border Gateway Protocol (BGP) described next.

➤ *Border Gateway Protocol (BGP)*—BGP is a more recent exterior routing protocol than EGP and, like EGP, is used to exchange routing table information between autonomous systems. Like the interior routing protocol OSPF, BGP exchanges only the routing table changes, and not the entire routing table, as EGP does. BGP makes use of Classless InterDomain Addresses (CIDR), which are described later in this chapter and allow more addresses to be assigned within the network than are available with IPv4. The latest version of BGP is BGP-4, which allows the metrics assigned to a route to be configured by the network administrator.

The Routing Table

At the heart of IPv4 routing is the route table, which contains a number of entries detailing how to get to various destinations. The route table is consulted when the exchange of data between two hosts is required. The `netstat -r` command is used to view the entries in the route table. The following example shows the route table for the hostname `ultra10`:

```
ultra10# netstat -r
Routing Table: IPv4
   Destination          Gateway              Flags  Ref   Use   Interface
-------------------- -------------------- ----- ----- ------ ---------
ultra-net            ultra10              U      1    177   hme0
multicast            ultra10              U      1      0   hme0
sparc-net            ultra-r1             UG     1    255   hme0
localhost            localhost            UH     3    635   lo0
```

Notice from this code that the first two columns are displaying names, rather than IP addresses. If you do not want any name resolution to be applied, then use the `-n` option as well. The following example shows the route table without any name resolution for the same host `ultra10`, which has an IP address of `192.168.28.28`:

```
ultra10# netstat -rn
Routing Table: IPv4
   Destination          Gateway              Flags  Ref   Use   Interface
-------------------- -------------------- ----- ----- ------ ---------
192.168.28.0         192.168.28.28        U      1    177   hme0
224.0.0.0            192.168.28.28        U      1      0   hme0
192.168.47.0         192.168.28.1         UG     1    255   hme0
127.0.0.1            127.0.0.1            UH     3    635   lo0
```

The standard behavior of the `netstat -r` command is to display only host, network, and default routes. To see all route table entries, including broadcast and local entries, use the `-a` option. The following example lists all routing entries, without any name resolution, for the same host:

```
# netstat -arn
Routing Table: IPv4
   Destination          Gateway              Flags  Ref   Use   Interface
-------------------- -------------------- ----- ----- ------ ---------
192.168.28.0         192.168.28.28        U      1     69   hme0
224.0.0.0            192.168.28.28        U      1      0   hme0
default              192.168.28.28        UG     1      0
0.0.0.0              192.168.28.28        UHB    1      0   hme0
0.0.0.0              192.168.28.28        UHB    1      0   hme0
192.168.28.19        --                   UHA    2     79   hme0
192.168.28.28        --                   UHL    5   1874   hme0
192.168.28.25        --                   UHA    1      1   hme0
192.168.28.0         192.168.28.28        UHB    1      0   hme0
192.168.28.0         192.168.28.28        UHB    1      0   hme0
192.168.28.255       192.168.28.28        UHB    1     29   hme0
192.168.28.255       192.168.28.28        UHB    1      0   hme0
255.255.255.255      192.168.28.28        UHB    1      0   hme0
255.255.255.255      192.168.28.28        UHB    1      0   hme0
127.0.0.1            127.0.0.1            UH     3     10   lo0
```

The output from the `netstat -r` command contains several fields, which are described as follows:

➤ *Destination*—The destination host or network.

➤ *Gateway*—The host or router that is being used to deliver data to an indirectly connected destination. When this field displays ‐‐, then the destination is on the same physical network and therefore a direct route is already known.

➤ *Flags*—The status of the route and some characteristics of the route. Valid values for this item are as follows:

➤ *D*—Denotes a route that was dynamically created by an ICMP redirect.

➤ *G*—Denotes that the route is to a gateway.

➤ *H*—Denotes that the route is to a host rather than a network.

➤ *U*—Denotes that the route is up and available.

If the `-a` option to `netstat` was used, then some additional flags are also displayed, which can be any of the following:

➤ *A*—Denotes combined routing and address resolution entries.

➤ *B*—Denotes a broadcast entry.

➤ *L*—Denotes a local address.

➤ *Ref*—This field shows the number of routes that use this network interface.

➤ *Use*—The number of packets that have used this route.

➤ *Interface*—The network interface that is used on the outgoing path to the destination host or network.

When you try to contact another system, whether it is on the local network or remote, the routing algorithm carries out a search of the route table in a specific order:

1. The local network is first checked for a match to see whether the destination host is directly connected. If a successful match is found, then the data is passed through the local network interface for delivery.

2. The route table is checked to see whether there is an IP address match in the destination field. If a successful match is found, the data is forwarded to the IP address designated in the gateway field for that route.

3. The route table is checked to see whether there is a network number match in the destination field. If a successful match is found, the data is

forwarded to the router that is associated with the route. This is not the final destination, so the router will have to forward the data on to either the destination network or another router.

4. The route table is checked to see whether a default route entry is present. If the entry exists, then the data is passed to this address for delivery.

5. No route has been found for the data, so an appropriate ICMP message is returned, such as `Destination network is unreachable`.

The **/etc/inet/networks** File

The `/etc/inet/networks` file is used to associate network numbers with network names, similar to the `/etc/inet/hosts` file that associates host IP addresses to hostnames. It is a convenient way to refer to networks by a familiar name, instead of remembering numerous IP addresses. The following is a sample `/etc/inet/networks` file:

```
ultra10# cat /etc/inet/networks
ultra-net       192.168.28.0
tech-net        192.168.42.0
sysadmin-net    192.168.66.0
market-net      192.168.145.0
```

If you need to add static routes to the routing table, then using this file enables you to use the familiar names—instead of the IP addresses—to add the route entries.

The file **/etc/networks** is a symbolic link to **/etc/inet/networks** and is included for BSD compatibility. The actual file is **/etc/inet/networks**, so be aware of this because it is a frequent exam question.

Static Route Configuration

Static routes are permanent entries that do not change. They can be configured in two ways: manually by using the `route` command, or through the use of two configuration files, `/etc/defaultrouter` and `/etc/gateways`. This section covers the use of the `route` command. The configuration files are discussed later in this chapter.

The **route** Command

The route command is used to manipulate the routing table manually. Routes can be added, deleted, and changed with this command. The general format of the route command is

```
route add | delete | change <destination> <gateway>
```

where *<destination>* is the host or network you are trying to reach and *<gateway>* is the router that will forward the packet to the destination.

The routing table can be flushed of all entries if you use the **route** command with the **flush** option as follows:

```
ultra10# route flush
```

The same can also be achieved by adding the **-f** option to the **route** command.

Figure 6.1 shows a sample configuration with three networks, connected through the use of two routers, which are used here to illustrate static routes.

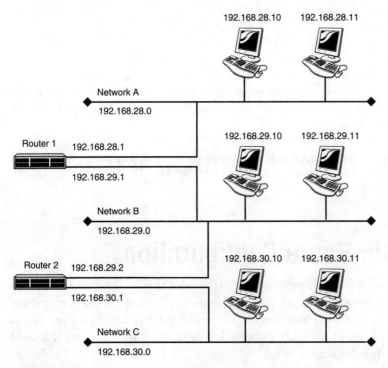

Figure 6.1 A sample network configuration using routers.

Notice that the hosts on network A can communicate with hosts on network B or network C, only if they use router 1 as an intermediate gateway. The connection to network C is not so apparent because it relies on router 1 forwarding data to router 2—that is, it would take three hops for a host on network A to communicate with a host on network C, namely host on network A to router 1, router 1 to router 2, and router 2 to host on network C.

Also, the hosts on network B can communicate with hosts on network A only if they use router 1 as an intermediate gateway. Similarly, the hosts on network B can communicate with hosts on network C only if they use router 2 as an intermediate gateway.

If a host were to be added to network B, for example, then a static route would be added for both network A and network C, using router 1 and router 2 as gateways, respectively. The commands to add these routes would be

```
ultra10# route add 192.168.28.0 192.168.29.1
add net 192.168.28.0: gateway 192.168.29.1
ultra10# route add 192.168.30.0 192.168.29.2
add net 192.168.30.0: gateway 192.168.29.2
```

When a host on network B sends a packet to a host on network A for example, it is passed to the router interface 192.168.29.1 for delivery. If the same host on network B sends a packet to a host on network C, it is passed to the router interface 192.168.29.2 for delivery.

To delete the route to the network 192.168.30.0, enter the following command:

```
ultra10# route delete 192.168.30.0 192.168.29.2
delete net 192.168.30.0: gateway 192.168.29.2
```

If the route to network A changes from 192.168.29.1 to 192.168.29.55, for example, enter the following command to modify the route:

```
ultra10# route change 192.168.28.0 192.168.29.55
change net 192.168.28.0: gateway 192.168.29.55
```

For hosts on network A, all communications will pass through router 1, using the IP address 192.168.28.1, so it would be easier to create a default route as follows:

```
ultra10# route add default 192.168.28.1
add net default: gateway 192.168.28.1
```

Static routes created with the **route** command at the command line are permanent entries, but do not exist across reboots of the system. If static routes are required to persist across reboots, then use the configuration files **/etc/defaultrouter** (for a default static route) or **/etc/gateways** (for other static routes). Alternatively, create a startup script containing the **route** commands, which will be executed each time the system reboots.

The route monitor command can be used see any changes that are made to the routing table. When you run this command, it informs you straight away of the changes. The following example code shows the addition and subsequent deletion of a route.

```
ultra10# route monitor
got message of size 124
RTM_ADD: Add Route: len 124, pid: 368, seq 1, errno 0, flags:<UP,GATEWAY, \
DONE,STATIC>
locks:  inits:
sockaddrs: <DST,GATEWAY,NETMASK>
 192.168.28.0 192.168.29.1 255.255.255.0
got message of size 124
RTM_DELETE: Delete Route: len 124, pid: 369, seq 1, errno 0, flags:<UP, \
GATEWAY,DONE,STATIC>
locks:  inits:
sockaddrs: <DST,GATEWAY,NETMASK>
 192.168.28.0 192.168.29.1 255.255.255.0
```

The manipulation of routing table entries can become quite complex when you have to deal with numerous IP addresses. A simpler way of doing this is to use the /etc/inet/networks file to assign names to the networks and the /etc/inet/hosts file to assign names to the router interfaces.

In the previous examples, you could add the following entries to /etc/inet/networks:

```
networkA     192.168.28.0
networkB     192.168.29.0
networkC     192.168.30.0
```

and add the following entries to /etc/inet/hosts:

```
192.168.28.1     routerA
192.168.29.1     routerBtoA
192.168.29.2     routerBtoC
192.168.30.1     routerC
```

Now, to add the route from a host on network B to any host on network A, use the following route command:

```
ultra10# route add networkA routerBtoA
add net networkA: gateway routerBtoA
```

Configuration Files

Two configuration files can be used to assign static routes: /etc/defaultrouter and /etc/gateways. Both of these files are described in this section:

➤ /etc/defaultrouter—This file normally contains a single IP address or hostname that identifies the default path that data should take when being transmitted across the network. The default route is used when no other specific route is identified for the destination. Hostnames can be used only if the relevant entry exists in the /etc/inet/hosts file. Although this file usually contains only one entry, multiple entries are permitted, one per line.

The use of default routes has some distinct advantages. These are

➤ The existence of the /etc/defaultrouter file stops the routing daemon (in.routed) and the dynamic router discovery daemon (in.rdisc) from starting when the system is booting. The startup script /etc/rc2.d/S69inet contains the check for the existence of the /etc/defaultrouter file.

➤ Using a single default route entry reduces the processing overhead because the routing table is smaller.

➤ Using multiple default route entries adds some resilience so that a potential single point of failure is avoided.

The use of default routes, however, has a few disadvantages, too:

➤ When using a single default route entry, a single point of failure is created, impacting the network connectivity if the default router becomes unavailable.

➤ The /etc/defaultrouter file must be present on every system. You can't use a naming service to manage this file centrally because it is read during the system startup process, before any naming service processes are running. On larger networks that change frequently, management of /etc/defaultrouter can incur a significant administration overhead.

➤ /etc/gateways—This file is an optional file that is read at system startup when the routing daemon (in.routed) starts up. It provides an alternative way of adding static routes. Each entry in the /etc/gateways file has the following format:

```
net | host <destination> gateway <gateway> metric <hopcount>
➥passive | active
```

The fields are described here:

➤ net | host—Using either net or host will identify whether the route is to a specific host or to a network. This precedes the address or name or the destination host or network.

➤ <destination>—The IP address, (or hostname or network name) of the destination, either a host or a network.

➤ gateway—This precedes the address, or name, of the gateway to be used.

➤ <gateway>—The IP address or hostname or the router to be used as the gateway.

➤ metric—This precedes the <hopcount> value.

➤ <hopcount>—The number of hops taken to reach the destination.

➤ passive | active—Use either passive for a static route or active for a dynamic route.

A typical entry for the /etc/gateways file that adds a static route to the network networkA via the router routerA, which takes two hops, is shown here:

```
net networkA gateway routerA metric 2 passive
```

Dynamic Route Configuration

Dynamic routing, in contrast to static routing, is where routing information is exchanged with other routers on the network. Entries in the routing table can change dynamically depending on the current status of the network. The protocols that are bundled with the Solaris 9 operating environment are Routing Information Protocol (RIP) versions 1 and 2 as well as the Router Discovery Protocol (RDISC).

Routing Information Protocol Version 1 (RIPv1)

RIP is a *distance vector protocol*, where the best route to use is calculated by the fewest hops taken to reach the destination. Each hop denotes a point where another router is used to forward a packet. The *hopcount* refers to the total number of hops taken to reach the final destination.

A number of routes might be available to use between two hosts, but RIP will keep a record of only the one that takes the fewest hops to reach. The dynamic nature of this protocol means that if an intermediate router becomes unavailable, then the best route can be modified to use the next best route.

RIP employs a number of features that help it cope with quickly changing networks:

➤ *Maximum hopcount*—RIP has a limit of 15 hops to prevent data traveling around the network endlessly. As a data packet traverses the network, the hopcount is incremented each time it passes through a router. If this value reaches 16 or more, the host is deemed unreachable.

➤ *Hold down timers*—When a router receives information about a failed router, a *hold down timer* starts. This prevents the receipt of further updates, which could result in an inconsistent network state. The time delay allows the network to stabilize with the new information before it calculates a new best route. It also allows the failed router time to recover. If a router has not yet received the failed router update, it continues to advertise the router as operational; the hold down timer prevents these invalid updates from being acted upon.

➤ *Split horizons*—This feature prevents a router from sending an update back to the same place it just came from. For example, if router A sends an update to router B, router B is prevented from advertising the information back to router A. Without this feature, two routers could become involved in an endless loop of information exchange.

➤ *Update triggers*—When a change to the network occurs, either because a new route has been found or an existing route has become unavailable, a router advertises this information immediately instead of waiting for the next scheduled advertisement—by default every 30 seconds.

➤ *Route poisoning*—When a route becomes unavailable, an update is triggered by the router to advertise the route with a hopcount of 16. This advertises the route as unreachable, making the other routers remove the route entry from the route table. In this way the failed route will not be used.

The Routing Daemon

The daemon process that manages routing in Solaris 9 is called `in.routed`. It is started at boot time by the startup script `/etc/rc2.d/S69inet` (which is a hard link to `/etc/init.d/inetinit`). Both routers and non-routers can run the `in.routed` process: Routers advertise their routing table entries to other hosts every 30 seconds, whereas non-routers learn the available routes by accessing the advertisements provided by other routers on the network.

 The time interval of 30 seconds between router advertisements is fixed and cannot be configured by the administrator.

The following are the most popular options for running this daemon:

➤ `-q`—Runs the daemon in "quiet" mode. Non-routers use this option to prevent the routing table from being advertised.

➤ `-s`—Runs the daemon in "speaking" mode, so that the routing table is broadcast (advertised) to other hosts every 30 seconds. This is the option a router uses.

➤ `-t`—Used in conjunction with the `-q` or `-s` options, this option causes all actions to be logged to the standard output. The following command starts the daemon process on a router and logs all activity to standard output.

```
ultra10# /usr/sbin/in.routed -s -t
```

➤ `-v <logfile>`—Used to log (with a timestamp) changes made to the routing table. The `<logfile>` location must also be entered. The following command starts the daemon process on a router and logs all changes to the file `/var/log/route.log`:

```
ultra10# /usr/sbin/in.routed -v /var/log/route.log
```

 When running the routing daemon, **in.routed**, with the **-v** option, the logfile that is specified must be created. The process does not automatically create it.

 The **in.routed** process is started at boot time only if the files **/etc/defaultrouter** and **/etc/notrouter** are not present. The **/etc/notrouter** file is used to prevent a system with more than one network interface card from being treated as a router automatically.

Router Discover Protocol (RDISC)

The RDISC protocol is used to provide default routes between a host and the routers on the network. The daemon process that is run to discover routers is `in.rdisc`. In a similar way to `in.routed`, `in.rdisc` has two forms of execution: one for routers and one for non-routers. A router advertises its presence on the network every 10 minutes (600 seconds) by default using the local multicast address (`224.0.0.1`), although this value can be changed. A non-router listens to the advertisements and populates its routing table with the default route entries for each router. The `in.rdisc` process is started from the startup script `/etc/rc2.d/S69inet`, only if the following conditions are satisfied:

➤ The system has multiple network interfaces configured.

➤ The files `/etc/defaultrouter` and `/etc/notrouter` are not present.

➤ The network interfaces are not being managed by the Dynamic Host Configuration Protocol (DHCP).

There are several advantages in using RDISC:

➤ Resilience can be added to the network because of the existence of multiple default routes.

➤ The default routes remove the need for multiple, often unnecessary, route entries, creating a smaller route table.

➤ RDISC is not tied to any particular routing protocol, such as RIP; it is independent.

➤ RDISC uses a multicast address rather than a broadcast address, resulting in less network traffic.

Routers running the RDISC protocol still need to run a routing protocol, such as RIP. RDISC only provides a default route from a host to a router; it does not advertise between routers as a routing protocol does.

A non-router runs the `in.rdisc` process with the `-s` option to request information from routers on the network, as shown here:

```
ultra10# /usr/sbin/in.rdisc -s
```

A router uses the `-r` option to the `in.rdisc` command to cause it to advertise its presence on the network every 600 seconds by default. You can modify the interval by using the -T option. To start in.rdisc as a router and change the interval to 60 seconds (every minute), enter the following command:

```
ultra10# /usr/sbin/in.rdisc -r -T 60
```

Configuring a Router on a Running System

The decision to start the routing daemon in.routed and the router discovery protocol daemon in.rdisc is taken when the startup script /etc/rc2.d/S69inet executes. You can also configure your system to act as a router without needing to reboot.

To configure a system as a router, it must have multiple network interfaces connected and configured.

Follow these steps to configure your system as a router:

1. Be sure the files /etc/defaultrouter and /etc/notrouter do not exist. If they do, remove them. Also, make sure that all network interfaces are correctly configured and have entries present in the /etc/inet/hosts file.

2. You need to enable the forwarding of IP packets, which is done using the ndd command. You can enable IP forwarding on all network interfaces or just a specific interface. To enable IP forwarding on all the network interfaces, enter the following:

```
ultra10# ndd -set /dev/ip ip_forwarding 1
```

Setting the value of the ip_forwarding parameter to 1 enables forwarding, and setting it to 0 disables it.

To enable IP forwarding on only a specific network interface, such as hme0, enter the following:

```
ultra10# ndd -set /dev/ip hme0:ip_forwarding 1
```

3. Stop and restart the in.routed process, if it is running, as follows:

```
ultra10# pkill in.routed; /usr/sbin/in.routed -s
```

4. Stop and restart the `in.rdisc` process, if it is running, as follows:

```
ultra10# pkill in.rdisc; /usr/sbin/in.rdisc -r
```

> You might also want to disable routing on a system with multiple network interfaces, which is often called a *multihomed host*. A system with multiple interfaces is automatically considered to be a router at boot time unless the file **/etc/notrouter** exists. To stop a system from functioning as a router, simply disable the **ip_forwarding** network parameter by setting it to **0**, using the **ndd** command, and then create the file **/etc/notrouter** as follows:
>
> ```
> ultra10# ndd -set /dev/ip ip_forwarding 0
> ultra10# touch /etc/notrouter
> ```
>
> When the system reboots, it will not function as a router.

Classless InterDomain Routing (CIDR)

Classless InterDomain Routing, or CIDR, is a way of grouping networks together for routing purposes across the Internet between domains. With the IPv4 address space running out, CIDR makes much more effective use of the available addresses. CIDR is also known as *supernetting*, where a number of network addresses are treated as a single address (as opposed to *subnetting*, where a single network address is divided into smaller networks).

CIDR works by using classless addresses, unlike IPv4, which uses classful addressing. For routing purposes, a single classless address can represent an aggregation of networks (in the same way that the telephone system uses area codes). A CIDR network address looks like this:

```
192.15.145.0/18
```

where `192.15.145.0` represents the network address itself and the `18` shows that the first 18 bits of the address are the network part of the address. The remaining 14 bits of the 32-bit IPv4 address are for specific host addresses.

CIDR uses netmasks—which are referred to as *network prefixes*—to create various network sizes, similar to the way that subnetworking uses network masks. The 18-bit network portion shown earlier is equivalent to a netmask of `255.255.192.0`.

Troubleshooting Routing

Routing problems are notoriously difficult to resolve, particularly when routers that are external to your organization—such as on the Internet—are used. As an administrator, though, you can verify that your configuration has been set up correctly and also demonstrate that the routers within your organization are working as expected. This section outlines some of the utilities that can be used, such as ping, netstat, and traceroute.

Verifying the Configuration

You should confirm that the system being used as a router is configured correctly. Start by running the ifconfig -a command to verify that the network interfaces have been configured correctly. If the interfaces are marked UP and RUNNING, then also check the IP addresses, the network masks, and the broadcast addresses. If the network mask is incorrectly set, the broadcast address will also be wrong. You can rectify this by checking the /etc/inet/netmasks file.

You should also verify that the /etc/inet/hosts and /etc/inet/networks files contain the correct IP addresses and names, as well as the contents of each network interface configuration file—that is, those files starting with /etc/hostname.<xxx>, where <xxx> represents the specific interface.

ping

The ping command is extremely useful for testing the reachability of other hosts on the network. Use this command to check that you can reach another system on the local network—this demonstrates connectivity to the network. You should also ping the default gateway. If this fails, then the default gateway could be down, but also check the /etc/defaultrouter file to make sure you have entered the correct IP address or hostname.

netstat

The netstat command is used with the -r option to view the routing table entries. It is often preferable, when diagnosing problems, to use the netstat -rn command, so that only IP addresses are displayed, rather than host and network names.

traceroute

Use the traceroute command to follow the path to the remote host you are trying to reach. The traceroute command sends three probes at 5-second intervals to each router that is encountered along the path. If any of these return asterisks, then it means there has been no response from the router, which can assist greatly with identifying where the problem is located. The following example traceroute output shown demonstrates a problem:

```
ultra10# traceroute www.mobile-ventures.net
Tracing route to mobile-ventures.net [209.67.50.203]
over a maximum of 30 hops:

   1     9 ms      8 ms      8 ms   10.25.0.1
   2    13 ms      8 ms      8 ms   gsr01-st.blueyonder.co.uk [62.30.65.1]
   3    12 ms     12 ms     12 ms   172.18.6.69
   4    13 ms     14 ms     12 ms   tele1-azt-pos.telewest.net [194.117.136.2]
   5    13 ms     13 ms     12 ms   pos50402hsd-gsr2-linx.cableinet.net
  ➥[194.117.154.190]
   6    12 ms     12 ms     11 ms   zcr1-so-5-0-0.London1nt.cw.net
  ➥[166.63.222.37]
   7    85 ms     83 ms     85 ms   *    *    *
   8    80 ms     78 ms     80 ms   *    *    *
...
```

This output demonstrates that the trace was successful through the routers provided in the U.K. by my ISP (entries 1 thru 6) and that the problem occurs when the next router following the international gateway in London is probed (entry 7). This information could be useful to the ISP if you raise a trouble ticket to report the problem, but it clearly shows that the problem is not on your own local network.

Exam Prep Questions

Question 1

> Which file is used to associate network names with network numbers?
>
> ○ A. **/etc/inet/hosts**
>
> ○ B. **/etc/inet/netmasks**
>
> ○ C. **/etc/inet/networks**
>
> ○ D. **/etc/defaultrouter**

Answer C is correct because /etc/inet/networks is the file used to associate network names with network numbers. Answer A is incorrect because /etc/inet/hosts is used to map IP addresses to hostnames. Answer B is incorrect because /etc/inet/netmasks is used to associate IPv4 network masks with IPv4 network numbers. Answer D is incorrect because /etc/defaultrouter is the file that contains the hostname or IP address of the default gateway.

Question 2

> If host A has an IP address of **192.168.28.28** and host B has an IP address of **192.168.28.12**, which type of routing takes place when host A sends an IP datagram to host B?
>
> ○ A. Static route
>
> ○ B. Dynamic route
>
> ○ C. Indirect route
>
> ○ D. Direct route

Answer D is correct because the two hosts are on the same physical network, so a direct route is used. Answers A and B are incorrect because static and dynamic routes are entries in the routing table, not routing types. Answer C is incorrect because an indirect route is used when the two hosts are on different physical networks, connected via a router.

Question 3

Your system is a non-router and you want to receive advertisement messages from other routers to determine the default routes. Which command would run the correct daemon process to do this?

○ A. **/usr/sbin/in.rdisc -r**

○ B. **/usr/sbin/in.rdisc -s**

○ C. **/usr/sbin/in.routed -q**

○ D. **/usr/sbin/in.routed -s**

Answer B is correct because the in.rdisc -s command would be used by a non-router to request information from other routers on the network about default routes. Answer A is incorrect because in.rdisc -r is the command that a router would run to advertise its presence on the network every 10 minutes. Answers C and D are incorrect because the in.routed command starts the routing daemon, but does not contain information about default routes.

Question 4

The Routing Information Protocol (RIP) uses a feature that advertises a failed route with a hop count of 16 to stop other systems from trying to use an unavailable route. What is this feature called?

○ A. Route poisoning

○ B. Split horizons

○ C. Hopcount limit

○ D. Update triggers

Answer A is correct because route poisoning is a feature that advertises a failed route with a hopcount of 16 to mark it as unreachable. This prevents other systems on the network from trying to use the failed route. Answer B is incorrect because split horizons is a feature that prevents a router from sending an advertisement back to the router from which the information came. This prevents routing loops between two systems. Answer C is incorrect because the hopcount limit feature sets a limit of 15 hops to stop continuous routing loops, but is not used to stop other systems from trying to use a specific route. Any route that contains a hopcount greater than 15 is deemed to be unreachable. This feature is used by route poisoning to force a route to breach the hopcount limit. Answer D is incorrect because update triggers is a feature that allows routing changes to be propagated quickly throughout the network, without waiting for the next scheduled advertisement.

Question 5

> Which command would manually add a default route by using the gateway named **gate01** as the router?
>
> ○ A. **route add gate01 default**
> ○ B. **route add default gate01**
> ○ C. **route default gate01**
> ○ D. **route default add gate01**

Answer B is correct because the correct command to add a default route that uses the host named `gate01` as the gateway is `route add default gate01`. Answers A, C, and D are incorrect because the syntax is incorrect for the `route` command.

Question 6

> Which of the following are interior gateway protocols? Choose 2.
>
> ❑ A. RIP
> ❑ B. EGP
> ❑ C. BGP
> ❑ D. OSPF

Answers A and D are correct because both the Routing Information Protocol (RIP) and the Open Shortest Path First (OSPF) are interior gateway protocols that are used to exchange routing information between IP routers within an autonomous system. Answers B and C are incorrect because the Exterior Gateway Protocol (EGP) and Border Gateway Protocol (BGP) are examples of exterior gateway protocols that exchange routing information between autonomous systems.

Question 7

If you are having trouble communicating with a remote host, which command would you use to follow the path taken to reach the host?

O A. **ping**

O B. **netstat**

O C. **traceroute**

O D. **ifconfig -a**

Answer C is correct because the traceroute command is used to follow the path taken to reach a specified remote host. Answer A is incorrect because the ping command is used to verify that a remote host is responding to communications, but does not trace the path taken to reach the remote host. Answer B is incorrect because the netstat command is used to provide network statistics. Answer D is incorrect because the ifconfig -a command is used to verify the network interface configuration.

Question 8

What command do you use to see any changes that are made to the routing table immediately?

O A. **route monitor**

O B. **netstat -r**

O C. **route change**

O D. **route flush**

Answer A is correct because the route monitor command is used to see changes made to the routing table immediately. Answer B is incorrect because the netstat -r command is used to view the routing table entries at a point in time; it does not show any subsequent updates to the routing table unless the command is run again. Answer C is incorrect because the route change command is used to modify a route entry. Answer D is incorrect because the route flush command is used to flush (delete) all routing entries from the routing table.

Need to Know More?

 Douglas Comer, *Internetworking with TCP/IP: Principles, Protocols and Architecture*. Prentice Hall, 2000.

 Malhotra, Ravi, *IP Routing*. (O'Reilly, 2002.)

 Sun Microsystems, *Solaris 9 System Administrator Collection—System Administration Guide: IP Services*. Available in printed form, on the Internet at http://docs.sun.com, and from the online documentation provided with the Solaris 9 operating system.

 Sun Microsystems, *System Reference Manual, Section 1M, System Administration Commands*. Available in printed form, on the Internet at http://docs.sun.com, and from the online documentation provided with the Solaris 9 operating system.

Basic IPv6

Terms you'll need to understand:

✓ Autoconfiguration
✓ Duplicate
✓ Interface Identifier
✓ **in.ndpd** Process
✓ **in.ripngd** Process
✓ Neighbor Discovery Protocol (NDP)
✓ Scope bits
✓ **/etc/hostname6.<*interface*>** File
✓ **/etc/inet/ipnodes** File

Concepts you'll need to master:

✓ Identify the purpose, features, and functionalities for different types of unicast, multicast, and anycast addressing, and auto-configuration as they relate to IPv6 addressing.
✓ Explain how to configure IPv6 on a router and non-router.

IPv6 is the latest version of the Internet Protocol (IP) that will eventually replace the current version of IP, IPv4. In the intervening years, both versions co-exist to make the transition easier. This chapter introduces the basics of IPv6, its features, the addressing types and structure, and how to implement IPv6.

IPv6 Features

IPv6 has added many new features, which together enhance the performance, security, and address space of the Internet protocol. The main features of IPv6 are

➤ *Extended address space*—The IP address size in IPv6 has increased to 128 bits compared to the 32-bit address in IPv4. As the number of available IPv4 addresses are becoming exhausted, IPv6 provides a vast increase in the number of addresses available.

➤ *Improved routing*—A simplified header in IPv6 reduces the routing complexity, increasing the performance of routers. Additionally, the inclusion of scope bits in multicast addresses improves routing by determining how far a multicast IP datagram is routed.

➤ *Simplified header format*—The number of fields in the IPv6 datagram header has been reduced, making the header section of the IPv6 datagram easier to inspect and hence, more efficient.

➤ *Autoconfiguration*—IPv6 includes the facility to assign IPv6 addresses automatically to interfaces and devices. Using IPv4, this is a manual process. Of course, the name-to-IPv6 address mapping still has to be done by the administrator, but a different file is used—`/etc/inet/ipnodes`. Note that `/etc/inet/ipnodes` can also be used in a naming service, such as NIS+ (ipnodes table), NIS (ipnodes map) or any other supported naming service. The file can also hold both IPv4 and IPv6 addresses.

➤ *Enhancements to header options*—Extension headers have been introduced in IPv6, which allow additional options to be specified, such as security authentication or special routing instructions, for example. They are not part of the IPv6 datagram header, so they can be added without affecting the router performance.

➤ *Enhanced security*—This feature is not yet implemented in Solaris 9, but will include an authentication header for authentication and an encapsulation security payload for privacy.

➤ *Quality of service*—IPv6 enables important data to be delivered more quickly with an enhanced priority. A "Flow Label" field in the IPv6 header enables the sender to request special handling of the data.

➤ *Anycast addresses*—IPv6 includes an extra address type, the *anycast* address. Similar to the multicast address where the communication is with a number of hosts that belong to the same group, an anycast address represents communication with a number of hosts belonging to the same group, but sends it to only the nearest member, not all the members.

IPv6 Addressing

IPv6 addresses are 128 bits long and, like IPv4, use three types of addresses, but they are not the same three types. IPv6 uses the following basic address types:

➤ *Unicast*—A unique address is assigned to a network interface, which communicates with a single host on the network.

➤ *Multicast*—A unique address is assigned to a group of systems. A message is sent from one host to all hosts that have the address assigned.

➤ *Anycast*—A unique address is assigned to a group of systems, but a message sent from one host is delivered to only the nearest host that has the address assigned, unlike the multicast address type, in which all hosts that have the address receive the message.

IPv6 does not use the broadcast address type as IPv4 does. With IPv6, a physical network interface can be assigned several types of IPv6 addresses. This is an important difference from IPv4. Remember also that IPv6 has introduced the anycast address type, which is not present in IPv4.

How IPv6 Addresses Are Represented

Each IPv6 address is divided into 8 octets, each consisting of 16 bits. An IPv6 address is written in hexadecimal, with each octet being separated by the colon (:) character. The general format is

```
nnnn:nnnn:nnnn:nnnn:nnnn:nnnn:nnnn:nnnn
```

where each nnnn group of characters represents four hexadecimal digits (16 bits). An example of an IPv6 address is

```
fe80:0000:0000:0000:0a00:20ff:feb3:4153
```

An IPv6 address can be written a number of ways because consecutive zeros can be shortened. The preceding address can be written in these ways:

➤ The standard way of representing an IPv6 address:

```
fe80:0000:0000:0000:0a00:20ff:feb3:4153
```

➤ Groups of 16-bits consisting of all zeros can be shortened to a single zero:

```
fe80:0:0:0:0a00:20ff:feb3:4153
```

➤ Groups of 16 bits consisting of all zeros can be compressed using a double colon (::) character:

```
fe80::0a00:20ff:feb3:4153
```

 The double colon (::) character that is used to compress 16-bit groups consisting of all zeros can be used only once in an IPv6 address. It is quite common to get a question on the exam that provides a number of IPv6 addresses and asks which ones are valid. For example, you might see something like the following IPv6 address:

```
fe80::0a::20ff:feb3:4153
```

This address is invalid because it uses the double colon (::) character twice in the address representation.

Format Prefixes (FP)

A format prefix at the beginning of each IPv6 address specifies the type of IPv6 address that is being used. Table 7.1 identifies some of the common format prefixes in use.

Table 7.1 Common IPv6 Format Prefixes		
Format Prefix (Binary)	**Format Prefix (Hexadecimal)**	**Address Type**
0000 0000	0	Reserved
1111 1111	FF	Multicast
001	2	Aggregatable global unicast
1111 1110 10	FE8	Link-local unicast
1111 1110 11	FEC	Site-local unicast

 Notice that the anycast address type is not included in Table 7.1. Anycast addresses are allocated from the unicast address space.

You might also see an IPv6 address written as follows:

`fe80:0000:0000:0000:0a00:20ff:feb3:4153/10`

The /10 at the end of the address signifies that 10 bits have been used to identify the address type. This is the format prefix, also known as the IPv6 subnet prefix. As you can see from Table 7.1, the address starts with fe8 and is a
unicast link-local address. When an address is specified with the format prefix attached, it is known as *prefix notation*.

Unicast Addresses

The unicast address type is used to send IP datagrams to a single host, or
interface. A number of unicast address types that each serve a particular purpose are described in the following sections.

Link-Local

The link-local address is intended to be used only on local network links;
that is, a system using this kind of address can send IPv6 datagrams only to
another system on the same physical network. A router will not forward this
type of packet onto another network.

Site-Local

The site-local address is very similar to the link-local address, but can be forwarded (routed) through an internal intranet. The limit for this kind of
address is the site rather than the same physical network.

Aggregatable Global

The aggregatable global address type is used for global communications,
such as across the Internet. Aggregatable global addresses contain a hierarchical structure of identifiers, as follows:

➤ *The format prefix*—A 3-bit field that identifies the address type as aggregatable global and is set to 001 hexadecimal.

➤ *A top-level aggregator (TLA)*—A 13-bit number that identifies the
Internet authority that assigned the next-level aggregator—the Internet
Assigned Numbers Authority (IANA), for example.

➤ *A next-level aggregator (NLA)*—A 32-bit number that is assigned to an
organization, normally by an Internet service provider (ISP).

➤ *A site-level aggregator (SLA)*—A 16-bit locally managed field that is used by an organization to create its own addressing and subnetworking hierarchy. This field is similar to the subnetwork mask in IPv4, except that the number of subnetworks is much greater—this field supports up to 65535 individual subnetworks.

➤ *An interface identifier*—The field that identifies individual interfaces on a network. This number must be unique and is normally based on the ethernet address associated with the particular interface. (The interface identifier calculation is discussed later in this chapter in the section "IPv6 Autoconfiguration.")

 On the exam, if you have to enter any of the unicast address types, remember that *link-local* and *site-local* are hyphenated. You could possibly lose a mark if you forget the hyphen. Also, *aggregatable global* is not hyphenated.

Embedded IPv4 Address

The transition to IPv6 is going to take many years, so a mechanism was necessary to allow IPv6 and IPv4 to work together while the migration to IPv6 carries on. IPv6 systems that use this mechanism use a special IPv6 unicast address, called an *IPv4-mapped IPv6 address*, that can accommodate an IPv4 address in the lower 32 bits of the address. This address is used to represent an IPv4 address within an IPv6 address space. The general format of an IPv4-mapped IPv6 address is

`0000:0000:0000:0000:0000:FFFF:X.X.X.X`

where

➤ The first 80 bits are zeros.

➤ FFFF is the flag that indicates that an embedded IPv4 address follows.

➤ x.x.x.x is the 32-bit IPv4 address, represented in decimal dot notation, as it is in IPv4.

As an example, the embedded IPv4 address 192.168.28.28 would appear as the following IPv6 address:

`0000:0000:0000:0000:0000:FFFF:192.168.28.28`

Additionally, an IPv4–compatible-IPv6 address consists of the first 96 bits being all zero, followed by the 32-bit IPv4 address, again in decimal dot notation. This address is used by hosts and routers to transfer IPv6 packets on an IPv4 infrastructure.

Unspecified Address Type

The unspecified address type is used when the sending system does not have an IP address assigned, such as when a diskless client starts up. The address consists of all zeros and can be represented as follows:

➤ `0000:0000:0000:0000:0000:0000:0000:0000`—Full representation.

➤ `0:0:0:0:0:0:0:0`—In a shortened zero format.

➤ `::`—In a compressed format.

Loopback Address Type

An IPv6 system, like an IPv4 system, uses a loopback address to send datagrams to itself. The IPv6 loopback address is shown in the three representations as follows:

➤ `0000:0000:0000:0000:0000:0000:0000:0001`—Full representation.

➤ `0:0:0:0:0:0:0:1`—In a shortened zero format.

➤ `::1`—In a compressed format.

This is equivalent to the IPv4 address `127.0.0.1`.

Multicast Addresses

The multicast address is used to address a number of hosts simultaneously. All hosts (or interfaces) that belong to the same multicast group receive the message.

Multicast addresses include a 4-bit field, called `scope bits`, that determines how far a multicast IPv6 datagram is routed. The contents of the first octet of the IPv6 multicast address determines the "scope" of the datagram. The format prefix for multicast addresses is `FF`. The next 4-bit field is used for flags that are normally set to zero. The final 4-bit field is the scope where:

➤ 1 indicates a node-local address—that is, the address is on the same host or system as the sender.

➤ 2 indicates a link-local address—that is, the destinations are all on the same network link as the sender.

➤ 5 indicates a site-local address—that is, the destinations are all on the same site as the sender.

➤ E indicates a global address—that is, the destinations are all on the Internet.

As an example, the IPv6 multicast address to send a datagram to all NTP servers located on the same site is

```
FF05:0:0:0:0:0:0:101
```

Anycast Addresses

The anycast address is an IPv6 address that is assigned to more than one interface. A packet sent to an anycast address is received only by the nearest interface that has the address assigned to it—nearest being interpreted by the routing protocol being used. (RIP, for example, would select the interface that can be reached in the fewest hops.)

Anycast IPv6 addresses are assigned from the unicast address space, so as soon as you assign a unicast address to more than one interface, it automatically becomes an anycast address.

IPv6 Header Format

The IPv6 datagram header has changed slightly from the IPv4 datagram header. The number of header fields has been reduced, making it simpler to process and also keeps the bandwidth use to a minimum. The most important change is the introduction of extension headers, which allow a variable number of additional options to be added, without any impact on the performance of the routing of IPv6 packets. Figure 7.1 shows the IPv6 datagram format.

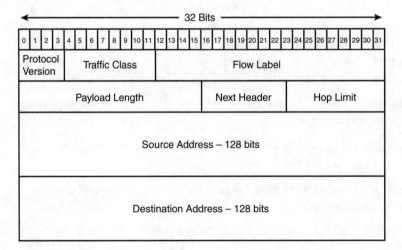

Figure 7.1 IPv6 datagram header format.

The header fields shown in the figure are as follows:

➤ *Version*—A 4-bit field identifying the IP version number. For IPv6, the value is 6; for IPv4, the value is 4.

➤ *Traffic class*—An 8-bit field that provides the means of identifying different classes or priorities of IPv6 packets.

➤ *Flow label*—A 20-bit field that enables the sender to identify sequences of packets for which special handling by IPv6 routers is required, such as "real-time" service. It allows important packets, for example, to be delivered immediately, possibly ahead of other lower-priority packets.

➤ *Payload length*—A 16-bit field that identifies the length of the IPv6 payload (the rest of the packet following the IPv6 header). Any extension headers that are included count toward the payload length, as well as the data itself.

➤ *Next header*—An 8-bit field that identifies the type of extension header that follows the primary IPv6 header. This is similar to the Protocol field in the IPv4 datagram header.

➤ *Hop limit*—An 8-bit integer field that is decremented by one each time the packet passes through a host that forwards it. If the value reaches zero, the packet is discarded.

➤ *Source address*—The sender's 128-bit address.

➤ *Destination address*—The destination's 128-bit address.

IPv6 headers also provide a second level of headers that contain optional Internet layer information. The extension header follows immediately after the primary IPv6 datagram header and is referred to by the Next header field. The advantage of using these headers is that the routers along the path that the packet takes do not examine the extension headers (with one exception: the hop-by-hop option, which defines a process that must be carried out each time the packet passes through a router), improving the performance of delivering the packet to its destination. Extension headers carry additional information relating to routing, fragmentation, or security.

IPv6 Autoconfiguration

Autoconfiguration is a new feature introduced with IPv6 that provides the facility for assigning an IPv6 address to a network interface without manual intervention by the administrator, as is currently necessary with IPv4. There are two types of autoconfiguration, stateless and stateful:

➤ *Stateless*—This mechanism enables a host to generate its own IPv6 address based on the ethernet address of the network interface being configured and advertisement information provided by local routers. The routers advertise the format prefixes for subnetworks on the local network and the host itself calculates an interface identifier, based on the ethernet address, to create a unique address for the interface. The IPv6 address is created through a combination of the interface identifier (discussed in the next section) and the prefix information provided by local routers.

When autoconfiguring an IPv6 address, if there are no local routers, then the only type of IPv6 address that can be assigned is the link-local address. The interface will be able to communicate only with other hosts on the same network.

➤ *Stateful*—This mechanism enables a host to obtain an address and other configuration information from a server, such as a Dynamic Host Configuration Protocol (DHCP) server. The server providing the addresses keeps track of which addresses have been assigned and to whom. It is not the preferred method of autoconfiguration because it requires additional resources to assign an IPv6 address.

A combination of stateful and stateless autoconfiguration can be used in the setup of an IPv6 interface. The stateless mechanism can be used for a host to configure its own interface, then stateful autoconfiguration can be used to obtain further information, such as format prefixes.

How to Calculate the Interface Identifier

The interface identifier provides the lower 64 bits of an autoconfigured IPv6 address. It is based on the ethernet address of the interface being configured. This section uses the ethernet address 08:00:20:b3:41:53 as the basis for creating the interface identifier.

The ethernet address is composed of two parts, each of 24 bits, where

➤ 08:00:20 is the company identifier (CID) assigned to Sun Microsystems for the majority of SPARC systems.

➤ b3:41:53 is the vendor-supplied identifier (VID) uniquely assigned by Sun Microsystems.

To calculate the interface identifier, the following steps are performed:

1. Obtain the ethernet address. This address can be found by running the `ifconfig -a` command as user root.

2. Convert the ethernet address to binary. Figure 7.2 shows the converted binary address as well as the hexadecimal representation.

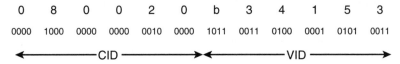

Figure 7.2　Converted ethernet address.

3. Swap bit 7 (from the left). This is the universal/local bit and is changed to create a locally assigned ethernet address. If it's currently a zero, change it to a 1, or vice versa. Figure 7.3 shows the modified address; bit 7 is shown in bold.

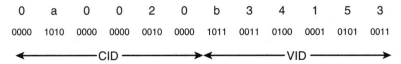

Figure 7.3　Ethernet address with bit 7 swapped.

4. Two additional octets need to be inserted into this address between the CID and the VID. These are FF and FE hexadecimal values. Figure 7.4 shows the address in both hexadecimal and binary, with these two octets added.

Figure 7.4　Ethernet address with two octets added.

5. The created interface identifier needs to be converted back to hexadecimal. Also, add the colon (:) characters as separators. This will give a final interface identifier of

```
0a00:20ff:feb3:4153
```

The unique interface identifier forms only 64 bits of the 128-bit IPv6 address. If this was a link-local IPv6 address, using the `fec` format prefix, the final autoconfigured IPv6 address would be

```
fec0:0000:0000:0000:0a00:20ff:feb3:4153
```

Duplicate Address Detection

One of the features of autoconfiguration is that of a duplicate address detection facility. This runs before an IPv6 address is assigned to ensure the address is unique. Duplicate detection checking is carried out regardless of whether stateful or stateless autoconfiguration is used to assign the IPv6 address.

The procedure works by sending a *neighbor solicitation* message to the network on which the address is going to be assigned. A *neighbor advertisement* will be received back from any systems that are using the address in question. If no response is received, it is assumed that the address is available to be used, and the assignment takes place.

Implementing IPv6

IPv6 is implemented at system bootup by the script `/etc/rc2.d/S69inet`. This script determines whether the system is a router or a host, and starts the relevant processes. This section describes the IPv6 processes and how to configure IPv6 interfaces.

Neighbor Discovery Protocol (NDP)

The neighbor discovery protocol (NDP) is implemented in IPv6 to provide the following facilities:

➤ *Address autoconfiguration*—Enables a host to automatically configure an IPv6 address for a network interface.

➤ *Address resolution*—Enables a host to determine the ethernet address of a neighbor, given the neighbor's IPv6 address. (The interface identifier part of the IPv6 address is based on the ethernet address.)

➤ *Neighbor unreachability detection*—Enables a host to determine that a neighbor is no longer reachable. This is important when the neighbor is acting as a router, so a different route can be found.

➤ *Duplicate address detection*—Enables a host to determine that the IPv6 address it wants to assign is not already in use by another interface on the network.

➤ *Parameter discovery*—Enables a host to learn network parameters of a neighbor, such as the maximum transfer unit (MTU).

➤ *Prefix discovery*—Enables a host to discover the address prefixes for desti-nation systems attached to the network. This information is used to find out which destination hosts are on the local network and which are only accessible via a router.

➤ *Router discovery*—Enables a host to locate routers that are attached to the local network.

The daemon process that implements NDP is `in.ndpd` and is started at boot time by the startup script `/etc/rc2.d/S69inet`. The script tests to see whether the system is acting as a router by checking for the existence of the configu-ration file `/etc/inet/ndpd.conf`. If the file is present, the system is assumed to be an IPv6 router, if not, an IPv6 host.

Routing in IPv6 is carried out by the **in.ripngd** process, which is initiated from the startup script **/etc/rc2.d/S69inet**. This process is started only if the system is assumed to be an IPv6 router; that is, if the configuration file **/etc/inet/ndpd.conf** exists.

IPv6 Configuration on a Non-Router

IPv6 addresses can be configured automatically with the autoconfiguration facility, or manually with the `ifconfig` command at the command-line. The two options can be described as follows:

➤ *Automatic*—To enable IPv6 on a network interface using the autoconfig-uration facility, create the file `/etc/hostname6.<interface>`, where `<interface>` corresponds to the specific network interface to be config-ured, such as `hme0` as shown here:

```
ultra10# touch /etc/hostname6.hme0
```

Now reboot the system and the interface will be configured auto-matically.

➤ *Manual*—To manually assign an IPv6 address to a network interface, such as hme0, use the ifconfig command as with IPv4, but you must specify the inet6 family to indicate that this is an IPv6 configuration. Note that the assignment does not persist across reboots of the system. The following piece of code initializes a link-local IPv6 address fec::abcd on the hme0 interface:

```
ultra10# ifconfig hme0 inet6 fec::abcd up
```

The file **/etc/inet/ipnodes** is used in IPv6 to associate IPv6 addresses with interface names, similar to the function of **/etc/inet/hosts** for IPv4 interfaces. Unlike **/etc/inet/hosts**, there is no symbolic link from **/etc/inet/ipnodes** to **/etc/ipnodes**, so don't be tricked if **/etc/ipnodes** is displayed as an option in an exam question.

View the status of IPv6 interfaces by using the ifconfig -a command, the same as for IPv4. If you want to see just IPv6 interface status, then specify the inet6 argument as follows:

```
ultra10# ifconfig -a inet6
lo0: flags=2000849<UP,LOOPBACK,RUNNING,MULTICAST,IPv6> mtu 8252 index 1
        inet6 ::1/128
hme0: flags=2000841<UP,RUNNING,MULTICAST,IPv6> mtu 1500 index 2
        inet6 fe80::a00:20ff:feb3:4153/10
```

IPv6 Configuration on a Router

IPv6 interfaces are defined in the same manner for a router as for a non-router, as described in the previous section.

To configure your system as an IPv6 router, create the configuration file /etc/inet/ndpd.conf. The file needs at least one entry, which turns on router advertisements. Enter the following into the file:

```
ifdefault AdvSendAdvertisements on
```

Further entries can be added to the configuration file to advertise prefixes. The following example entries advertise a global and site-local prefix for the 192.168 network:

```
prefix 2:0:0:c0a8::0/64        hme0
prefix fec0:0:0:c0a8::0/64     hme0
```

Reboot the system. When the system starts up, it will be configured as an IPv6 router and, as well as running the neighbor discovery protocol daemon in.ndpd, it will also be running the IPv6 routing daemon in.ripngd.

Configuring IPv6 Logical Interfaces

Logical interfaces can be created in IPv6, just as in IPv4. To configure a logical IPv6 interface `hme0:3`, for example, with an IPv6 address of `fe80::1111:abcd`, enter the following command:

```
ifconfig hme0:3 inet6 plumb fe80::1111:abcd/10 up
```

The /10 at the end of the IPv6 address specifies that the address uses the first 10 bits as the format prefix, making the address a link-local unicast address.

To remove an IPv6 logical interface, the same procedure is used as with IPv4. The following command removes the `hme0:3` logical interface created in the previous example:

```
ifconfig hme0:3 inet6 down unplumb
```

 You must always specify the **inet6** argument when configuring or removing an IPv6 interface. If you omit this argument, the system will assume it is an IPv4 interface and will carry out the required operation on the relevant IPv4 interface.

Exam Prep Questions

Question 1

Which command displays the status of IPv6 interfaces only?

- ○ A. **ifconfig -a**
- ○ B. **ifconfig -a IPv6**
- ○ C. **ifconfig -a inet6**
- ○ D. **ifconfig -a ip6**

Answer C is correct because the command `ifconfig -a inet6` displays the status of IPv6 interfaces, ignoring IPv4 interfaces. Answer A is incorrect because `ifconfig -a` displays the status of all interfaces, both IPv4 and IPv6. Answer B and D are incorrect because the arguments `IPv6` and `ip6` are invalid and not part of the syntax.

Question 2

Which of the following are features of IPv6? Choose 3.

- ❑ A. Longer header formats provide a greater amount of information to be contained within the header.
- ❑ B. IPv6 provides expanded addressing, increasing the address size from 32-bit addresses to 128-bit addresses.
- ❑ C. Quality of service allows a sequence of packets to be labeled for priority handling.
- ❑ D. Extension headers have been removed to allow the primary header to be processed more efficiently.
- ❑ E. IPv6 addresses can be automatically assigned with the new autoconfiguration feature.

Answers B, C, and E are correct because IPv6 addresses have expanded from 32 bits in IPv4 to 128 bits in IPv6. Also, IPv6 provides a quality of service feature that allows a sequence of datagrams that require priority handling to be identified. The addition of autoconfiguration enables IPv6 addresses to be assigned automatically. Answer A is incorrect because the IPv6 header has been simplified; the number of fields has been reduced. Answer D is incorrect because extension headers have been added to IPv6 to improve routing performance. Additional information can be contained within the datagram that is intended for the recipient, so each router the datagram passes through doesn't have to examine the contents, and subsequently consume more resources.

Question 3

> Which IPv6 address type involves an address being assigned to a number of interfaces, with IPv6 datagrams being delivered to the nearest interface member, rather than to all interfaces that have the address assigned?
>
> ○ A. Anycast
> ○ B. Broadcast
> ○ C. Multicast
> ○ D. Unicast

Answer A is correct because the anycast address type involves an address being assigned to a number of interfaces, but the datagrams are delivered to only the nearest member with the address assigned. Answer B is incorrect because broadcast addresses are not used in IPv6. Answer C is incorrect because a multicast address involves an address being assigned to a number of interfaces, but the datagrams are delivered to all members with the address assigned. Answer D is incorrect because a unicast address involves a single address being assigned to a single interface and is used when a host communicates with another host on the network.

Question 4

> Which of the following IPv6 addresses is invalid?
>
> ○ A. **fe80:0000:0000:0000:0a00:20ff:feb3:4153**
> ○ B. **fe80:0:0:0:a00:20ff:feb3:4153**
> ○ C. **fe80::0000::0a00:20ff:feb3:4153**
> ○ D. **fe80::a00:20ff:feb3:4153**

Answer C is correct because the IPv6 address `fe80::0000::0a00:20ff:feb3:4153` makes use of the double colon (::) character twice. This can be used only once in an IPv6 address. Answers A, B, and D are incorrect because these are all valid IPv6 addresses.

Question 5

> Which type of unicast address would you use if the address needs to be routed through the Internet?
>
> ○ A. Aggregatable global address
>
> ○ B. Link-local address
>
> ○ C. Loopback address
>
> ○ D. Site-local address

Answer A is correct because an aggregatable global unicast address is the type that can be routed through the Internet. Answer B is incorrect because a link-local address is used to provide communication between single hosts on a local link and cannot be routed. Answer C is incorrect because a loopback address is used by an IPv6 system to send datagrams to itself. Answer D is incorrect because a site-local address can be routed only through an intranet and is limited to the same site. It cannot be routed externally through the Internet.

Question 6

> In an IPv6 datagram header, what does the **Payload length** field describe?
>
> ○ A. The length of the data portion of the datagram
>
> ○ B. The length of the data and IPv6 header
>
> ○ C. The length of the data, IPv6 header, and extension headers, if present
>
> ○ D. The length of the data and any extension headers, but not the IPv6 header itself

Answer D is correct because the Payload length field of an IPv6 header identifies the length of the data and any extension headers that follow the IPv6 datagram header, but not the IPv6 header itself. Answers A, B, and C are incorrect because the Payload length field contains the length of the data and extension headers only, not the IPv6 header.

Need to Know More?

 Douglas Comer, *Internetworking with TCP/IP: Principles, Protocols and Architecture*. Prentice Hall, 2000.

 Sun Microsystems, *Solaris 9 9/02 (and later) System Administrator Collection—IPv6 Administration Guide*. Available in printed form, on the Internet at `http://docs.sun.com`, and from the online documentation provided with the Solaris 9 operating system.

 Sun Microsystems, *Solaris 9 System Administrator Collection—System Administration Guide*, "IP Services." Available in printed form, on the Internet at `http://docs.sun.com`, and from the online documentation provided with the Solaris 9 operating system.

 RFC 2460, which describes the specification for IPv6. Available on the Internet at `http://www.ietf.org/rfc/rfc2460.txt`.

8

Advanced IPv6

Terms you'll need to understand:

✓ **in.mpathd** process
✓ IPv6-over-IPv4 Tunnel
✓ Multicast group
✓ Tunnel
✓ Tunnel Destination
✓ Tunnel Source

Concepts you'll need to master:

✓ Explain how to configure IPv6-over-IPv4 tunnels and IPv6 multipathing.
✓ Explain how to troubleshoot IPv6 configuration and interface problems.

This chapter carries on from the previous chapter and covers multipathing with IPv6 and a mechanism for enabling two IPv6 interfaces to communicate over an IPv4 network. This is known as *tunnelling*. The chapter also looks at troubleshooting IPv6.

IPv6 Multipathing

IP multipathing was introduced in Chapter 5, "IP Multipathing." To use multipathing with IPv6, the setup is very similar to that of IPv4, although there are some important differences. The most notable are that the test addresses are created on the same network interface, such as hme0, without the need for additional logical interfaces, and that the test address can also be used for normal operation. With IPv4 setup, the test address is used only to enable the in.mpathd process to probe its status.

Like IPv4, IPv6 multipathing can be set up via a command line or through the use of configuration files.

Remember that if you set up multipathing on the command line, the configuration will be lost on the next reboot. To make your changes persist across reboots, you must use configuration files so that multipathing is implemented each time the system reboots.

Using Configuration Files

To use IP multipathing with existing IPv6 interfaces, you simply edit the relevant /etc/hostname6.<*interface*> files for the network interfaces you want to participate in multipathing and then reboot the system.

To set up IPv6 multipathing for a system that has two interfaces—hme0 and hme1—and uses a multipath group called ip6test, you would edit the files /etc/hostname6.hme0 and /etc/hostname6.hme1 and add the following entry to each:

```
-failover group ip6test up
```

Using the configuration files to configure IPv6 multipathing assumes that the IPv6 interfaces already exist—that is, they have already been configured for normal use. This process merely modifies the interface's functionality to participate in multipathing.

When the system is rebooted, view the configuration with the `ifconfig -a` command:

```
ultra10# ifconfig -a
lo0: flags=1000849<UP,LOOPBACK,RUNNING,MULTICAST,IPv4> mtu 8232 index 1
        inet 127.0.0.1 netmask ff000000
hme0: flags=1000843<UP,BROADCAST,RUNNING,MULTICAST,IPv4> mtu 1500 index 2
        inet 192.168.28.28 netmask ffffff00 broadcast 192.168.28.255
        groupname ip6test
        ether 8:0:20:b3:41:53
lo0: flags=2000849<UP,LOOPBACK,RUNNING,MULTICAST,IPv6> mtu 8252 index 1
        inet6 ::1/128
hme0: flags=a000841<UP,RUNNING,MULTICAST,IPv6,NOFAILOVER> mtu 1500 index 2
        ether 8:0:20:b3:41:53
        inet6 fe80::a00:20ff:feb3:4153/10
        groupname ip6test
hme1: flags=1000843<UP,BROADCAST,RUNNING,MULTICAST,IPv4> mtu 1500 index 3
        inet 192.168.28.29 netmask ffffff00 broadcast 192.168.28.255
        groupname ip6test
        ether 8:0:20:b3:41:52
hme1: flags=a000841<UP,RUNNING,MULTICAST,IPv6,NOFAILOVER> mtu 1500 index 3
        ether 8:0:20:b3:41:52
        inet6 fe80::a00:20ff:feb3:4152/10
        groupname ip6test
```

Notice from this code that

➤ The multipath group has been applied to the IPv6 interfaces and the IPv4 interfaces.

➤ The `inet6` lines for both `hme0` and `hme1` are now configured as test addresses for the IP multipathing daemon, `in.mpathd`, to monitor.

Using the Command Line

Multipathing with IPv6 can also be set up on the command line manually, but any changes made are lost at the next reboot of the system. Like IPv4, you need to be running at least Solaris 8 10/00, and your system needs to be able to support local ethernet addresses. This was described in Chapter 1, "Local Area Networks," in the section "Assigning a Port-Based Ethernet Address."

To set up IPv6 multipathing manually on a system with two network interfaces—`hme0` and `hme1`—and a multipath group of `ip6test`, the following needs to be done:

1. Run the `ifconfig -a` command to view the current interface setup:

```
ultra10# ifconfig -a
lo0: flags=1000849<UP,LOOPBACK,RUNNING,MULTICAST,IPv4> mtu 8232 index 1
        inet 127.0.0.1 netmask ff000000
hme0: flags=1000843<UP,BROADCAST,RUNNING,MULTICAST,IPv4> mtu 1500 \
➥index 2
```

```
        inet 192.168.28.28 netmask ffffff00 broadcast 192.168.28.255
        ether 8:0:20:b3:41:53
lo0: flags=2000849<UP,LOOPBACK,RUNNING,MULTICAST,IPv6> mtu 8252 index 1
        inet6 ::1/128
hme0: flags=a000841<UP,RUNNING,MULTICAST,IPv6> mtu 1500 index 2
        ether 8:0:20:b3:41:53
        inet6 fe80::a00:20ff:feb3:4153/10
hme1: flags=1000843<UP,BROADCAST,RUNNING,MULTICAST,IPv4> mtu 1500 \
➥index 3
        inet 192.168.28.29 netmask ffffff00 broadcast 192.168.28.255
        ether 8:0:20:b3:41:52
hme1: flags=a000841<UP,RUNNING,MULTICAST,IPv6> mtu 1500 index 3
        ether 8:0:20:b3:41:52
        inet6 fe80::a00:20ff:feb3:4152/10
```

The current configuration shows that both hme0 and hme1 have IPv6 addresses assigned—these are the hexadecimal values for the inet6 lines relating to hme0 and hme1 in the code shown in step 1.

2. Assign the hme0 interface to the multicast group ip6test.

```
ultra10# ifconfig hme0 group ip6test
```

3. Repeat step 2 for the hme1 interface, so that both interfaces are associated with the multicast group ip6test.

4. Configure a test address for both the hme0 and hme1 IPv6 interfaces, so that in.mpathd can monitor their status.

```
ultra10# ifconfig hme0 inet6 -failover
ultra10# ifconfig hme1 inet6 -failover
```

5. Start the in.mpathd process (if it is not already running), to start monitoring the network interfaces. Check whether the daemon is running by entering the following command:

```
ultra10# ps -ef lgrep mpath
    root   366   354  0 10:41:07 pts/2     0:00 grep mpath
    root   365     1  0 10:41:03 ?         0:00 /sbin/in.mpathd
```

The result shows that the daemon is running. If the process is not running, you can either reboot the system or start it manually by entering

```
ultra10# /sbin/in.mpathd
```

6. Multipathing is now running.

 A multipathing test address for an IPv6 interface does not have to be marked as **deprecated** (to prevent normal applications from using the address) as it does when you are implementing IP multipathing in IPv4.

IPv6-Over-IPv4 Tunnels

During the transition period from IPv4 to IPv6, there are going to be occasions where two hosts on a network are configured with IPv6 addresses, but the intervening hosts and routers are part of an IPv4 network. This section describes how to use a tunnel to overcome this problem.

What Is an IPv6-Over-IPv4 Tunnel?

An IPv6-over-IPv4 tunnel is a mechanism by which IPv6 datagrams can be transported over an IPv4 network. The sender and the receiver both support IPv6 (and IPv4), but the hosts and routers along the path the datagram takes support only IPv4. As an example, consider encryption as an analogy. Only the sender and the intended recipient know how to get at the data, such as your credit card details. While this sensitive information is transported across the Internet, for example, the actual data is not accessible and is passed on to the destination, where it is extracted correctly. With an IPv6-over-IPv4 tunnel, the data is encapsulated into IPv4 datagrams at the sender side, and then transported across the network as normal IPv4 datagrams are. When the datagram reaches the destination, the IPv6 data is extracted (decapsulated).

Configuring a Tunnel

This section describes how to configure an IPv6-over-IPv4 tunnel between two hosts (ultra10 and systema), each having an hme0 network interface.

The following steps describe how to create the tunnel.

1. A new IPv4 logical interface needs to be configured on both systems. On the host ultra10, enter the following:

```
ultra10# ifconfig hme0 addif 192.168.23.23 up
Created new logical interface hme0:1
```

On the host systema enter the following:

```
systema# ifconfig hme0 addif 192.168.24.24 up
Created new logical interface hme0:1
```

2. On host ultra10, define the IPv6 tunnel and then configure it to join the two IPv4 logical interfaces just created, as follows:

```
ultra10# ifconfig ip.tun0 inet6 plumb
ultra10# ifconfig ip.tun0 inet6 tsrc 192.168.23.23 tdst 192.168.24.24 up
```

The first command creates the tunnel and the second line configures it with the source and destination IP addresses.

The initialization and configuration of the IPv6-over-IPv4 tunnel could be carried out in one step by doing the following:

```
ultra10# ifconfig ip.tun0 inet6 plumb tsrc 192.168.23.23 tdst \
➥192.168.24.24 up
```

3. On host systema, define the IPv6 tunnel and then configure it to join the two IPv4 logical interfaces just created. This time the source and destination addresses are swapped because the tunnel is being created at the other end:

```
systema# ifconfig ip.tun0 inet6 plumb
systema# ifconfig ip.tun0 inet6 tsrc 192.168.24.24 tdst 192.168.23.23 up
```

The first command creates the tunnel and the second line configures it with the source and destination IP addresses.

4. The tunnel is now created and can be verified by running the ifconfig -a command. The following output shows the result of running this command on the host ultra10:

```
ultra10# ifconfig -a
lo0: flags=1000849<UP,LOOPBACK,RUNNING,MULTICAST,IPv4> mtu 8232 index 1
        inet 127.0.0.1 netmask ff000000
hme0: flags=1000843<UP,BROADCAST,RUNNING,MULTICAST,IPv4> mtu 1500 \
➥index 2
        inet 192.168.23.28 netmask ffffff00 broadcast 192.168.23.255
        ether 8:0:20:b3:41:53
hme0:1: flags=1000843<UP,BROADCAST,RUNNING,MULTICAST,IPv4> mtu 1500 \
➥index 2
        inet 192.168.23.23 netmask ffffff00 broadcast 192.168.23.255
ip.tun0: flags=2200851<UP,POINTOPOINT,RUNNING,MULTICAST,NONUD,IPv6> \
mtu 1480 index 3
        inet tunnel src 192.168.23.23   tunnel dst 192.168.24.24
        inet6 fe80::c0a8:1717/10 --> fe80::c0a8:1818
```

Notice that both the tunnel source and tunnel destination have been automatically configured with IPv6 addresses. The IPv6 addresses will be used for communiation between the two hosts when utilizing the tunnel, but the IPv4 addresses will be used to actually transport the data across the IPv4 network.

5. Verify the tunnel is working by issuing a ping command to the tunnel destination (IPv6 address fe80::c0a8:1818) as follows:

```
ultra10# ping fe80::c0a8:1818
fe80::c0a8:1818 is alive
```

A tunnel is removed like any other network interface. The following **ifconfig** command would remove the tunnel **ip.tun0**:

```
ultra10# ifconfig ip.tun0 inet6 down unplumb
```

Routing Between Tunnels

When an IPv6-over-IPv4 tunnel is configured, the routing entry is automatically added to the routing table. Verify that the routing is correct by issuing the following command:

```
ultra10# netstat -r -f inet6
Routing Table: IPv6
  Destination/Mask          Gateway             Flags Ref   Use   If
---------------------- ------------------- ----- --- ------ -----
fe80::c0a8:1818          fe80::c0a8:1717      UH    1     1 ip.tun0
```

Notice that the -f inet6 argument was used when running the netstat command to show only IPv6 routing entries.

Troubleshooting IPv6

If you have problems on an IPv6 network interface, you use the same troubleshooting commands as with IPv4, namely ifconfig, ping, and traceroute. The only difference between the two is that you use the inet6 option to display only IPv6 interface information. The following ifconfig command displays only the IPv6 interfaces on a system:

```
ultra10# ifconfig -a inet6
lo0: flags=2000849<UP,LOOPBACK,RUNNING,MULTICAST,IPv6> mtu 8252 index 1
        inet6 ::1/128
hme0: flags=2000841<UP,RUNNING,MULTICAST,IPv6> mtu 1500 index 2
        inet6 fe80::a00:20ff:feb3:4153/10
hme0:1: flags=1000843<UP,BROADCAST,RUNNING,MULTICAST,IPv4> mtu 1500 index 2
        inet 192.168.23.23 netmask ffffff00 broadcast 192.168.23.255
ip.tun0: flags=2200851<UP,POINTOPOINT,RUNNING,MULTICAST,NONUD,IPv6> \
mtu 1480 index 3
        inet tunnel src 192.168.23.23   tunnel dst 192.168.24.24
        inet6 fe80::c0a8:1717/10 --> fe80::c0a8:1818
```

As with IPv4 multipathing problems, error messages are written to the /var/adm/messages file, so this should be inspected if problems occur.

The majority of problems with IPv6-over-IPv4 tunnels results from incorrect configuration and can be detected with the ifconfig command. You should make sure that you have entered the correct addresses for both the source and destination of the tunnel. The following extract from the ifconfig -a command shows a tunnel that has been configured, but no

destination address has been specified. Even though the tunnel will be created, it will not function at all. In this case, the solution is to remove the tunnel completely and reconfigure it with the correct addresses:

```
ultra10# ifconfig -a
ip.tun2: flags=2200851<UP,POINTOPOINT,RUNNING,MULTICAST,NONUD,IPv6> \
mtu 1480 index 5
        inet tunnel src 192.168.28.66
        inet6 fe80::c0a8:1c42/10 --> ::
```

Notice from the code that the IPv4 destination address is missing. Also, the
inet6 line of output demonstrates that the tunnel is pointing to an unspecified IPv6 address (::).

Exam Prep Questions

Question 1

> Which of the following commands creates a test address for the network interface **hme0** so that it can be used in IPv6 multipathing?
>
> ○ A. ifconfig hme0 -failover
> ○ B. ifconfig hme0 inet6 -failover
> ○ C. ifconfig hme0 inet6 deprecated -failover
> ○ D. ifconfig inet6 hme0 -failover

Answer B is correct because the command ifconfig hme0 inet6 -failover creates a test address for the network interface hme0 so that it can be used as part of the IPv6 multipathing mechanism. Answer A is incorrect because this would modify the IPv4 network interface and not the IPv6 interface. Answer C is incorrect because IPv6 multipathing does not require the interface to be marked as deprecated. Answer D is incorrect because the syntax is wrong—the interface name must be entered immediately following the ifconfig command, as the first argument.

Question 2

> Which command verifies the status of only the IPv6 network interfaces?
>
> ○ A. ifconfig -a inet6
> ○ B. ifconfig inet6
> ○ C. ifconfig inet6 -a
> ○ D. ifconfig -a ip6

Answer A is correct because the command ifconfig -a inet6 verifies the status of IPv6 network interfaces. It does not show the status of any IPv4 interfaces. Answer B is incorrect because the syntax of the ifconfig command is wrong. The first argument must be a valid command option, such as -a, or a network interface, such as hme0. Answer C is incorrect because the syntax is wrong. Answer D is incorrect because there is no such network family as ip6.

Question 3

> Why would you need to configure an IPv6-over-IPv4 tunnel?
>
> ○ A. To allow IPv4 hosts to communicate over an IPv6 network.
>
> ○ B. To allow IPv6 hosts to communicate over an IPv4 network.
>
> ○ C. To connect an IPv6 network to an IPv4 network.
>
> ○ D. To provide an additional network path for IPv4 hosts on the network.

Answer B is correct because an IPv6-over-IPv4 tunnel is used to allow IPv6 hosts to communicate with each other through the use of an IPv4 network. Answer A is incorrect because an IPv6-over-IPv4 tunnel does not allow IPv4 hosts to communicate over an IPv6 network—the tunnel has been introduced to aid the transition from IPv4 to IPv6. Answer C is incorrect because an IPv6-over-IPv4 tunnel is not used to connect networks together; it is used to allow IPv6 hosts to communicate over an IPv4 network. Answer D is incorrect; IPv4 hosts do not make use of an IPv6-over-IPv4 tunnel. The purpose of the tunnel is to allow IPv6 hosts to communicate with each other within the existing IPv4 network.

Question 4

> You are creating an IPv6-over-IPv4 tunnel, called **ip.tunz**. To make the tunnel configuration persist across reboots, which configuration file would you create?
>
> ○ A. **/etc/hostname.ip.tunz**
>
> ○ B. **/etc/hostname6.hme0**
>
> ○ C. **/etc/hostname6.ip.tunz**
>
> ○ D. **/etc/hostname.hme0**

Answer C is correct because the configuration file `/etc/hostname6.ip.tunz` would be used to create a permanent tunnel called `ip.tunz`. Answer A is incorrect because the configuration file `/etc/hostname.ip.tunz` would refer to an IPv4 interface. Answer B is incorrect because the configuration file `/etc/hostname6.hme0` is the file that would be used to configure a primary network interface for use with IPv6. It would not be used for an IPv6-over-IPv4 tunnel. Answer D is incorrect because the configuration file `/etc/hostname.hme0` would be used to configure the primary network interface for use with IPv4.

Question 5

Which command would successfully unconfigure and remove the IPv6-over-IPv4 tunnel, **ip.tun0**?

- ○ A. **ifconfig inet6 down ip.tun0**
- ○ B. **ifconfig ip.tun0 inet6 down unplumb**
- ○ C. **ifconfig down unplumb ip.tun0 inet6**
- ○ D. **ifconfig inet6 ip.tun0 down unplumb**

Answer B is correct because the command `ifconfig ip.tun0 inet6 down unplumb` would successfully unconfigure and remove the tunnel `ip.tun0`. Answers A, C, and D are incorrect because the syntax for the `ifconfig` command is wrong.

Question 6

Which of the following statements are true with regard to IPv6-over-IPv4 tunnels? Choose 2.

- ❏ A. The sender and the receiver support both IPv4 and IPv6, but the intervening routers and hosts only need to support IPv4.
- ❏ B. All hosts and routers between the sender and receiver support IPv6.
- ❏ C. The IPv6 data is transported across the network in special IPv6 datagrams, which are recognized by the IPv4 network.
- ❏ D. The IPv6 data is encapsulated into IPv4 datagrams and transported across the network.
- ❏ E. The sender and the receiver need to support only IPv4, because the data is encapsulated into IPv4 datagrams.

Answers A and D are correct because the sender and the receiver support both IPv4 and IPv6. The intervening hosts and routers along the path between the sender and receiver need to support only IPv4. The IPv6 data is encapsulated into IPv4 datagrams for transportation across the IPv4 network. Answer B is incorrect because the hosts and routers along the path between the sender and the receiver need to support only IPv4 because the data is transported in IPv4 datagrams. Answer C is incorrect because the IPv6 data is transported across the network in IPv4 datagrams. Answer E is incorrect because the sender and the receiver need to support both IPv4 and IPv6—the IPv6 data is encapsulated into IPv4 datagrams for transportation across the network.

Need to Know More?

Sun Microsystems, *Solaris 9 9/02 and later System Administrator Collection—IPv6 Administration Guide*. Available in printed form, on the Web at http://docs.sun.com, and from the online documentation provided with the Solaris 9 operating system.

Sun Microsystems, *Solaris 9 System Administrator Collection—System Administration Guide: IP Services*. Available in printed form, on the Web at http://docs.sun.com, and from the online documentation provided with the Solaris 9 operating system.

Sun Microsystems, *System Reference Manual*, Section 1M—"System Administration Commands." Available in printed form, on the Web at http://docs.sun.com, and from the online documentation provided with the Solaris 9 operating system.

TCP and UDP

Terms you'll need to understand:

✓ Buffered Transfer
✓ Congestion Window
✓ Full-Duplex
✓ Large Window
✓ Piggybacking
✓ TCP Segment
✓ Three-Way Handshake
✓ Virtual Circuit
✓ Window Advertisement

Concepts you'll need to master:

✓ Distinguish among protocol characteristics of the transport layer
✓ Explain the fundamentals of TCP and UDP

TCP and UDP are the two main protocols that operate at the Transport layer of the TCP/IP model. The Transport layer provides an end-to-end service for application data—that is, from the source to the destination. TCP and UDP are both delivered as part of the Solaris 9 operating system kernel.

Transport layer protocols communicate via port numbers, unlike the Internet layer, which uses IP addresses, and the Network Interface layer, which uses ethernet addresses. Well known ports are established for a number of applications, on both the sending and receiving hosts, such as port 23, which is used by Telnet. The full list of well known ports and the associated applications is contained in the file **/etc/inet/services**.

TCP

The Transmission Control Protocol (TCP) is a connection-oriented, stateful, and reliable protocol that handles the delivery of data packets across a network. Packets can be routed via different destinations, and TCP also handles the reassembly of packets at the destination end. It is used typically for larger volumes of data that need to be exchanged between hosts. TCP has the following features:

> *Virtual circuit*—Both the sending and receiving host must establish a connection before data transmission can commence. This connection is called a virtual circuit because it is a logical connection, not a physical one.

> *Full-duplex*—TCP connections allow data to be transferred in both directions at the same time, increasing the amount of data that can be carried on the network at a given time. The application views a TCP connection as two paths moving in opposite directions. Full-duplex also makes use of *piggybacking*, where control information, such as acknowledgements, are sent inside data segments traveling in the opposite direction. This reduces the amount of traffic on the network.

> *Streams*—An application passes data to TCP for transmission as a stream of bytes. TCP divides the stream into *segments*, which comprise a header, containing control information (discussed in the next section) and data.

> *Buffers*—TCP uses both input and output buffers to regulate the flow of traffic between the sending and receiving hosts. The default value for the maximum size of the buffers is 1MB (1048576 bytes). This parameter can be viewed, or tuned, by using the ndd command as shown here:

```
# ndd /dev/tcp tcp_max_buf
1048576
```

When TCP establishes a connection, it carries out what is called a *three-way handshake,* in which the sending host sends a SYN (synchronize) message, and then the receiver sends an acknowledgement (ACK) of the SYN and also sends a SYN message of its own. The sender then receives the SYN and the ACK and sends a final ACK. The sender can now start to send data. Figure 9.1 shows how this works.

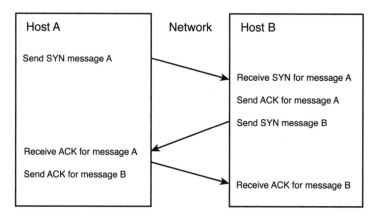

Figure 9.1   Three-way handshake.

 Some examples of applications that use TCP are Telnet, FTP, HTTP, and the Solaris **r** commands, such as **rlogin** and **rsh**.

TCP Header

TCP uses segments as its basic unit of transfer, as IP uses datagrams and ethernet uses packets. A TCP header consists of a number of 32-bit words (4 bytes). The header must be a minimum of 5 words or 20 bytes, and contains a number of fields that control the delivery of the data across the network. The format of the TCP segment header is shown in Figure 9.2.

The following are TCP header fields:

➤ *Source Port*—Identifies the TCP application program on the sending side.

➤ *Destination Port*—Identifies the TCP application program on the receiving side.

➤ *Sequence Number*—Identifies the position of this segment in the data stream—the sending and receiving hosts synchronize the sequence number when the connection is established. The receiving host rejects segments that arrive too late or are lost.

➤ *Acknowledgement Number*—Identifies how much of the data stream has been received successfully. When a host is sending an acknowledgement, the ACK flag has to be set for the value to be treated as valid. (ACK is discussed later in this chapter in "Code Flags.")

➤ *Offset*—Identifies the position in the segment where the data starts. This is necessary because the options field can vary in length.

➤ *Reserved*—This field is reserved and is not used.

➤ *Code Flags*—This 6-bit field is used to determine the purpose and contents of the TCP segment. Each flag is a single bit and is listed from left to right:

  ➤ *URG*—When this bit is set, the Urgent Pointer field becomes valid. TCP enables the sender to specify "urgent" data that should be delivered as quickly as possible.

  ➤ *ACK*—When this bit is set, the Acknowledgement field becomes valid.

  ➤ *PSH*—When this bit is set, the segment requests a push, that is, to transmit the data immediately.

  ➤ *RST*—When this bit is set, reset the connection.

  ➤ *SYN*—When this bit is set, synchronize the sequence numbers— used when establishing a connection.

  ➤ *FIN*—Indicates that the sender has finished sending—used when terminating a connection.

➤ *Window*—This field specifies how much data the receiving side can accept. This is part of the TCP flow control, discussed in the next section.

➤ *Checksum*—A 16-bit integer used to verify the integrity of the TCP segment header and the data.

➤ *Urgent Pointer*—This field specifies a position in the data stream where "urgent" data ends. The field is used only when the URG code flag bit is set to 1.

➤ *Options*—TCP uses this field to communicate with the TCP software at the other end of the connection. A maximum segment size is specified in this field.

➤ *Padding*—Padding to fill the header out to the minimum size and to ensure that the header ends on a 32-bit boundary. Padding is composed of zeros.

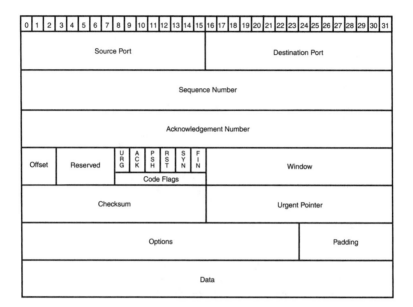

Figure 9.2   TCP header format.

TCP Flow Control

TCP is not only a reliable protocol, able to guarantee the delivery of data through an acknowledgement and retransmit mechanism; it also regulates the flow of data at both the sender and receiver side. The flow control mechanism is known as a *sliding window* because it is variable and can change in size according to how many packets have been received and processed. The window dictates how much data can be read-ahead; the window reduces when data can't be processed fast enough by the local application, and increases when the local application processes data at the rate it's being transferred.

Window Advertisements (Receiver)

The receiving side sends a window advertisement back to the sender, along with an acknowledgement. This tells the sender how many more bytes can be sent before the sender has to wait for further acknowledgements. Figure 9.3 shows how the receiving station controls how many bytes are sent and manages the flow of data between the two hosts. Notice that as the window moves through the packets to send, the size of the window varies according to how many acknowledgements have been received. In Figure 9.3 (a), the window size is set to 4, but in (b), some acknowledgements have obviously not been received, hence the window size is reduced. As acknowledgements are received, Figure 9.3 (c) shows the window size increasing, allowing the sender to transmit more packets.

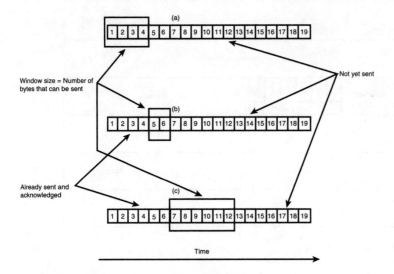

Figure 9.3   TCP sliding window using window advertisements.

Note from Figure 9.3 that the sending window is constantly updated with the current size of the window and, as time progresses, the window slides along (varying in size), dictating how many packets can be sent—hence the name, *sliding window*.

Congestion Window (Sender)

The sending side also manages the flow of data across the network by adjusting the amount of data it can send according to the number of segments that have recently been acknowledged or lost. Congestion is identified by the sending side in the form of lost packets. When this occurs, the sender halves the size of the congestion window, allowing less data to be transmitted (and thereby easing the congestion). When acknowledgements are received for segments recently sent, it is an indication that the congestion has cleared, so the congestion window doubles in size, allowing more data to be sent.

TCP Large Window

The standard TCP segment header, as you have seen, contains a 16-bit field for the window, giving a maximum window size of 64K (or 2^{16}). RFC 1323 provides TCP extensions to allow a larger window size, up to 1GB (or 2^{30}). For this extension to function correctly, both the sender and the receiver must support RFC 1323 extensions. Further details on RFC 1323 can be found on the Web at www.ietf.org/rfc.html.

UDP

User Datagram Protocol (UDP) is a connectionless, stateless, and unreliable protocol that was designed for applications that do not need to have a reliable transport mechanism, such as NTP, DNS (for lookup queries), and NFS. UDP relies on the network to provide the reliability, and the actual application handles any retransmission of lost data. Consequently, UDP requires less processing overhead than TCP, because there is no setup and termination of a virtual connection and no acknowledgement mechanism.

UDP uses datagrams as its basic units of transfer, which are shorter than TCP segment headers and contain fewer fields. The format of the UDP datagram header is shown in Figure 9.4.

0	1	2	3	4	5	6	7	8	9	10	11	12	13	14	15	16	17	18	19	20	21	22	23	24	25	26	27	28	29	30	31
Source Port																Destination Port															
Length																Checksum															
Data																															

Figure 9.4 UDP header format.

UDP uses the following UDP header fields:

➤ *Source Port*—Identifies the UDP application program on the sending side.

➤ *Destination Port*—Identifies the UDP application program on the receiving side.

➤ *Length*—A 16-bit integer for the length of the datagram (in bytes), including the data portion.

➤ *Checksum*—A 16-bit integer used to verify the integrity of the UDP datagram header and the data.

Exam Prep Questions

Question 1

Which two protocols operate at the Transport layer of the TCP/IP model? Choose 2.

- ❏ A. ICMP
- ❏ B. TCP
- ❏ C. IP
- ❏ D. UDP
- ❏ E. HTTP

Answers B and D are correct because TCP and UDP are both protocols that operate at the Transport layer of the TCP/IP model. Answers A and C are incorrect because ICMP and IP are both protocols that operate at the Internet layer of the TCP/IP model. Answer E is incorrect because HTTP is a protocol that operates at the Application layer of the TCP/IP model.

Question 2

Which of the following are characteristics of UDP? Choose 2.

- ❏ A. UDP has a high overhead.
- ❏ B. UDP is designed for applications that require a reliable Transport Layer mechanism.
- ❏ C. UDP is designed for applications that run on reliable networks.
- ❏ D. UDP is a connectionless, stateless, and unreliable protocol.

Answers C and D are correct because UDP is designed for applications that run on reliable networks and it is a connectionless, stateless, and unreliable protocol. Answer A is incorrect because UDP has a low overhead. Answer B is incorrect because TCP, not UDP, is designed for applications that require a reliable Transport layer mechanism.

Question 3

In a TCP segment header, what function does the **window** field carry out?

- ○ A. It is reserved and is not used.
- ○ B. It informs the sending system how many bytes can be sent.
- ○ C. It informs the receiving system how many bytes can be sent.
- ○ D. It defines the starting point of the data portion.

Answer B is correct because the window field contains the number of bytes that the sending system can send. Answer A is incorrect because the reserved field is not used. Answer C is incorrect because there is no field that informs the receiving system how many bytes can be sent. Answer D is incorrect because it is the offset field that denotes the starting point of the data portion of a TCP segment.

Question 4

This protocol is used at the Transport layer of the TCP/IP model and guarantees delivery of messages by using a virtual connection and an acknowledgement mechanism. Which protocol is being described?

- ○ A. UDP
- ○ B. ICMP
- ○ C. TCP
- ○ D. IP

Answer C is correct because TCP is a Transport layer protocol that guarantees delivery of messages by using a virtual connection and an acknowledgement mechanism. Answer A is incorrect because UDP, although it is a Transport layer protocol, is connectionless and unreliable—that is, it does not implement any acknowledgement mechanism. Answers B and D are incorrect because ICMP and IP are Internet layer protocols.

Question 5

Which file contains the well known ports and the applications associated with them?

- ○ A. **/etc/inet/networks**
- ○ B. **/etc/inet/services**
- ○ C. **/etc/inet/hosts**
- ○ D. **/etc/nodename**

Answer B is correct because the file /etc/inet/services contains the well known ports and the applications associated with them. Answer A is incorrect because the file /etc/inet/networks is used for mapping network numbers to network names. Answer C is incorrect because /etc/inet/hosts is used to provide IPv4 address to hostname mapping. Answer D is incorrect because /etc/nodename contains the canonical hostname for the system.

Question 6

When TCP initiates a connection, a number of messages and acknowledgements are sent and received to establish a viable link. What is this procedure called?

- ○ A. A one-way handshake
- ○ B. A two-way handshake
- ○ C. A three-way handshake
- ○ D. A four-way handshake

Answer C is correct because the procedure to establish a TCP connection is known as a three-way handshake, making answers A, B, and D obviously incorrect.

Question 7

In a UDP datagram header, what does the **length** field denote?

- ○ A. The length of the datagram header, not including the data
- ○ B. The length of the datagram, including the header and the data
- ○ C. The length of the data portion of the datagram
- ○ D. The length of the checksum field

Answer B is correct because the `length` field of a UDP datagram header denotes the length of the datagram, including the header and the data, making answers A, C, and D incorrect.

Question 8

Which of the following are valid fields in the TCP segment header? Choose 3.

❑ A. Source IP address

❑ B. Checksum

❑ C. Sequence number

❑ D. Acknowledgement number

❑ E. Maximum transfer unit

❑ F. Length

Answers B, C, and D are correct because checksum, sequence number, and acknowledgement number fields are all valid fields in a TCP segment header. Answer A is incorrect because the Source IP address field is present in an IP datagram header and not in a TCP segment header. Answer E is incorrect because the maximum transfer unit (MTU) is a valid field in an Ethernet frame and is not present in a TCP segment header. Answer F is incorrect because the length field is a valid field in a UDP datagram header.

Question 9

Which of the following are characteristics of TCP? Choose 2.

❑ A. TCP has a lower overhead than UDP.

❑ B. TCP is designed for applications that require a reliable Transport layer mechanism.

❑ C. TCP is designed for applications that run on reliable networks.

❑ D. TCP is a connection-oriented, stateful, and reliable protocol.

Answers B and D are correct because TCP is designed for applications that require a reliable Transport layer mechanism and TCP is a connection-oriented, stateful, and reliable protocol. Answers A and C are incorrect because these are features of UDP and not TCP.

Need to Know More?

 Comer, Douglas. *Internetworking with TCP/IP: Principles, Protocols and Architecture.* (Prentice Hall, 2000.)

 Hunt, Craig. TCP/IP Network Administration (3rd Edition). (O'Reilly & Associates, 2002.)

 Stevens, Richard W. *TCP/IP Illustrated, Volume 1—The Protocols.* (Addison-Wesley, 1994.)

 Sun Microsystems, *Solaris 9 System Administrator Collection,* "*Solaris Tunable Parameters Reference Manual (Chapter 4).*" Available in printed form, on the Internet at http://docs.sun.com, and from the online documentation provided with the Solaris 9 operating system.

Domain Name System (DNS)

Terms you'll need to understand:

✓ Berkeley Internet Name Daemon (BIND)

✓ **/etc/resolv.conf**

✓ **/etc/named.conf**

✓ Fully qualified domain name (FQDN)

✓ **in.named**

✓ Name resolution

✓ Primary server

✓ Resource records

✓ Root domain

✓ Secondary server

✓ Top-level domain

✓ Zone of authority

Concepts you'll need to master:

✓ Explain the purpose of DNS in a network environment.

✓ Explain how to configure a primary and secondary DNS server and a DNS client.

✓ Given DNS server output for a problem scenario, identify strategies to resolve the problem.

Domain name system (DNS) is the mechanism by which IP addresses are resolved from domain names and vice versa. The primary use for DNS is on the Internet, where it resolves any hostname to its relevant IP address. For example, you could navigate to Sun's Web site by typing in `www.sun.com`. After you type in this DNS name, Internet DNS servers resolve this name to Sun's IP address, which is returned to your computer so that you navigate to it. This chapter describes the basics of DNS: how to configure a server and a client as well as how to troubleshoot DNS problems.

> You wouldn't need DNS if you only communicated with a small number of hosts on your local network. The **/etc/inet/hosts** file would contain the necessary information to resolve IP addresses from hostnames.

DNS Fundamentals

DNS works in a hierarchical fashion with the root at the top. Queries cascade down through the branches until a server is found that can provide a resolution. The collection of machines that use DNS is called the *namespace*. The namespace is made up of a number of domains, each consisting of a number of machines that contain information about hosts, or of other servers that might contain the required information. The domains are organized in a similar way to a Unix file system, which is an inverted tree, with a root at the top and numerous branches extending from the root.

Top-Level Domains

If you are connected to the Internet, then the root domain is the highest level of domain, identified by a . (dot). It is often called the "Nameless root" and acts as a placeholder for the top-level domains that are administered centrally by the Internet Assigned Numbers Authority (IANA). When you specify a URL, such as `www.sun.com`, the last word (furthest right) is the top-level domain, in this case `com`, which identifies the domain as a commercial organization. Top-level domains are broken down into organizational and geographical structures. Table 10.1 shows the most popular organizational top-level domains.

Table 10.1 Organizational Top-Level Domains	
Domain Name	**Description**
com	Commercial organizations (mainly U.S. based)
org	Non-commercial or non-profit organizations
edu	Educational organizations, such as schools and universities
net	Networking organizations and Internet Service Providers (ISPs)
mil	US Military domain names
gov	Government departments and organizations
int	International organizations, such as NATO, for example

Geographical domains are assigned to each country, normally with two letters relating to the country. Table 10.2 shows some of the geographical top-level domains.

Table 10.2 Geographical Top-Level Domains	
Domain Name	**Description**
ca	Canada
de	Germany
es	Spain
fr	France
jp	Japan
uk	United Kingdom (Great Britain)
us	United States

Second-Level Domains

Second-level domains come below the top-level domains and are administered by the organizations themselves. In the domain name www.sun.com, for example, sun is the second-level domain name and is administered by Sun Microsystems. An organization is free to split its second-level domain into further subdomains, if required, and so delegate responsibility of the subdomains to specific departments or sections. There is a restriction, however, that a complete domain name, including all its subdomain names and the top-level domain name (known as a *Fully Qualified Domain Name — FQDN*), cannot be longer than 255 characters. Also, each single domain name cannot be longer than 63 characters.

Zones

A zone represents the extent of the authority of a name server. A single DNS name server might manage a single domain, or it might include a number of subdomains. A DNS name server maintains its own zone files, which are referenced when a resolution request is received from a client. Figure 10.1 shows a conceptual picture of an organization, xyz.com—this is the domain name that would be registered on the Internet. There are four subdomains: accounts, marketing, systems, and staff. The top-level domain and the accounts subdomain are part of the same zone of authority; the other three subdomains are located in their own zone of authority.

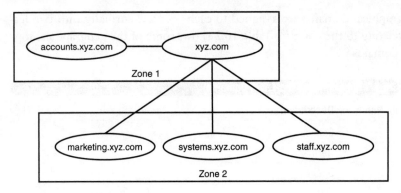

Figure 10.1   DNS zones of authority.

If a query is received for a host in the systems.xyz.com subdomain, it is passed to the DNS server responsible for the zone. The server responsible for xyz.com does not answer the DNS request because it is outside the server's authority.

DNS Server Types

There are a number of DNS server types, which carry out different functions within the DNS namespace. The most common types are root, primary, secondary, caching-only, and forwarding servers:

➤ *Root*—These servers maintain the data about the top-level domains. There are currently 13 root servers on the Internet. A list of the root servers can be obtained on the Web from ftp://ftp.rs.internic.net/ domain/named.root.

➤ *Primary*—Every DNS zone requires a primary server to act as the master. There is normally only one primary server in a zone. You can have more than one, but there is a corresponding administration overhead and a greater risk of errors. Primary servers specifically:

➤ Specify the delegation of authority for subdomains.

➤ Are the place where all changes are made to the zone, such as the addition of a secondary server.

➤ Are the authoritative servers for the specific zone.

➤ Provide updates to secondary servers and synchronize the information held on them.

➤ *Secondary*—These servers act as a backup for the primary server and are updated, through zone transfers, by the primary server. There can be multiple secondary servers in a domain.

➤ *Caching-only*—DNS servers cache the information they receive on domains for which they have no authority. A caching-only server does not have any authority for any domain, providing only cached information about the most commonly accessed namespace queries. Caching-only servers reduce the overhead of a secondary server because there are no zone transfers from the primary server.

➤ *Forwarding*—A forwarding server is used when a query requires off-site resolution; that is, it can't be resolved by the local DNS servers because it is remote.

Forwarding servers have the following features:

➤ They handle all remote queries.

➤ They build up a cache of remote queries, so that frequently used queries can be answered very quickly.

➤ They are simple to set up—a directive in the configuration file is all that's needed.

➤ If the forwarder fails to respond with an answer, the local DNS server proceeds to contact remote servers itself, unless the `forward only` directive is used, which prevents local name servers from contacting remote servers.

Two terms that could come up in the exam are *recursive DNS* and *iterative DNS*. Recursive DNS refers to a query that is sent to a DNS server, and if it is not resolved locally, the server will contact further servers until it is resolved. In other words, "Here's a query—you do all the work." With iterative DNS, if a query is not resolved by the DNS server, either the address of another DNS server to try is returned or an error message is returned, but no further searching is carried out by the server. In other words, "Here's a query—give me your best answer and I'll do all the work."

Name Resolution

DNS resolution is done in several steps, all of which are transparent to the DNS client making the request. The following list outlines the steps to resolving a client request.

1. A client issues a command, or query, that requires name-to-address resolution, such as `ping sun.com`.

2. The name service switch file, `/etc/nsswitch.conf`, is referenced for the search order and name service to use. This file determines whether or not DNS is used. The following entry

   ```
   hosts:    files dns
   ```

   signifies that the local `/etc` files should be searched first and then DNS should be used if the local files do not provide the resolution.

3. Assuming the local `/etc/inet/hosts` file did not answer the query, the local DNS server is consulted.

4. The client consults the file `/etc/resolv.conf` to determine the IP addresses of up to three name servers to contact.

5. The client sends a recursive DNS query to the server. This means that DNS will continue to try to resolve the query if it doesn't have the information itself. The local DNS server will contact remote servers on the client's behalf.

6. The local DNS server checks its own cache to see whether the query has been resolved recently. If it can't resolve the query itself, it sends an iterative request to one of the root DNS servers. The iterative request states that the root server should simply return any information it has and not pursue the query itself. The local DNS server will continue to try to resolve the query, not the root server.

7. The root server normally responds with the IP address of another server to contact. This server is sent an iterative request. The response is the IP address that resolves the query, the IP address of another server to try, or an error message stating that no information could be found.

8. The process continues until, eventually, the IP address is returned to the local DNS server, and subsequently returned to the client. If the IP address cannot be found, an error message is issued to the client.

Configuring a Primary DNS Server

To configure a DNS server, you must first gather the necessary information to be able to provide a service. This includes:

➤ The names and IP addresses of root servers, if connected to the Internet. If your organization is not connected to the Internet, then you still need to know the names and addresses of root servers for the organization.

➤ The names and IP addresses of any DNS servers to which authority is delegated—in other words, subdomains that are not part of the zone of responsibility for this server.

➤ Hostnames and IP addresses of all hosts for which this server is going to be the authority. This information is used when name-to-address resolution is required.

➤ Reverse lookup information for all hosts for which this server is going to be the authority. This information is used when address-to-name resolution is required.

The `in.named` process is started at boot time to provide DNS services. The startup script that initializes DNS is `/etc/rc2.d/S72inetsvc`. The process is started only if the configuration file, `/etc/named.conf`, is present. `/etc/named.conf` is the main configuration file for a DNS server and does not exist by default: It must be created manually. `/etc/named.conf` does the following:

➤ Identifies the DNS server and its function (that is master, slave, cache, and so on).

➤ Specifies the zones of authority for the server.

➤ Specifies the pathname of the file that contains details of the root servers.

➤ Contains security information for the zones of authority so that restrictions can be enforced to limit zone transfers of data to secondary servers, for example.

➤ Specifies the pathnames of the zone data files.

You should note that in the **/etc/named.conf** file, domain names do not contain a trailing . (dot) in the zone name. The trailing dot is required in the zone file itself, but not in this file. Inserting the dot in this file is a common mistake.

A sample /etc/named.conf file is shown here for a master DNS server:

```
ultra10# cat /etc/named.conf
options {
        directory "/var/named";
};

acl "slaves" {
        {192.168.28.0/24 ; };
};

zone "." in {
        type hint;
        file "named.ca";
};

zone "xyz.com" in {
        type master;
        file "db.xyz";
        allow-transfer {"slaves";}};
};

zone "28.168.192.in-addr.arpa" in {
        type master;
        file "xyz.rev";
};

zone "0.0.127.in-addr.arpa" in {
        type master;
        file "named.local";
};
```

Note the following about the preceding code:

➤ Under the options directive, a directory is specified, /var/named. This is the default location for all the data files for this DNS server.

➤ A special domain called . (dot) identifies the root DNS servers and the filename that contains their names and addresses—the default filename to use for this is named.ca, although any meaningful name can be used if you wish. Note that the type for this entry is hint because the DNS server contacts one of the root servers listed in this file to obtain a current list of root servers, which is then held in the server's cache. The filename is not consulted again until the cached list reaches its expiry time, when the data is refreshed.

➤ This is a master (primary) DNS server, as depicted by the type master directive for each of the files listed. A secondary DNS server would have each of these values set to slave.

➤ An access control list has been created that uses the alias slaves, which is referred to later in the file. It enables IP addresses to be grouped together for ease of reference.

➤ A number of zone files are specified, along with the locations of the data files. The `allow-transfer` directive makes use of the access control list `slaves` so that zone data can be transferred only to servers that are on the specified network, in this case `192.168.28.x`. It enforces security so that an unauthorized host cannot obtain the name and address information.

➤ The zone file `28.168.192.in-addr.arpa` refers to the reverse lookup file for the zone. The domain `in-addr.arpa` is a conceptual domain used for reverse resolution—that is, IP address-to-hostname. It is frequently used for authentication purposes to verify the identity of a remote host.

 There are no forward references allowed in the **/etc/named.conf** file, so any alias definitions must be set up before they can be referenced. You might get a question showing an invalid configuration file where a reference is used before it is defined.

The named.ca File

The `named.ca` file contains the list of root servers. This file is particularly important if your DNS server is connected to the Internet because it contains the names and IP addresses of the servers managing the top-level domains, such as `com` and `gov`, for example. The file is managed by IANA and is globally accessible. Periodically—say, every two months—this file should be checked on the Internet to see whether any changes have been made, and downloaded to keep it up to date.

The list of root servers can be obtained from `ftp://ftp.rs.internic.net/domain/named.root`.

The current file looks like this:

```
ultra10# cat /var/named/named.ca
;       This file holds the information on root name servers needed to
;       initialize cache of Internet domain name servers
;       (e.g. reference this file in the "cache.  "
;       configuration file of BIND domain name servers).
;
;       This file is made available by InterNIC
;       under anonymous FTP as
;           file            /domain/named.root
;           on server       FTP.INTERNIC.NET
;
;       last update:    Nov 5, 2002
;       related version of root zone: 2002110501
;
;
; formerly NS.INTERNIC.NET
;
.                       3600000  IN  NS    A.ROOT-SERVERS.NET.
A.ROOT-SERVERS.NET.     3600000      A     198.41.0.4
;
```

```
; formerly NS1.ISI.EDU
;
.                               3600000         NS      B.ROOT-SERVERS.NET.
B.ROOT-SERVERS.NET.             3600000         A       128.9.0.107
;
; formerly C.PSI.NET
;
.                               3600000         NS      C.ROOT-SERVERS.NET.
C.ROOT-SERVERS.NET.             3600000         A       192.33.4.12
;
; formerly TERP.UMD.EDU
;
.                               3600000         NS      D.ROOT-SERVERS.NET.
D.ROOT-SERVERS.NET.             3600000         A       128.8.10.90
;
; formerly NS.NASA.GOV
;
.                               3600000         NS      E.ROOT-SERVERS.NET.
E.ROOT-SERVERS.NET.             3600000         A       192.203.230.10
;
; formerly NS.ISC.ORG
;
.                               3600000         NS      F.ROOT-SERVERS.NET.
F.ROOT-SERVERS.NET.             3600000         A       192.5.5.241
;
; formerly NS.NIC.DDN.MIL
;
.                               3600000         NS      G.ROOT-SERVERS.NET.
G.ROOT-SERVERS.NET.             3600000         A       192.112.36.4
;
; formerly AOS.ARL.ARMY.MIL
;
.                               3600000         NS      H.ROOT-SERVERS.NET.
H.ROOT-SERVERS.NET.             3600000         A       128.63.2.53
;
; formerly NIC.NORDU.NET
;
.                               3600000         NS      I.ROOT-SERVERS.NET.
I.ROOT-SERVERS.NET.             3600000         A       192.36.148.17
;
; operated by VeriSign, Inc.
;
.                               3600000         NS      J.ROOT-SERVERS.NET.
J.ROOT-SERVERS.NET.             3600000         A       192.58.128.30
;
; housed in LINX, operated by RIPE NCC
;
.                               3600000         NS      K.ROOT-SERVERS.NET.
K.ROOT-SERVERS.NET.             3600000         A       193.0.14.129
;
; operated by IANA
;
.                               3600000         NS      L.ROOT-SERVERS.NET.
L.ROOT-SERVERS.NET.             3600000         A       198.32.64.12
;
; housed in Japan, operated by WIDE
;
.                               3600000         NS      M.ROOT-SERVERS.NET.
M.ROOT-SERVERS.NET.             3600000         A       202.12.27.33
; End of File
```

If your DNS server is not connected to the Internet, then you should create a `named.ca` file similar to the one shown in this section, but with the names and IP addresses of the root DNS servers for your organization. This will allow organizationwide DNS queries to be resolved.

Zone Files

At least one zone is specified in the master configuration file `/etc/named.conf`, along with the location of the relevant zone file. The actual name and IP address details of the hosts for which the DNS server has authority are stored in the zone file. Zones are used to distribute authority, which is particularly useful in large organizations, where the delegation of zones makes the process of keeping the information up to date much easier and more manageable.

Information in the zone file is stored in a particular format, known as *resource records*. Each resource record serves a specific purpose.

Resource records exist within the zone files of a server and contain all of the information pertaining to the zone of authority. There are a number of resource record types, each having special meaning and a number of keywords. The more common types are detailed in the following list:

➤ *Start Of Authority (SOA)*—This marks the start of the zone data and defines default parameters for the entire zone. This entry must be present in a zone file. A typical SOA entry follows:

```
@   IN SOA master.xyz.com. root.master.xyz.com. (
            2003061001;  Serial Number
            10800;       Refresh timer - 3 hours
            1800;        Retry - 30 minutes
            604800;      Expiry - 1 week
            43200);       Minimum TTL - 12 hours
```

The following notes apply to this entry:

➤ The @ symbol is a placeholder for the domain name, in this case `xyz.com`.

➤ The record is of the class IN, Internet class.

➤ `master.xyz.com` identifies the primary DNS server.

➤ `root.master.xyz.com` identifies the email contact address for messages. Note that there is no @ symbol after the email name because this symbol is used elsewhere as already described.

➤ The serial number field is important because secondary DNS servers use it to detect any changes that have been made to the zone and to update their own copies of the data files via a zone transfer. When the administrator makes a change to the zone data, this value should be incremented. A popular method of maintaining the serial number is to use the current date, in the form YYYYMMDD with two digits on the end that can be incremented by the administrator each time a change is made. This allows 100 updates to be made each day. You can choose any method to maintain the serial number, such as starting at number 1 and incrementing each time a change is made, but it is imperative that the secondary DNS servers detect the change and update accordingly.

➤ The refresh timer, currently set to 3 hours, is the time at which a secondary server attempts to refresh its database from the primary DNS server. At this time, the primary server's serial number value is checked, and if it has been changed, the secondary server needs to update its database.

➤ The retry entry specifies how long a secondary server should wait before retrying a failed contact to the primary DNS server.

➤ The expiry entry, set to 1 week, stipulates how long a secondary DNS server's database can remain valid if no updates have been received. After this time, if there have been no updates, the secondary server updates its database from the primary DNS server.

➤ The minimum time-to-live (TTL), set to 12 hours, specifies how long a hostname remains valid in the cache. After this time, the entry is discarded.

➤ Everything after the ; (semicolon) character on each line is a comment and is not part of the configuration.

➤ *Name Server (NS)*—This lists the name servers for the zone and also includes any subdomains that have been delegated to other DNS servers. A typical NS entry follows:

```
xyz.com.          IN   NS    master.xyz.com.
                  IN   NS    slave.xyz.com.
sales.xyz.com     IN   NS    saleserv.xyz.com.
```

In this entry, the sales.xyz.com. subdomain has been delegated to the DNS server saleserv.xyz.com.

➤ *Address (A)*—This is where the hostnames and IP addresses are listed for the zone, the functionality being similar to a /etc/hosts file. The following sample entries identify a host named test and a host named fulltest:

```
test                IN   A    192.168.28.67
fulltest.xyz.com.   IN   A    192.168.28.45
```

The preceding two entries show that both relative and fully qualified hostnames can be entered as address records. If a relative hostname is used, the domain name is automatically appended.

> Relative hostnames do not have a trailing . (dot) because the domain name is appended to the hostname. It is a common mistake to make because the fully qualified hostnames do have the trailing . (dot) present.

➤ *IPv6 Address (AAAA)*—Similar to the address resource record, but the quad A record identifies IPv6 addresses for hostnames. The quad A record is similar in function to the /etc/inet/ipnodes file.

➤ *Canonical Name (CNAME)*—This record is used to define aliases for a hostname. For example, you might have a server providing several applications, each of which requires its own hostname. It is also commonly used for access to Web servers via a WWW hostname. A sample CNAME entry is shown here:

```
appl_1            IN   A      192.168.28.67
appl_accounts     IN   CNAME  appl_1
```

This type of entry is extremely useful when relocating services to another server. All that is required is a modification of the CNAME entry to point to a different hostname.

➤ *Mail Exchanger (MX)*—This record identifies a mail server or a number of mail servers that handle email for the domain. The MX resource record contains a preference field to allow a primary server to be used first, with a backup server to be used if the primary server is not available. The server with the lowest preference value is tried first. The following example shows two email servers, with their addresses and the relevant MX records:

```
mailmaster    IN   A    192.168.28.68
mailslave     IN   A    192.168.28.78
              IN   MX   2    mailmaster
              IN   MX   8    mailslave
```

➤ *Host Info (HINFO)*—This record provides information about the host, such as the hardware and operating system. For security purposes, it is not recommended to include this type of record, especially if the server is connected to the Internet, because it could provide an intruder with additional information. A sample entry is shown here:

```
mailmaster  IN  HINFO   Enterprise-450  Solaris-9
```

➤ *Text (TXT)*—This record provides textual comments about the DNS server. For security purposes, it is not recommended to include this type of record, especially if the server is connected to the Internet, because it could provide an intruder with additional information. A sample entry is shown here:

```
mailmaster  IN  TXT    "Connected directly to 192.168.23.23 firewall"
```

➤ *Well-Known Services (WKS)*—This record describes the well-known services that are supported by a protocol on a particular server. For security purposes, it is not recommended to include this type of record, especially if the server is connected to the Internet, because it could provide an intruder with the necessary information to attack the server. Most sites do not use this record, but you should be aware of its existence. A sample entry is shown here:

```
mailmaster  IN  WKS    192.168.28.78   TCP (smtp rpc)
```

➤ *Pointer (PTR)*—This type of record is used for reverse hostname resolution—that is, when you want to find the IP address for a specified hostname. Typically, zone files used for reverse resolution append the .rev extension to the filename so that they are easily distinguishable. A special zone is used for reverse resolution, namely in-addr.arpa. The two sample entries shown here are equivalent, one using a relative address and one using the full address:

```
68                          IN  PTR  mailmaster
68.28.168.192.in-addr.arpa. IN  PTR  mailmaster
```

Note that the first entry includes only the host portion of the address because the remainder is automatically inserted. The second address is specified in full, but you should note that it is entered in reverse order with the in-addr.arpa. domain name appended to it, including the trailing . (dot) .

Configuring a Secondary DNS Server

The configuration of a secondary DNS server is similar to that of a primary DNS server, although there are some important differences:

➤ There are no zone files to create. These are automatically copied from the primary DNS server when the secondary server is configured and started for the first time.

➤ The status of this server for all zone entries in /etc/named.conf is slave, except for the root domain.

➤ There is an extra entry in the /etc/named.conf file that identifies the master server IP address. This specifies from where the zone files are to be copied.

In the previous section, the domain xyz.com was used to configure a primary DNS server. The sample /etc/named.conf file shown here is for a secondary DNS server in the same domain:

```
options {
        directory "/var/named";
};

zone "." in {
        type hint;
        file "named.ca";
};

zone "xyz.com" in {
        type slave;
        file "db.xyz";
        masters { 192.168.28.28; };
};

zone "28.168.192.in-addr.arpa" in {
        type slave;
        file "xyz.rev";
        masters { 192.168.28.28; };
};

zone "0.0.127.in-addr.arpa" in {
        type master;
        file "named.local";
};
```

 Each DNS server is always the master for the loopback reverse resolution zone (**0.0.127.in-addr.arpa**) because it refers to the local loopback address. This would not be copied from a primary DNS server. You should be aware of this in case you have to analyze a **/etc/named.conf** file in the exam.

Note that the root domain file, named.ca, is not automatically copied from the primary DNS server; it should be manually copied once during the configuration.

Configuring a Caching-Only DNS Server

A caching-only DNS server is much simpler to set up and contains no zone data files, except for the root domain file—named.ca (which should be manually copied to the server during the initial configuration)—and the loopback reverse resolution file. The local server is always the master for this conceptual zone. A typical caching-only configuration file, /etc/named.conf, is shown here:

```
directory "/var/named";
cache                     named.ca
master     0.0.127.in-addr.arpa   named.local;
```

Note that the named.ca root domain file should be manually copied from the primary DNS server during the initial configuration.

Configuring a DNS Client

A DNS client uses the DNS servers to carry out name resolution. DNS servers are also configured as DNS clients because they can also issue queries to be resolved. The client configuration process consists of two separate steps: one to configure the system to use DNS as a mechanism for name resolution and the second to identify the DNS servers that should be contacted to carry out the resolution. The first step involves the file /etc/nsswitch.conf, and the second involves the file /etc/resolv.conf>. Both are covered in the following sections.

/etc/nsswitch.conf

This file is the name service switch file that allows the use of flat files or other name services (such as NIS, NIS+, or LDAP) to resolve various queries. For DNS purposes, there is only one entry in this file of interest: the hosts: entry. When a system is installed with Solaris 9, the default hosts: entry uses only the flat files for name resolution, namely /etc/inet/hosts. To change this entry to include DNS, modify the entry to the following:

```
hosts:       files    dns
```

Solaris 9 provides a number of switch file templates, one of which is **/etc/nsswitch.dns**. This file can simply be copied to **/etc/nsswitch.conf** so that DNS resolution can apply. Be careful, though, if another name service is already in use (such as NIS) because doing this would overwrite the current configuration file and cause NIS problems. Read any exam question thoroughly to see whether any other name service is running before contemplating this as your answer.

The order of the entries in the switch file is important because DNS entries could be masked by entries in the local hosts file. A rogue entry in the hosts file could prevent DNS from being used to look up an IP address. You can also include a conditional statement that interprets the result of the query and takes a specific action based on the code returned from the query. There are four possible return codes, shown in Table 10.3.

Table 10.3	Name Resolution Return Codes
Code	**Description**
NOTFOUND	The required hostname entry was not found.
SUCCESS	The required hostname entry was found and resolved.
TRYAGAIN	The service was busy. Trying again might prove successful.
UNAVAIL	The service did not respond.

Two actions can be taken after the return code has been interpreted, namely continue or return. The continue action enables the query to try the next resolution method in the hosts: entry of the file, whereas the return action does not; it simply stops and the process fails.

As an example, consider what would happen if you had the following hosts: entry in your /etc/nsswitch.conf file:

```
hosts:        files [NOTFOUND=return]  dns
```

The result is that if a hostname could not be resolved with the /etc/inet/hosts file, then the process would stop and not use DNS at all.

You should be prepared for various scenarios involving the **/etc/nsswitch.conf** file. There are often questions that ask you to identify the resolution steps that would take place based on different **hosts:** entries. Make sure you understand the return codes and actions.

/etc/resolv.conf

This file specifies the DNS servers that the client can use to resolve host-names/IP addresses. A sample /etc/resolv.conf is shown here with the most popular options:

```
domain xyz.com
search xyz.com
nameserver 192.168.28.28;  Primary DNS server
nameserver 192.168.28.72;  Secondary DNS server
```

The domain entry identifies the current DNS domain name. The search entry identifies the domain name to append to queries that were not specified as fully qualified, such as if you queried the host sales rather than sales.xyz.com. The next two entries specify the IP addresses of two DNS servers that will attempt to resolve the query. You can enter up to three nameservers to consult, although it is normal to place the server that is physically nearest to you at the top so that it is always tried first.

NOTE

If there are no **nameserver** entries, or if the file **/etc/resolv.conf** does not exist, the client tries to use its own loopback address to resolve the query.

Troubleshooting

Some basic Solaris utilities can be used to troubleshoot DNS problems. This section shows how to deal with the most common problems.

Error Messages

The first place to look for DNS server error messages is /var/adm/messages. All errors relating to the DNS server are written to this file. The following extract shows that there is a configuration error in /etc/named.conf (normally a bracket or semi-colon has been omitted), and that the expiry time might need to be increased to at least 1 week, because it is currently less:

```
Jun  6 18:03:51 ultra10 named[597]: [ID 295310 daemon.error] \
/etc/named.conf:4: syntax error near '}'
Jun  6 18:03:51 ultra10 named[597]: [ID 295310 daemon.warning] db.xyz: \
WARNING SOA expire value is less than 7 days (432000)
Jun  6 18:03:51 ultra10 named[597]: [ID 295310 daemon.warning] xyz.rev: \
WARNING SOA expire value is less than 7 days (432000)
Jun  6 18:03:51 ultra10 named[597]: [ID 295310 daemon.warning] named.local:
\
WARNING SOA expire value is less than 7 days (432000)
Jun  6 18:03:51 ultra10 named[598]: [ID 295310 daemon.notice] \
Ready to answer queries.
```

telnet

You can easily test whether the `in.named` process is accepting requests by using the `telnet` command. DNS uses port 53, so connect to this port. If you establish a connection, it is working; if you don't, the process isn't running or there is a problem with it. The following code shows a `telnet` session to port 53, which connects successfully. Use the `Ctrl + ]` key to return to the `telnet` prompt and `close` to quit.

```
ultra5# telnet ultra10 53
Trying 192.168.28.28...
Connected to ultra10.
Escape character is '^]'.
^]
telnet> close
Connection to ultra10 closed.
```

nslookup

The `nslookup` command is useful for testing the DNS process. `nslookup` can be used as a single query command, or interactively where a number of additional functions can be carried out.

It is always a useful test to look up a host that you know is not present in your `/etc/inet/hosts` file, but you know exists on the network. The `nslookup` command returns the resolved information as well as the DNS server used to execute the query, as shown here:

```
ultra5# nslookup systemb
Server:  ultra10.xyz.com
Address:  192.168.28.28

Name:    systemb.xyz.com
Address:  192.168.28.127
```

You can also test another server, such as a secondary DNS server, by using the `nslookup` command. The following session output shows the interactive use of `nslookup` to resolve the same hostname as the preceding example:

```
ultra5# nslookup
Default Server:  ultra10.xyz.com
Address:  192.168.28.28

> server ultra5.xyz.com
Default Server:  ultra5.xyz.com.com
Address:  192.168.28.29
> systemb
Server:  ultra5.xyz.com
Address:  192.168.28.29

Name:    systemb.xyz.com
Address:  192.168.28.127
> #
```

Note that the interactive nslookup facility requires a Ctrl + D keystroke to exit to the command prompt.

Taking a Snapshot of the DNS Database

If there are problems with the DNS server, then taking a snapshot of the DNS database might help to diagnose the cause. You can take a snapshot of the database, which is being cached in the system memory, and write it to an ASCII file for later examination. The snapshot is stored in the file /var/named/named_dump.db and can be useful for finding errors in zone files, for example.

To take a snapshot, enter the following command as root from the command line:

```
ultra10# pkill -INT in.named
```

The action is logged in the /var/adm/messages file as shown here:

```
Jun 06 22:44:00 ultra10 named[173]: [ID 295310 daemon.notice] \
dumping nameserver data
Jun 06 22:44:00 ultra10 named[173]: [ID 295310 daemon.notice] \
finished dumping nameserver data
```

Debugging the **in.named** Daemon

To debug the in.named process, you can force it to provide a greater amount of output. Debugging is disabled by default, but you can initiate it and increase the debug level incrementally by running the following command a number of times:

```
ultra10# pkill -USR1 in.named
```

Each time you send in.named the USR1 signal, the debug level is increased, producing more output. Debug output is stored in the file /var/named/named.run.

The following output extract shows the debug output while the nslookup command is being run. It demonstrates how the additional output provides more detailed information about how the resolution process is working:

```
ultra10# cat /var/named/named.run
Debug level 1
Version = in.named BIND 8.2.4 Sat Apr  6 14:44:58 PST 2002
        Generic-5.9-May 2002
conffile = /etc/named.conf
Debug level 2
Debug level 3
datagram from [192.168.28.28].32829, fd 23, len 44
```

```
req: nlookup(28.28.168.192.in-addr.arpa) id 45076 type=12 class=1
req: found '28.28.168.192.in-addr.arpa' as '28.28.168.192.in-addr.arpa' \
(cname=0)
wanted(0xa0318, IN PTR) [IN PTR]
wantedtsig(0xa0318, IN PTR) [IN PTR]
finddata: added 1 class 1 type 12 RRs
req: foundname=1, count=1, founddata=1, cname=0
findns: SOA found
req: leaving (28.28.168.192.in-addr.arpa, rcode 0)
free_nsp: ultra10.xyz.com rcnt 1
findns: 2 NS's added for '28'
free_nsp: ultra10.xyz.com rcnt 1
free_nsp: systemb.xyz.com rcnt 1
doaddinfo() addcount = 3
do additional "ultra10.xyz.com" (from "28.168.192.in-addr.arpa")
found it
do additional "systemb.xyz.com" (from "28.168.192.in-addr.arpa")
found it
do additional "28.168.192.in-addr.arpa" (from "28.168.192.in-addr.arpa")
found it
ns_req: answer -> [192.168.28.28].32829 fd=23 id=45076 size=146 rc=0
datagram from [192.168.28.28].32830, fd 23, len 39
req: nlookup(systemb.xyz.com) id 45077 type=1 class=1
req: found 'systemb.xyz.com' as 'systemb.xyz.com' (cname=0)
wanted(0x9e2d4, IN A) [IN A]
wantedtsig(0x9e2d4, IN A) [IN A]
finddata: added 1 class 1 type 1 RRs
req: foundname=1, count=1, founddata=1, cname=0
findns: SOA found
req: leaving (systemb.xyz.com, rcode 0)
free_nsp: ultra10.xyz.com rcnt 1
findns: 2 NS's added for 'xyz'
free_nsp: ultra10.xyz.com rcnt 1
free_nsp: systemb.xyz.com rcnt 1
doaddinfo() addcount = 4
do additional "ultra10.xyz.com" (from "xyz.com")
found it
do additional "systemb.xyz.com" (from "xyz.com")
found it
do additional "systemb.xyz.com" (from "systemb.xyz.com")
found it
do additional "xyz.com" (from "xyz.com")
found it
ns_req: answer -> [192.168.28.28].32830 fd=23 id=45077 size=122 rc=0
```

Notice that the debug level was increased three times; that is, the USR1 signal was sent to the in.named process three times.

To turn off the debugging facility, send the in.named process the -USR2 signal. This sets the debug level to zero, effectively turning the facility off, as shown here:

```
ultra10# pkill -USR2 in.named
```

A short message is appended to the debug file /var/named/named.run to confirm that debugging has been turned off.

Causing the **in.named** Daemon to Reread Its Configuration Files

In a similar way to the `inetd` daemon, you can make `in.named` reread all its configuration files, without having to stop and start the daemon process itself. The advantage to taking this action is that you don't lose the information held in cache. To make the process reread its configuration files, send `in.named` the `HUP` signal, as shown here:

```
ultra10# pkill -HUP in.named
```

The following information messages are written to the `/var/adm/messages` file to confirm that the action has been carried out:

```
Jun  6 18:06:29 ultra10 named[598]: [ID 295310 daemon.notice] \
reloading nameserver
Jun  6 18:06:29 ultra10 named[598]: [ID 295310 daemon.notice] \
Ready to answer queries.
```

Using **ndc**

The `ndc` utility can be used to monitor and modify the DNS server and provides an alternative to sending various signals to the `in.named` process. It can be used either directly from the command-line prompt, or interactively. `ndc` provides much greater control over a DNS server from within a single utility, which enables you to stop and start the server, change or disable the debug levels, and examine the current status, among other things. Run the `ndc` command and type **help** to see a list of options. The following session shows an example use of `ndc` specifying the `help` and `status` options:

```
ultra10# ndc
Type  help  -or-  /h   if you need help.
ndc> help
(builtin) start - start the server
(builtin) restart - stop server if any, start a new one
getpid
status
stop
exec
reload [zone] ...
reconfig [-noexpired] (just sees new/gone zones)
dumpdb
stats [clear]
trace [level]
notrace
querylog
qrylog
help
quit
ndc> status
```

```
in.named BIND 8.2.4 Sat Apr  6 14:44:58 PST 2002  Generic-5.9-May 2002
config (/etc/named.conf) last loaded at age: Fri Jun  6 18:06:22 2003
number of zones allocated: 64
debug level: 0
xfers running: 0
xfers deferred: 0
soa queries in progress: 0
query logging is OFF
server is up and running
ndc> quit
```

The status option in this code shows the version of the BIND software in use and that debugging is currently at level 0; that is, debugging is disabled. It also shows that the DNS server is available and running and that there are no queries outstanding.

Exam Prep Questions

Question 1

Which well-known network port number does DNS use?

○ A. 21
○ B. 23
○ C. 53
○ D. 25

Answer C is correct because DNS uses well-known port number 53 for its network communication. Answer A is incorrect because port 21 is used by ftp. Answer B is incorrect because port 23 is used by telnet. Answer D is incorrect because port 25 is used by smtp for email purposes.

Question 2

Which signal would you send to the **in.named** process to turn off debugging?

○ A. **HUP**
○ B. **USR1**
○ C. **INT**
○ D. **USR2**

Answer D is correct because the USR2 signal is sent to the in.named process to turn off debugging. Answer A is incorrect because the HUP signal causes in.named to reread its configuration files. Answer B is incorrect because the USR1 signal increases the debug level incrementally each time it is sent. Answer C is incorrect because the INT signal causes in.named to dump a snapshot of the DNS database to an ASCII file.

Question 3

Which two files are involved in the configuration of a DNS client? Choose 2.

❑ A. /etc/named.conf
❑ B. /etc/nsswitch.conf
❑ C. /etc/resolv.conf
❑ D. /etc/inet/hosts

Answers B and C are correct because the two files involved in configuring a DNS client are /etc/nsswitch.conf and /etc/resolv.conf. Answer A is incorrect because the /etc/named.conf file is the master configuration file used to configure a DNS server; it is not used to configure a DNS client. Answer D is incorrect because the /etc/inet/hosts file is used to provide hostname resolution through the use of local files; it is not used by DNS.

Question 4

In a DNS zone data file, what does the resource record type **AAAA** mean?

- ○ A. It identifies a name server for the domain
- ○ B. It identifies a hostname entry with an IPv4 address.
- ○ C. It identifies a hostname entry with an IPv6 address.
- ○ D. It identifies an alias for a hostname.

Answer C is correct because the AAAA resource record type (or quad A) identifies a hostname entry with an IPv6 address. Answer A is incorrect because this describes the NS record type. Answer B is incorrect because this describes the A record type. Answer D is incorrect because this describes the CNAME record type.

Question 5

The DNS daemon process **in.named** is started only if which file exists?

- ○ A. **/etc/named.conf**
- ○ B. **/var/named/named.run**
- ○ C. **/var/named/named_dump.db**
- ○ D. **/etc/nsswitch.conf**

Answer A is correct because the file /etc/named.conf is the DNS server master configuration file and must exist before the daemon process will start. Answer B is incorrect because the file /var/named/named.run is used to store DNS server debug output. Answer C is incorrect because /var/named/named_dump.db is the file used to store a DNS database snapshot. Answer D is incorrect because /etc/nsswitch is used by the DNS client; it has no effect on whether the DNS server process starts.

Question 6

What is the maximum number of DNS nameservers that can be specified in the **/etc/resolv.conf** file?

- ○ A. 1
- ○ B. 2
- ○ C. 3
- ○ D. 4

Answer C is correct because a maximum of 3 DNS nameservers can be specified in the /etc/resolv.conf file, making answers A, B and D incorrect.

Question 7

Which signal would you send to the **in.named** process to reread its configuration file?

- ○ A. **HUP**
- ○ B. **USR2**
- ○ C. **INT**
- ○ D. **USR1**

Answer A is correct because the HUP signal causes in.named to reread its configuration files. Answer B is incorrect because the USR2 signal is sent to the in.named process to turn off debugging. Answer C is incorrect because the INT signal causes in.named to dump a snapshot of the DNS database to an ASCII file. Answer D is incorrect because the USR1 signal increases the debug level incrementally each time it is sent.

Need to Know More?

 Albitz, Paul and Liu, Cricket, et al. *DNS and BIND*. O'Reilly & Associates, 2001.

 Sun Microsystems. *Solaris 9 System Administrator Collection—System Administration Guide* "Naming and Directory Services (DNS, NIS and LDAP)." Available in printed form, on the Web at www.docs.sun.com, and from the online documentation provided with the Solaris 9 operating system.

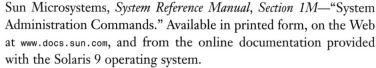 Sun Microsystems, *System Reference Manual, Section 1M*—"System Administration Commands." Available in printed form, on the Web at www.docs.sun.com, and from the online documentation provided with the Solaris 9 operating system.

Basic Dynamic Host Configuration Protocol (DHCP)

Terms you'll need to understand:

✓ Datastore
✓ **dhcpagent** Process
✓ **dhcptab** Table
✓ DHCP Client
✓ DHCP Scope
✓ DHCP Server
✓ **/etc/inet/dhcpsvc.conf**
✓ Lease
✓ Relay

Concepts you'll need to master:

✓ Describing the purposes and features of DHCP client and server functions
✓ Describing how to configure a DHCP server and use associated utilities
✓ Explaining how to configure and manage a DHCP client to either request a dynamic hostname or use its own hostname

This chapter introduces the Dynamic Host Configuration Protocol (DHCP) and explains basically how it works, what it is used for, and how to configure a server and client.

DHCP Fundamentals

DHCP allows the automatic assignment of network parameters, such as IP addresses, to a number of hosts or devices. Previously, networks were smaller and contained a number of hosts that used static addresses. These networks were easy to manage and administer, but with the proliferation of laptops and network devices, coupled with the increase in user mobility, the administrator could not cope with the demand for short-term address management. DHCP addresses this issue by managing ranges of IP addresses, which can be allocated as required. When an address is no longer needed by a client, it is released and becomes free to be allocated to another client.

Why Use DHCP?

DHCP facilitates the distribution and allocation of IP addresses dynamically, from a central location, the DHCP server. When a client is configured to use DHCP, it automatically obtains a short-term lease of an IP address when it boots up. If the same computer moves to another network, it is automatically assigned a new IP address relevant to that network, without the need for an administrator to manually configure the network interface.

Without the use of DHCP, all IP addresses would have to be manually configured, a task that would quickly become unmanageable in today's large network environments.

What Does a DHCP Server Do?

A DHCP server manages a range of IP addresses. When a request is received from a booting client, known as a DHCPDISCOVER request, the server responds with an offer of an IP address to lease from the server for a finite period of time, known as a DHCPOFFER. The client can receive multiple offers if there are a number of DHCP servers on the network (as long as the servers all manage a different range of IP addresses). The client then selects an offer to receive, which is passed back to the server in the form of a DHCPREQUEST message. The server finally sends a DHCPACK message to confirm the lease. The process that runs on a DHCP server is called `in.dhcpd`.

What Does a DHCP Client Do?

A DHCP client is responsible for obtaining sufficient information to enable it to configure the network interface so that network communication can occur. The client runs a process called dhcpagent, which listens for a response from a DHCP server, handles the renewing or relinquishing of a lease for an IP address, and configures the network interface when an IP address has been assigned to the client, after checking that no other host on the network is using the assigned IP address.

Configuring a DHCP Server

DHCP server configuration consists of two steps: configuring the server and then starting it. There are two ways of configuring the server: a command-line method that uses the dhcpconfig command and the use of a graphical utility, dhcpmgr. The dhcpconfig command method is the fastest way to configure a server, but it requires more detailed knowledge of the process and is more advanced, whereas the dhcpmgr utility is easier to use, validates the input values as they are entered, and uses default values automatically—unlike dhcpconfig, where the values must be specified.

dhcpmgr

The dhcpmgr command runs in an X Windows environment, such as CDE, and is located in the /usr/sadm/admin/bin directory.

The following steps describe the server configuration process when you use the dhcpmgr graphical utility:

1. Start the dhcpmgr utility by running the following command in the background from the command line in any window:

```
ultra10# /usr/sadm/admin/bin/dhcpmgr &
```

The following window appears, enabling you to configure either a DHCP server or a BOOTP relay server. A BOOTP relay server is one that acts on behalf of a DHCP server and forwards requests from a DHCP client onto a DHCP server. These steps concentrate on configuring a DHCP server, so click the Configure as DHCP Server button and then the OK button to do this, as shown in Figure 11.1.

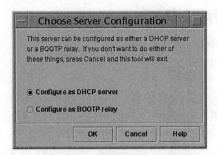

Figure 11.1 Initial DHCP Server Configuration window.

2. The next window determines the format of the datastore. There are three formats available in Solaris 9:

➤ *Text Files*—The datastore is stored as ASCII files, which are readable with standard Unix utilities. This is the default option.

➤ *Binary Files*—The datastore is stored as binary files, requiring you to use either the dhcpmgr utility or the dhtadm or pntadm commands to view the data. This option provides better performance, particularly for large networks.

➤ *NIS+*—The datastore is stored as an NIS+ table and requires that the NIS+ naming service be available and the DHCP server must be configured as an NIS+ client.

Select the Text Files option and click the > button to continue, as shown in Figure 11.2.

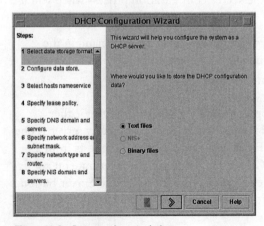

Figure 11.2 Datastore format window.

3. Now that you have determined the format of the datastore, the next window prompts for the directory in which the contents of the datastore are to be located. The default value is /var/dhcp. Accept this by clicking the > button to continue, as shown in Figure 11.3.

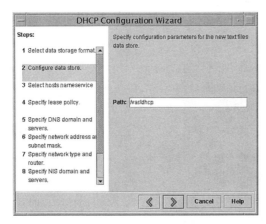

Figure 11.3   Datastore location window.

4. The next window determines where the client DHCP host records will be stored. If you were solely using DNS for host resolution, then you would select this option and enter the name of the DNS domain that manages these hosts. For this example, the local /etc/hosts file is being selected to manage the local DHCP clients, with DNS being available for remote name resolution, as shown in Figure 11.4. Click the > button to continue.

Figure 11.4   Host record storage window.

5. The lease policy in the next window determines how long a leased IP address will be valid. The default of one day is normally sufficient and is being used here. Another important option on this screen is whether clients can renew their leases. The default is to leave this enabled so that a client can renew a lease when it expires and retain the same IP address. Figure 11.5 shows this window with the desired values. Click the > button to continue.

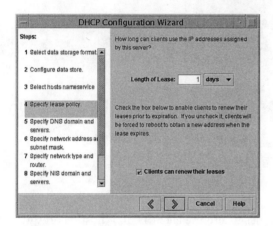

Figure 11.5   Lease policy window.

6. The specification of any DNS domain and relevant DNS servers is configured next. If you are not using DNS, then there is no need to enter anything here. If you are using DNS, then the utility attempts to insert the domain name and server IP addresses of any servers that are known. Figure 11.6 shows the DNS domain xyz.com with a DNS server IP address of 192.168.28.28. Click the > button to continue.

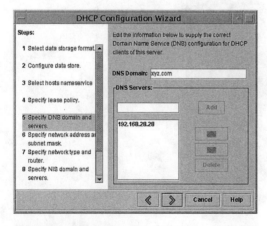

Figure 11.6   DNS configuration window.

7. The next window specifies the network on which IP addresses are to be allocated. Known networks are displayed in a pull-down menu along with the relevant network mask. For this example, the network 192.168.29.0 is going to be the network for which IP addresses will be allocated. Figure 11.7 demonstrates this. Click the > button to proceed.

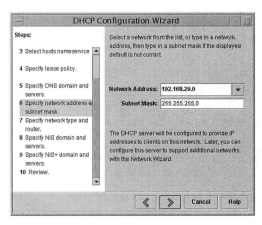

Figure 11.7 Network address window.

8. The next window specifies the type of network you are using, either a LAN or a point-to-point network. Also, you configure the routing, either by using the Router Discovery Protocol (RDISC) or, if you have a dedicated default router, you can enter the router's IP address. Figure 11.8 shows that the router discovery protocol is being used to dynamically determine the routers on the network. Click the > button to proceed.

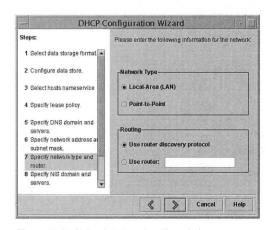

Figure 11.8 Network type and routing window.

9. If you are using the NIS naming service, then the next window is the place to enter the NIS domain name and the IP addresses of your NIS servers. If you are not using NIS, then you should leave the fields blank, as shown in Figure 11.9, and proceed to the next screen.

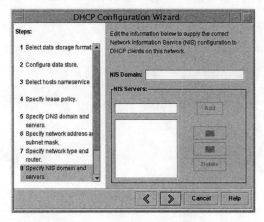

Figure 11.9 NIS configuration window.

10. If you are using the NIS+ naming service, then the next window is the place to enter the NIS+ domain name and the IP addresses of your NIS+ servers. If you are not using NIS+, then you should leave the fields blank and proceed to the next screen. Figure 11.10 shows that NIS+ is not being used.

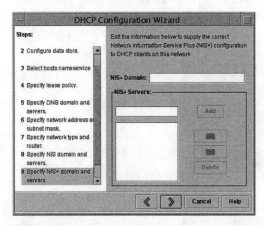

Figure 11.10 NIS+ configuration window.

11. The final DHCP server configuration window shows a summary of the information entered so far. Confirm that the configuration is acceptable and click the Finish button as shown in Figure 11.11.

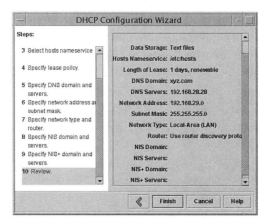

Figure 11.11   DHCP server configuration summary window.

12. A popup window appears because even though the DHCP server configuration is complete, there is no list of IP addresses to use. To begin allocating IP addresses to clients, the DHCP tables must be configured. Click Yes in the window to begin populating the tables. Figure 11.12 shows this window.

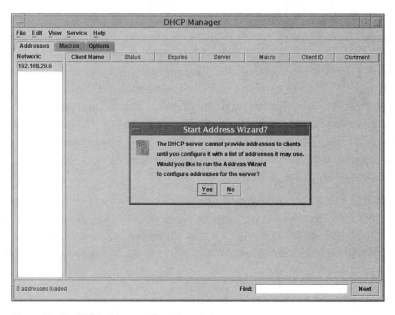

Figure 11.12   DHCP address configuration window.

13. When you select the Yes option in the preceding step, the address configuration wizard starts, which guides you through the remainder of the setup. Figure 11.13 displays a window where the range of addresses is defined, as well as comments for the administrator. For this example, a block of 50 IP addresses is going to be reserved for use by DHCP and a comment will remind the administrator that these addresses are to be used by hosts on the Alpha site located on the 3rd floor. Click the > button to continue.

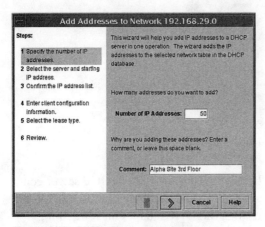

Figure 11.13 DHCP address scope window.

14. Having defined the block of IP addresses as 50, you are now prompted to specify the starting IP address. The block of 50 IP addresses is allocated sequentially, starting at the address entered here. For this example, 192.168.29.31 is to be the first address. The server name is inserted into this window as the name of the server that will manage the IP addresses. The last part of this window identifies a root for the hostnames that will be assigned to clients that use these IP addresses. In this example, the root name alpha3 is used to represent the 3rd floor of the Alpha site. The first hostname in this block of IP addresses will therefore be alpha3-31. Figure 11.14 demonstrates these values. Click the > button to continue.

15. A scrolling list of the allocatable IP addresses and associated hostnames is displayed. You have to confirm that these details are to be added to the DHCP database. Click the > button to proceed and accept the values, as shown in Figure 11.15.

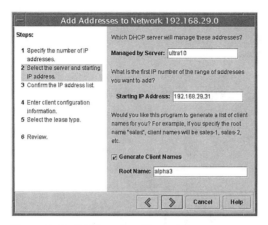

Figure 11.14   DHCP starting address window.

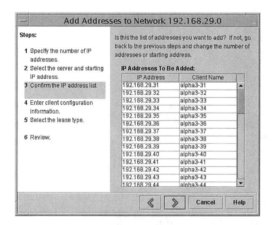

Figure 11.15   DHCP allocatable address confirmation window.

16. When you have confirmed that the IP addresses are correct, you are prompted for information on how to configure the clients. A pull-down menu lists a number of macros that can be selected. The default option is to select the one with the hostname of the DHCP server. This macro would normally contain all of the information a DHCP client requires and was created as part of the server configuration process. Figure 11.16 shows this window.

17. To view the contents of any of the macros, click the View button and another window appears detailing the contents of the values that will be applied to the clients that use this DHCP server. Figure 11.17 displays the macro relating to the DHCP server that has just been configured—ultra10.

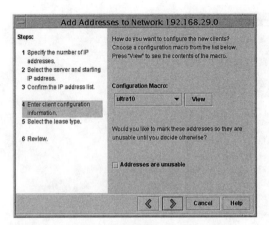

Figure 11.16 DHCP client macro selection window.

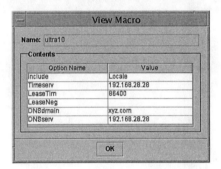

Figure 11.17 DHCP client macro window.

18. The last thing to do is to specify the type of lease that is going to be provided for each of the IP addresses in the block that has been added to the DHCP database. There are two choices: dynamic, where the IP addresses are allocated on a first-come first-served basis, and permanent, where a client reserves the same IP address each time it connects to the network. For this example, dynamic leasing is being used, as demonstrated in Figure 11.18. Click the > button to proceed to the final confirmation window.

19. There is a final confirmation window that appears, showing a summary of the information entered so far. Click the Finish button to accept these values and exit from the address configuration wizard. Figure 11.19 shows the confirmation window for the values entered in the example.

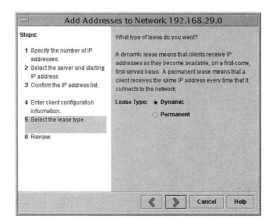

Figure 11.18   DHCP lease type window.

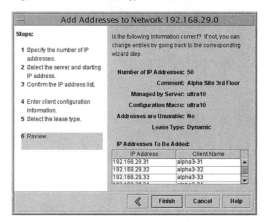

Figure 11.19   DHCP address confirmation window.

20. The main DHCP manager window appears again, which now includes the addresses that have been added to the database. Figure 11.20 shows the window as it appears following the example configuration. From the `File` menu, select `Exit` to close `dhcpmgr`. The DHCP server is now configured and ready to use.

DHCP lease types cannot be mixed within the same block of allocated IP addresses. If you needed both permanent leases and dynamic leases, you would have to create a separate block of addresses for each.

DHCP Manager

File Edit View Service Help

Addresses **Macros** **Options**

Network:	Client Name	Status	Expires	Server	Macro	Client ID	Comment
192.168.29.0	alpha3-31	Dynamic		ultra10	ultra10	00	Alpha Site 3rd Floor
	alpha3-32	Dynamic		ultra10	ultra10	00	Alpha Site 3rd Floor
	alpha3-33	Dynamic		ultra10	ultra10	00	Alpha Site 3rd Floor
	alpha3-34	Dynamic		ultra10	ultra10	00	Alpha Site 3rd Floor
	alpha3-35	Dynamic		ultra10	ultra10	00	Alpha Site 3rd Floor
	alpha3-36	Dynamic		ultra10	ultra10	00	Alpha Site 3rd Floor
	alpha3-37	Dynamic		ultra10	ultra10	00	Alpha Site 3rd Floor
	alpha3-38	Dynamic		ultra10	ultra10	00	Alpha Site 3rd Floor
	alpha3-39	Dynamic		ultra10	ultra10	00	Alpha Site 3rd Floor
	alpha3-40	Dynamic		ultra10	ultra10	00	Alpha Site 3rd Floor
	alpha3-41	Dynamic		ultra10	ultra10	00	Alpha Site 3rd Floor
	alpha3-42	Dynamic		ultra10	ultra10	00	Alpha Site 3rd Floor
	alpha3-43	Dynamic		ultra10	ultra10	00	Alpha Site 3rd Floor
	alpha3-44	Dynamic		ultra10	ultra10	00	Alpha Site 3rd Floor
	alpha3-45	Dynamic		ultra10	ultra10	00	Alpha Site 3rd Floor
	alpha3-46	Dynamic		ultra10	ultra10	00	Alpha Site 3rd Floor
	alpha3-47	Dynamic		ultra10	ultra10	00	Alpha Site 3rd Floor
	alpha3-48	Dynamic		ultra10	ultra10	00	Alpha Site 3rd Floor
	alpha3-49	Dynamic		ultra10	ultra10	00	Alpha Site 3rd Floor
	alpha3-50	Dynamic		ultra10	ultra10	00	Alpha Site 3rd Floor
	alpha3-51	Dynamic		ultra10	ultra10	00	Alpha Site 3rd Floor
	alpha3-52	Dynamic		ultra10	ultra10	00	Alpha Site 3rd Floor
	alpha3-53	Dynamic		ultra10	ultra10	00	Alpha Site 3rd Floor
	alpha3-54	Dynamic		ultra10	ultra10	00	Alpha Site 3rd Floor
	alpha3-55	Dynamic		ultra10	ultra10	00	Alpha Site 3rd Floor
	alpha3-56	Dynamic		ultra10	ultra10	00	Alpha Site 3rd Floor
	alpha3-57	Dynamic		ultra10	ultra10	00	Alpha Site 3rd Floor
	alpha3-58	Dynamic		ultra10	ultra10	00	Alpha Site 3rd Floor

50 addresses loaded   Find: Next

Figure 11.20 DHCP Manager window.

A configuration file is created when you run the server configuration utility. This file is located in /etc/inet/dhcpsvc.conf and should not be edited by hand. The configuration file created during this session is shown here:

```
ultra10# cat /etc/inet/dhcpsvc.conf
DAEMON_ENABLED=TRUE
RUN_MODE=server
RESOURCE=SUNWfiles
PATH=/var/dhcp
CONVER=1
HOSTS_RESOURCE=files
```

The DHCP server configuration file, **/etc/inet/dhcpsvc.conf**, was stored in **/etc/default/dhcp** in previous Solaris releases. In an exam question, it could be an option that distracts you from the correct answer.

dhcpconfig

The dhcpconfig utility is intended for use by more advanced system administrators and lends itself well to configuration using scripts. It is a command-line tool for configuring the DHCP server and is a much quicker way of creating the server than using the graphical utility, dhcpmgr. Specifically, dhcpconfig provides options to

➤ Configure a new DHCP server.

➤ Convert an existing datastore to a different format, making the new format ready for use.

➤ Import data from other DHCP servers and export data to other DHCP servers.

➤ Unconfigure an existing DHCP server, with additional options to remove host entries and the DHCP database files.

In previous releases of Solaris, **dhcpconfig** was a menu-driven utility. This has changed with Solaris 9, where it is now a command-line utility. Also, an additional datastore format, binary files (**SUNWbinfiles**), was released with Solaris 9—previous releases had only two formats, text files (**SUNWfiles**) and NIS+ table (**SUNWnisplus**).

To configure the DHCP server, you must first define the datastore type and the directory to be used for storing the database tables. Additionally, you can specify a DNS domain name and a DNS server. The following example shows the command which configures a DHCP server to use a text file datastore (SUNWfiles), with /var/dhcp being the repository directory (-p option). It also identifies the DNS domain (-d option) and a DNS server (-a option) and that the local /etc/inet/hosts file (-h option) is to store hostname and IP address details:

```
ultra10# dhcpconfig -D -r SUNWfiles -p /var/dhcp -d xyz.com
➥-a 192.168.28.28 -h files
Created DHCP configuration file.
Created dhcptab.
Added "Locale" macro to dhcptab.
Added server macro to dhcptab - ultra10.
DHCP server started.
```

Note that the messages received on the screen as the configuration proceeds let you know what is happening. The configuration file /etc/inet/dhcpsvc.conf is created along with the dhcptab table. Two macros have been defined in the table and the server process, in.dhcpd, is now running.

This server doesn't actually do anything at this point because it is not managing any specific network and does not have a list of IP addresses under its control. This is done next.

Use the dhcpconfig command again to specify the network for which the DHCP server is going to provide a service. The following example also uses a single router, specified with the -t option:

```
ultra10# dhcpconfig -N 192.168.28.0 -t 192.168.28.28
Added network macro to dhcptab - 192.168.28.0.
Created network table.
```

Note that an additional macro has been added to the `dhcptab` table. This table is described in greater detail later in this chapter.

An advantage of using the ASCII file type of datastore is that the tables are easily viewed, just like any other file. The contents of the `dhcptab` file at this point in the configuration process are shown here:

```
ultra10# cat /var/dhcp/SUNWfiles1_dhcptab
# SUNWfiles1_dhcptab
#
# Do NOT edit this file by hand -- use dhtadm(1M) or dhcpmgr(1M) instead
#
Locale|m|62231302600958935051:UTCoffst=0:
ultra10|m|46933137616734781451:Include=Locale:Timeserv=192.168.28.28 \
:LeaseTim=86400:LeaseNeg:DNSdmain="xyz.com":DNSserv=192.168.28.28:
192.168.28.0|m|160311258235787018251:Subnet=255.255.255.0: \
Router=192.168.28.28:Broadcst=192.168.28.255:
```

Note that the `ultra10` macro has been defined so that it provides standard setup information for clients, such as the locale, the default lease time, DNS information and so on.

The network macro (`192.168.28.0`) contains a subnet mask. If this value is not specified on the command line, the `/etc/inet/netmasks` file is automatically consulted.

The dhcp_network File

The next step in the manual configuration of the DHCP server is to add the range of IP addresses the server is going to be responsible for allocating to clients. The `dhcp_network` file is used to contain the range of addresses.

A separate file is created for each network that is specified with the `-N` option to the `dhcpconfig` command. The example used in this section specifies the network `192.168.28.0`. In the repository directory, there is a file called `SUNWfiles1_192_168_28_0`. The filename is based on the datastore type and the IP address of the network it serves. When the file is created initially, it looks like this:

```
ultra10# cat SUNWfiles1_192_168_28_0
# SUNWfiles1_192_168_28_0
#
# Do NOT edit this file by hand -- use pntadm(1M) or dhcpmgr(1M) instead
#
```

Note that there are no IP addresses for the DHCP server to manage yet. You add these in the next section, by using `pntadm`.

The pntadm Command

The pntadm command is used to manage the DHCP network table, specifically to add, modify, or delete IP addresses that the DHCP server is going to manage; to add or remove networks that come under the control of the DHCP server; and to inspect the network tables themselves.

The most common use for this command is to add the range of IP addresses the DHCP server is responsible for allocating to clients. Each address has to be added manually to the table, which is one reason why this method of configuring a DHCP server is well suited to the use of scripts to loop through a defined block of numbers, eliminating the need to add each one manually.

The following command adds the IP address 192.168.28.31 to the 192.168.28.0 network table. It also identifies a hostname (alpha3_31), which will automatically be added to the local /etc/inet/hosts file:

```
ultra10# pntadm -A 192.168.28.31 -h alpha3_31 192.168.28.0
```

This command uses the default configuration information, such as the datastore type and the repository directory. The following command is identical to it, but instead of accepting default values, it specifies them on the command line:

```
ultra10# pntadm -r SUNWfiles -p /var/dhcp -A 192.168.28.31 -h alpha3_31
➥192.168.28.0
```

The database now contains an IP address to manage that looks like this:

```
ultra10# cat /var/dhcp/SUNWfiles1_192_168_28_0
# SUNWfiles1_192_168_28_0
#
# Do NOT edit this file by hand -- use pntadm(1M) or dhcpmgr(1M) instead
#
192.168.28.31|00|00|192.168.28.28|0|7336363792986537986|UNKNOWN|
```

The manual pages for the pntadm command and for the dhcp_network file describe the full range of options and the file format.

The dhcptab Table and dhtadm

The dhcptab table is used to store the configuration parameters, which will be passed to clients that use DHCP. The parameters are stored as macros in this table, where symbols can also be created to hold specific values. A symbol functions in a similar way to a variable.

The dhcptab table should not be edited manually; use either the DHCP manager (dhcpmgr) or the dhtadm command. This section describes the use of the dhtadm command.

```
# dhtadm -P
Name                      Type           Value
========================================================
192.168.28.0              Macro          :Subnet=255.255.255.0: \
Router=192.168.28.28:Broadcst=192.168.28.255:
ultra10                   Macro          :Include=Locale:Timeserv= \
192.168.28.28:LeaseTim=86400:LeaseNeg:DNSdmain="xyz.com":DNSserv= \
192.168.28.28:
Locale                    Macro          :UTCoffst=0:
```

Notice that the the `dhtadm -P` command results in the same output as using the `cat` command, for example, to view the file `SUNWfiles1_dhcptab`. The `dhcptab` table is readable only because an ASCII file based `datastore` type is being used.

Any changes that are made to the **dhcptab** table need to be read by the DHCP server. Remember that a SIGHUP (**-HUP**) needs to be sent to the **in.dhcpd** process so that it rereads the **dhcptab** table and implements any changes that have been made.

The most common `dhtadm` options are

➤ -A—Use this option to add and define a symbol or macro to the table.

➤ -M—Use this option to modify an existing symbol or macro in the table.

➤ -D—Use this option to delete an existing symbol or macro from the table.

➤ -P—Use this option to print (view) the contents of the `dhcptab` table.

Starting and Stopping the DHCP Server

The DHCP server is started at system boot time by the startup script `/etc/rc3.d/S34dhcp`. The `in.dhcpd` process starts only if the configuration file `/etc/inet/dhcpsvc.conf` exists and if the `DAEMON_ENABLED` variable in the configuration file is set to `TRUE`.

To stop a running DHCP server, enter the following command:

```
ultra10# /etc/rc3.d/S34dhcp stop
```

This cleanly shuts down the DHCP server manually.

To start the DHCP server manually, enter the following command:

```
ultra10# /etc/rc3.d/S34dhcp start
```

Uninstalling a DHCP Server

If DHCP is no longer required, or you wish to remove the DHCP server from your system, then you can use the `dhcpconfig` command to uninstall the server and optionally remove the host entries and the DHCP database tables as shown here:

```
ultra10# dhcpconfig -U -x -h -f
```

The options are described here:

➤ -U—This is the option to uninstall the DHCP server.

➤ -f—This sub-option states that no confirmation of the operation is required. If this sub-option is omitted, you get a confirmation message to reply to before the DHCP server is removed.

➤ -x—This sub-option removes the DHCP database tables.

➤ -h—This sub-option removes the host entries that were added for each managed IP address.

The following example shows how to uninstall a DHCP server, omitting the -f option, so that the confirmation message is displayed:

```
ultra10# dhcpconfig -U -x -h
Unconfigure will stop the DHCP service and remove the DHCP configuration
➥ file.
Are you SURE you want to unconfigure the DHCP service? ([Y]/N):y
DHCP server shutdown.
Deleted the server macro from dhcptab.
Deleted table for network 192.168.28.0.
Deleted the dhcptab.
Deleted the DHCP configuration file.
```

The first thing the command does is to stop the server process. The DHCP database tables are then removed, along with the host entries, and finally the configuration file is removed.

NOTE

Note that the host entries are removed from the local **/etc/inet/hosts** file because this option was specified when the DHCP server was initially configured.

Configuring a DHCP Client

The DHCP client configuration procedure is much simpler than that of the DHCP server, where most of the work has to be done. If you elected to use

DHCP when installing Solaris 9 on your system, then there is nothing more to do and the DHCP client software will be enabled.

By default, the DHCP client is enabled to request a hostname dynamically, depending on how the DHCP server has been set up.

To start using DHCP on a system already running Solaris 9, create an empty file for the primary interface and edit the /etc/default/dhcpagent file so that any IP address assigned to the client is relinquished when the client is shut down or is rebooted:

1. Log in as root on the client.

2. Edit the client DHCP default parameter file, /etc/default/dhcpagent.

3. Go to the entry RELEASE_ON_SIGTERM=yes. This entry is commented out by default, so uncomment it to make the client relinquish its IP address when it shuts down or reboots.

4. Create the appropriate interface file to enable DHCP. For example, if your system has an hme0 interface, create the file /etc/dhcp.hme0 as shown here:

```
ultra5# touch /etc/dhcp.hme0
```

5. Reboot the client.

When you create the empty interface file, such as **/etc/dhcp.hme0**, you do not have to delete the original corresponding interface file, such as **/etc/hostname.hme0**. It would still be needed if you disabled DHCP on the client.

The DHCP client process dhcpagent manages DHCP on the client side and interacts with the DHCP server. When the process starts, it waits for a request from the ifconfig command during the boot process to configure the primary network interface, at which point it starts DHCP. The process also handles the renewing of leases from a DHCP server transparently. The default parameter file, /etc/default/dhcpagent, is read when the process starts and determines the default behavior of the client with regard to DHCP.

Configuring a DHCP Client to Request a Specific Hostname

The configuration for a client to request a specific hostname, rather than to request a dynamic hostname from the DHCP server, is slightly different, and the procedure to follow is shown here for a system using an `hme0` network interface and a hostname of `ultra_test`:

1. Log in as `root` on the client.

2. Edit the default parameter file, `/etc/default/dhcpagent`.

3. Go to the entry `REQUEST_HOSTNAME=no`. By default this entry is commented out, so uncomment it and modify the entry to `REQUEST_HOSTNAME=yes`.

4. Edit the hostname interface file, such as `/etc/hostname.hme0`, and insert the following entry to identify the system hostname as `ultra_test`, as follows:

   ```
   inet ultra_test
   ```

5. Disable the `dhcpagent` process and remove the state file if one exists, as follows:

   ```
   ultra5# pkill dhcpagent
   ultra5# rm /etc/dhcp/hme0.dhc
   ```

6. Reboot the client.

> You should note that you still need the file **/etc/dhcp.<*interface*>** to be present if you want to use DHCP when the client boots up. If this file is deleted, then DHCP doesn't start up. Also, when specifying a hostname, it must already be configured on the DHCP server as a valid hostname with a valid IP address—you can't just choose any hostname.

When you elect to specify a hostname, the DHCP server first checks to make sure the hostname is not already in use on the network, before assigning it to the client.

How to Update DNS Dynamically

When a client is assigned an IP address and hostname by the DHCP server, the server can also update DNS, so that the new hostname is visible from outside the local domain. To configure DNS dynamic updates, both the DNS server and the DHCP server need to be modified.

The following procedure shows how to enable dynamic DNS updates from the DHCP server with an IP address of 192.168.28.28.

1. On the DNS server, log in as root and edit the /etc/named.conf file. For the relevant zone, update both the zone file entry and the reverse lookup entry, adding the following line:

```
allow-update { 127.0.0.1; 192.168.28.28; };
```

Note that both zone entries must be updated to allow the A records and PTR records to be updated.

The modified /etc/named.conf file from Chapter 10, "Domain Name System (DNS)," is shown here to demonstrate the application of dynamic DNS updates:

```
ultra10# cat /etc/named.conf
options {
        directory "/var/named";
};

acl "slaves" {
        {192.168.28.0/24 ; };
};

zone "." in {
        type hint;
        file "named.ca";
};

zone "xyz.com" in {
        type master;
        file "db.xyz";
        allow-transfer {"slaves";};
        allow-update { 127.0.0.1; 192.168.28.28; };
};

zone "28.168.192.in-addr.arpa" in {
        type master;
        file "xyz.rev";
         allow-update { 127.0.0.1; 192.168.28.28; };
};

zone "0.0.127.in-addr.arpa" in {
        type master;
        file "named.local";
};
```

2. Restart the DNS server process, in.named as follows:

```
ultra10# pkill -HUP in.named
```

3. On the DHCP server, start the DHCP server manager by entering the following command in a CDE window:

```
ultra10# /usr/sadm/admin/bin/dhcpmgr &
```

The DHCP manager window appears. Figure 11.21 shows a sample DHCP server with only two IP addresses configured on the `192.168.28.0` network.

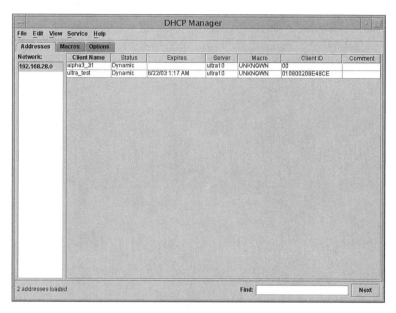

Figure 11.21   DHCP Manager window with two IP addresses.

4. Select the `Service` menu and the `Modify` option. Figure 11.22 shows the Modify Service Options window.

Figure 11.22   DHCP Modify Service Options window.

5. Check the Update DNS Host Information Upon Client Request check box. This configures the DHCP server to update the DNS server with newly assigned client information. The default timeout value of 15 seconds should be acceptable, but this can be changed as well, if required.

6. Make sure the Restart Server box is also checked at the bottom of the window, so that the changes take effect immediately.

7. Click on the OK button to apply the modifications.

8. Quit dhcpmgr.

Exam Prep Questions

Question 1

> Which two commands can be used to configure a DHCP server? Choose 2.
>
> ❑ A. **dhcpconfig**
> ❑ B. **in.dhcpd**
> ❑ C. **dhcpmgr**
> ❑ D. **dhcpagent**
> ❑ E. **pntadm**

Answers A and C are correct because dhcpconfig is a command-line utility used to configure a DHCP server and dhcpmgr is a graphical (GUI) utility used to carry out the same process. Answer B is incorrect because in.dhcpd is the process that runs on a DHCP server when it has been configured. Answer D is incorrect because dhcpagent is the process that runs on a DHCP client when it has been configured. Answer E is incorrect because pntadm is a command that manages the DHCP network table and is typically used to add, modify, or remove IP addresses being managed by DHCP.

Question 2

> Which file would be created on a client with an **hme0** network interface to enable it to use DHCP with a dynamically assigned hostname when it is rebooted?
>
> ○ A. **/etc/default/dhcpagent**
> ○ B. **/etc/dhcp.hme0**
> ○ C. **/etc/hostname.hme0**
> ○ D. **/etc/inet/dhcpsvc.conf**

Answer B is correct because you would create the file /etc/dhcp.hme0 to enable DHCP with a dynamically assigned hostname. Answer A is incorrect because /etc/default/dhcpagent is the file that controls the default behavior of the dhcpagent process on a DHCP client. Answer C is incorrect because /etc/hostname.hme0 is the file that is used to configure the primary network interface and would be used only if a specific hostname were being specified, not a dynamically assigned one. Answer D is incorrect because /etc/inet/dhcpsvc.conf is the DHCP server configuration file.

Question 3

Which command would you use to add an IP address to be managed by a DHCP server?

- ○ A. **pntadm**
- ○ B. **dhtadm**
- ○ C. **dhcpconfig**
- ○ D. **in.dhcpd**

Answer A is correct because the pntadm command is used to manage the network table and is used to add an IP address to the list of addresses managed by a DHCP server. Answer B is incorrect because the dhtadm command manages the DHCP service configuration table, dhcptab. Answer C is incorrect because dhcpconfig is the command-line utility to configure a DHCP server. Answer D is incorrect because in.dhcpd is the process that runs on a DHCP server.

Question 4

You have a DHCP server using a datastore with a binary file format and managing the **192.168.45.0** network. What would the filename be for this network table?

- ○ A. **SUNWfiles1_192_168_45_0**
- ○ B. **SUNWbinfiles1_192_168_45_0**
- ○ C. **192_168_45_0_SUNWbinfiles1**
- ○ D. **SUNWbinfiles1_dhcptab**

Answer B is correct because the correct filename for a binary file datastore managing the 192.168.45.0 network would be SUNWbinfiles1_192_168_45_0. Answer A is incorrect because this filename indicates the use of an ASCII file datastore type. Answer C is incorrect because the filename consists of the datastore type followed by the IP address of the network being managed—this answer is syntactically incorrect. Answer D is incorrect because the dhcptab file contains the DHCP service configuration information, not details about networks being managed by DHCP.

Question 5

You have a client that is going to use DHCP as its means of obtaining an IP address. The client has an **hme0** network interface and is going to specify a particular hostname to use—**ultra99**. Which of the following entries would you add to the **/etc/hostname.hme0** file to achieve this?

○ A. **ultra99**

○ B. **dhcp ultra99**

○ C. **hostname ultra99**

○ D. **inet ultra99**

Answer D is correct because the file /etc/hostname.hme0 would have the entry inet ultra99 added to it to request the use of hostname ultra99. Answer A is incorrect because the entry ultra99 would specify the hostname, but would not use DHCP to configure the interface. Answers B and C are incorrect because these entries are invalid for this file.

Question 6

Which option to the **dhcpconfig** command is used to initially configure a DHCP server?

○ A. **-D**

○ B. **-N**

○ C. **-U**

○ D. **-C**

Answer A is correct because the -D option is used to initially configure the DHCP service on a server. Answer B is incorrect because the -N option is used to define a network that the DHCP server is to manage. Answer C is incorrect because the -U option is used to unconfigure a DHCP server. Answer D is incorrect because the -C option is used to convert an existing datastore to a different format.

Question 7

> When a DHCP client is booted, it sends a message to locate a DHCP server and request an IP address. Which of the following message types is sent, in response, by the DHCP server with details of an IP address that is available to be leased?
>
> ○ A. **DHCPREQUEST**
>
> ○ B. **DHCPACK**
>
> ○ C. **DHCPOFFER**
>
> ○ D. **DHCPDISCOVER**

Answer C is correct because the DHCPOFFER message type is returned by a DHCP server offering an IP address for the client to lease. Answer A is incorrect because the DHCPREQUEST message type is sent by the DHCP client in response to a DHCPOFFER message from the server. This request accepts the offer made by the DHCP server. Answer B is incorrect because the DHCPACK message type is sent by the DHCP server acknowledging the client's acceptance of an offer. Answer D is incorrect because the DHCPDISCOVER message type is sent by a booting DHCP client to locate a DHCP server and request an IP address.

Need to Know More?

 Sun Microsystems, technical whitepaper, "DHCP." Available on the Web at wwws.sun.com/software/whitepapers/solaris9/dhcp.pdf.

 Sun Microsystems, *Solaris 9 System Administrator Collection—System Administration Guide: IP Services*. Available in printed form, on the Web at http://docs.sun.com, and from the online documentation provided with the Solaris 9 operating system.

 Sun Microsystems, *System Reference Manual, Section 1M—System Administration Commands*. Available in printed form, on the Web at http://docs.sun.com, and from the online documentation provided with the Solaris 9 operating system.

Advanced Dynamic Host Configuration Protocol (DHCP)

. . . .

Terms you'll need to understand:

✓ **add_install_client**

✓ Debug mode

✓ DHCP server macro

✓ DHCP server symbol

✓ Hostname acquisition

✓ JumpStart client

Concepts you'll need to master:

✓ Explain how to configure a DHCP server to support JumpStart clients.

✓ Given DHCP debug output, deduce resolution strategies.

JumpStart is a facility provided with the Solaris OE that allows the operating environment to be installed automatically on numerous hosts. The JumpStart process is not discussed in this book because it is part of the Solaris 9 system administrator certification, a prerequisite for the exam covered in this book. It is therefore assumed that the reader is already familiar with JumpStart. This chapter describes how to perform advanced DHCP functions such as configuring a DHCP server to support JumpStart clients and troubleshooting both the DHCP server and client.

JumpStart and DHCP

The DHCP server can be configured so that a JumpStart client can use DHCP, rather than the traditional JumpStart mechanism using RARP, when it boots up. Using the DHCP method is advantageous because DHCP packets pass through a router, eliminating the need for a client to have a JumpStart boot server present on the same subnet—a boot server on the same subnet as the client is currently required under standard JumpStart procedures because the RARP protocol used by clients does not pass through a router.

 JumpStart with DHCP is currently supported only on Intel and Ultra workstations. The boot PROM version must be at least 3.25 on an Ultra workstation. If these requirements are not met, then the client cannot perform a DHCP boot. There is often an exam question that asks for the minimum requirements.

Symbols and Macros

The add_install_client script, which is provided with the Solaris OE, is used to register JumpStart clients on the JumpStart configuration server. The -d option to this script specifies that the client is a DHCP client. At the point of running the script, your JumpStart server should already be configured, but there are a number of symbols that need to be configured before the DHCP server can support the JumpStart client. The following example uses the host ultra10 as the JumpStart server and adds support for the SUNW.Ultra5_10 platform.

```
ultra10# ./add_install_client -d -s ultra10:/export/install -c ultra10: \
/export/jumpstart -p ultra10:/export/install SUNW.Ultra5_10 sun4u
copying inetboot to /tftpboot

To enable SUNW.Ultra5_10 in the DHCP server,
add an entry to the server with the following data:

  Install server      (SinstNM)  : ultra10
  Install server IP   (SinstIP4) : 192.168.28.28
```

```
Install server path (SinstPTH) : /export/install
Root server name    (SrootNM)  : ultra10
Root server IP      (SrootIP4) : 192.168.28.28
Root server path    (SrootPTH) : /export/install/Solaris_9/Tools/Boot
Profile location    (SjumpsCF) : ultra10:/export/jumpstart
sysidcfg location   (SsysidCF) : ultra10:/export/install
```

Notice that a number of items, such as sinstNM, appear within parentheses. These represent vendor symbols that need to be added to the DHCP server, so that when a client boots, it is provided with the necessary information to install the Solaris OE over the network. When the symbols have been created, they can be added to a macro, which in turn is executed when the client boots up. Table 12.1 identifies the most common vendor symbols:

Table 12.1	Vendor Symbols for SUN DHCP Clients				
Symbol Name	**Code**	**Type**	**Granularity**	**Max**	**Description**
SrootOpt	1	ASCII Text	1	0	The options that NFS will use for the client's root file system
SrootIP4	2	IP Address	1	1	The root server's IP address
SrootNM	3	ASCII Text	1	0	The root server's hostname
SrootPTH	4	ASCII Text	1	0	The path to the client's root directory on the root server
SswapIP4	5	IP Address	1	0	The IP address of a swap server
SswapPTH	6	ASCII Text	1	0	The client's swap file path on a swap server
SbootFIL	7	ASCII Text	1	0	The client's boot file path
Stz	8	ASCII Text	1	0	The time zone the client will use
SbootRS	9	Number	2	1	The read size that NFS will use when the client is booting
SinstIP4	10	IP Address	1	1	The JumpStart install server's IP address
SinstNM	11	ASCII Text	1	0	The JumpStart install server's hostname
SinstPTH	12	ASCII Text	1	0	The path to the installation image on the JumpStart install server

(continued)

Table 12.1   Vendor Symbols for SUN DHCP Clients *(continued)*

Symbol Name	Code	Type	Granularity	Max	Description
SsysidCF	13	ASCII Text	1	0	JumpStart **sysidcfg** file path, in the form **server:/path**
SjumpsCF	14	ASCII Text	1	0	JumpStart config file path, in the form **server:/path**
Sterm	15	ASCII Text	1	0	Terminal Type

The fields are described here:

➤ *Symbol Name*—The name of the symbol.

➤ *Code*—A unique code number assigned to the symbol. The code number must be unique within the category.

➤ *Type*—The entry's data type.

➤ *Granularity*—The number of instances. For example, a symbol with a data type of IP Address and a granularity of 2 means that the entry must contain 2 IP addresses.

➤ *Max*—The maximum number of values. For example, a symbol with a data type of IP Address, granularity of 2 and maximum of 2 can contain a maximum of 2 pairs of IP addresses.

➤ *Description*—A textual description of the symbol.

Modifying a DHCP Server to Support JumpStart

In the preceding section, `add_install_client` was run, which reported a number of symbols that need to be created, namely:

➤ SinstNM

➤ SinstIP4

➤ SinstPTH

➤ SrootNM

➤ SrootIP4

➤ SrootPTH

➤ SjumpsCF

➤ SsysidCF

The symbols need to be created so that they can be used in macros. The following example shows how to create the symbol SinstNM and to include it in the ultra10 macro.

1. Start dhcpmgr from any CDE window. The DHCP manager window appears as shown in Figure 12.1.

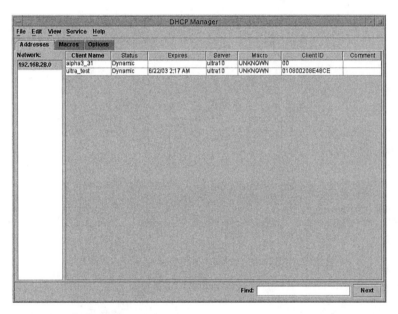

Figure 12.1   DHCP Manager window.

2. Select the Options tab and the Options window appears. From the Edit menu, select Create as shown in Figure 12.2.

3. A new window appears to create the option. Enter the name SinstNM in the Name field. The next field is a pull-down menu; select Vendor from this menu, as shown in Figure 12.3.

4. Refer back to Table 12.1, which lists the valid values for the symbols to be added. In this case, the code value for the symbol SinstNM is 11. The type is currently set to IP Address. Table 12.1 shows this symbol should be of type ASCII Text, so select this from the pull-down menu. Table 12.1 also states the values for granularity and maximum; enter these accordingly.

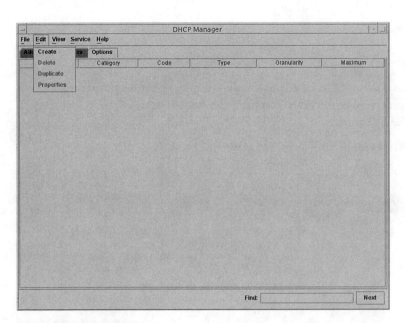

Figure 12.2 DHCP Options window.

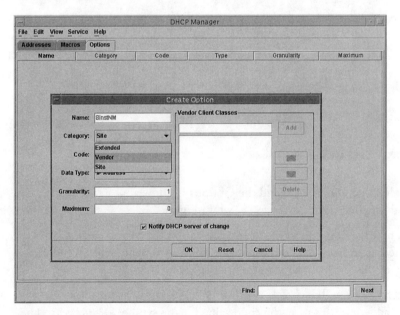

Figure 12.3 DHCP Create Options window.

5. On the right side of the window is the Vendor Client Classes box. This is where you specify to which class of systems the option applies. For this example, because a Sun Ultra10 is being used, the client class is

SUNW.Ultra5_10. Enter this in the box provided and click Add. The class now appears in the list as shown in Figure 12.4.

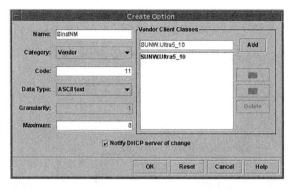

Figure 12.4   DHCP completed Create Option window.

6. Make sure the box marked Notify DHCP Server of Change is checked and click OK to complete the operation.

7. You are returned to the Options window, which now includes the symbol just created. Figure 12.5 shows this.

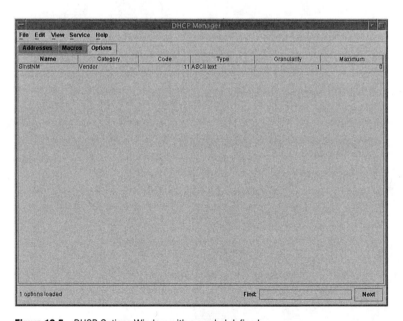

Figure 12.5   DHCP Options Window with a symbol defined.

8. Further symbols can be added by repeating the preceding steps.

9. To add the symbol sinstNM that was just created to the ultra10 macro, select the Macro tab and the ultra10 macro from the list on the left. Figure 12.6 shows the current contents of this macro.

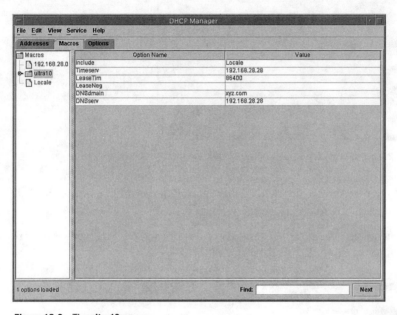

Figure 12.6   The **ultra10** macro.

10. From the Edit menu, select Properties. Figure 12.7 shows the Macro Properties window.

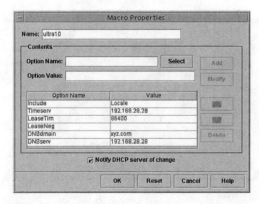

Figure 12.7   The Macro Properties window.

11. You need to locate the symbol that you want to add, so click on Select to the right of the Option Name field. The Select Option window appears, as shown in Figure 12.8.

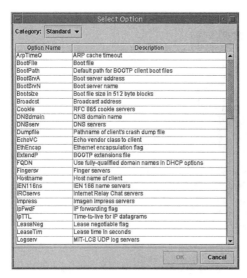

Figure 12.8 The Select Option (standard) window.

12. The symbol just created is a Vendor class symbol but the options being displayed are symbols in the standard category. The category field is a pull-down menu, so click on the menu and choose Vendor. The symbol SinstNM is now displayed, as shown in Figure 12.9.

Figure 12.9 The Select Option (vendor) window.

13. Click on the symbol sinstNM and then click OK to display the Macro Properties window. This symbol identifies the hostname of the JumpStart install server, which is ultra10. Enter this in the Option Value field, as shown in Figure 12.10.

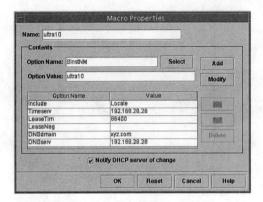

Figure 12.10 The Macro Properties window.

14. Click Add to insert the symbol and value into the macro properties. Figure 12.11 demonstrates that the symbol sinstNM has been added to the macro.

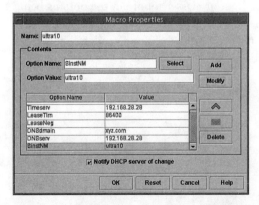

Figure 12.11 The Macro Properties window with symbol added.

15. When you click OK to complete the operation, you are returned to the Macros tab of the DHCP Manager window, showing the contents of the ultra10 macro. Figure 12.12 shows the completed operation.

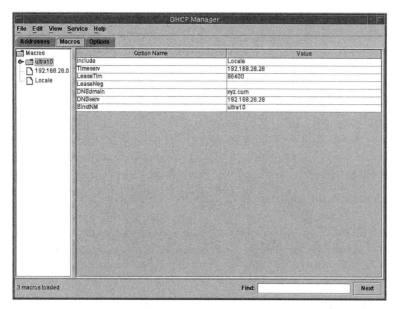

Figure 12.12   The **ultra10** macro with symbol added.

16. Repeat steps 12–15 for the other symbols that the DHCP server requires to support JumpStart.

17. If the DHCP server is located on a different network from the client, then the Router symbol must also be added to the macro. Additionally, another symbol, TFTPsrvN, needs to be added to identify the TFTP boot server—this is the DHCP server IP address and responds to a TFTP request from the client. Add both these options from the standard list of symbols, shown earlier in Figure 12.8.

A client can find out the platform class by running the command **uname -i**. A sparc **ultra10**, for example, returns **SUNW,Ultra5_10**. Note that the classname used in a DHCP macro replaces the , (comma) with a . (dot), making the classname **SUNW.Ultra5_10**.

When you have configured the DHCP server to support JumpStart clients, test it by booting a client to use DHCP. From the ok prompt, that is, with the client shut down, enter the following boot command:

```
ok boot net:dhcp - install
```

The client should successfully boot from the server and start the Solaris 9 installation process. The client boots by using TFTP with numbers flashing on the client console. If the numbers stop flashing at 23e00, then the DHCP server has been configured correctly and the boot process has been successful.

Troubleshooting the DHCP Server

When problems occur on a DHCP server, it is worth checking whether the server itself is functioning before assuming the DHCP configuration is at fault. Use standard Solaris commands to verify that the server is working, such as ping, ifconfig, and snoop.

You can also stop and start the DHCP server process, in.dhcpd, as described in Chapter 11, "Basic DHCP." Doing this can often solve a number of problems, particularly when the process has hung and is not responding to client requests, or when you are using either the binary or nisplus format for the DHCP datastore, neither of which is human readable.

Error Messages

There are a number of reasons why a DHCP client might be unable to obtain an IP address from a DHCP server. Table 12.2 lists some of the more common errors encountered, along with a brief explanation of what the cause of the error is and also the required resolution. Note that the IP addresses will be different from those shown here.

Table 12.2 Common DHCP Error Messages

Message	Description	Resolution
No more IP addresses on 192.168.28.0 network	All the IP addresses that are managed by DHCP are in use for the specified network.	Use **dhcpmgr** or **dhcpconfig** to create additional IP addresses to allocate to clients.
Client: 010800208E48CE is trying to renew 192.168.28.32, an IP address it has not leased	The IP address held by the server for this client does not match the IP address specified by the client. This is often caused by a client's record being deleted while the IP address is still in use.	Use **dhcpmgr** or **pntadm** to view the network table and correct.

(continued)

Table 12.2   Common DHCP Error Messages *(continued)*

Message	Description	Resolution
Offer expired for client: 192.168.28.32	The DHCP made an offer of an IP address, but the client did not respond in time.	The cache offer timeout on the DHCP server may be set too low. Increase the value by using **dhcpmgr**.
192.168.28.32 currently marked as unuseable	The IP address has been marked in the network table as unuseable.	Use **dhcpmgr** or **pntadm** to make the address useable.
There is no 192.168.28.0 dhcp-network table for DHCP client's network	A client is requesting an IP address, but the DHCP server cannot find the network table for the address, usually because the network table has been deleted.	Re-create the network table by using **dhcpmgr** or **dhcpconfig**.
DHCP network record for 192.168.28.32 is unavailable, ignoring request	The specified IP address is not present in the network table.	Use **dhcpmgr** or **pntadm** to view the table and create the record if necessary.
ICMP ECHO reply to OFFER candidate: 192.168.28.32, disabling	The IP address is already in use. The server carries out this check before finally allocating the IP address to the client.	You need to establish whether the specified IP address should be managed by DHCP, or whether it is a static IP that is outside the scope of DHCP addresses.

Running the DHCP Server in Debug Mode

If there are problems with the DHCP server that cannot be easily resolved, it is useful to run the server process, in.dhcpd, in debug mode to receive additional messages on the server console. The following example shows the process running in debug mode, using the -d option, and also with verbose output, using the -v option. The lines of interest appear in bold.

```
# /usr/lib/inet/in.dhcpd -d -v
3ef739e5:  Daemon Version: 3.5
3ef739e5:  Maximum relay hops: 4
```

```
3ef739e5:   Run mode is: DHCP Server Mode.
3ef739e5:   Datastore resource: SUNWfiles
3ef739e5:   Location: /var/dhcp
3ef739e5:   DHCP offer TTL: 10
3ef739e5:   ICMP validation timeout: 1000 milliseconds, Attempts: 1.
3ef739e5:   Name service update enabled, timeout: 15 seconds
3ef739e5:   Maximum concurrent clients: 1024
3ef739e5:   Maximum threads: 256
3ef739e5:   Read 3 entries from DHCP macro database on Mon Jun 16 18:33:25
➥ 2003
3ef739e5:   Monitor (0003/hme0) started...
3ef739e5:   Thread Id: 0003 - Monitoring Interface: hme0 *****
3ef739e5:   MTU: 1500    Type: SOCKET
3ef739e5:   Broadcast: 192.168.28.255
3ef739e5:   Netmask: 255.255.255.0
3ef739e5:   Address: 192.168.28.28
3ef73a71:   Datagram received on network device: hme0
3ef73a71:   Reserved offer: 192.168.28.32
3ef73a72:   Unicasting datagram to 192.168.28.32 address.
3ef73a72:   Adding ARP entry: 192.168.28.32 == 0800208E48CE
3ef73a72:   Updated offer: 192.168.28.32
3ef73a73:   Datagram received on network device: hme0
3ef73a73:   Client: 010800208E48CE maps to IP: 192.168.28.32
3ef73a73:   Unicasting datagram to 192.168.28.32 address.
3ef73a73:   Adding ARP entry: 192.168.28.32 == 0800208E48CE
```

The lines in bold show the messages received when a DHCP client requests an IP address. In this case, the IP address allocation worked because the client was mapped to the IP address successfully.

Later on, when the client is shut down, the debug output shows the same IP address being released:

```
3ef73b2d:   Freeing offer: 192.168.28.32
3ef73b2d:   Datagram received on network device: hme0
3ef73b2d:   Client: 010800208E48CE RELEASED address: 192.168.28.32
3ef73b2d:   RELEASE: client message: DHCP agent is exiting
```

Troubleshooting the DHCP Client

The majority of problems that will be found on a DHCP client involve a DHCP server that can't be reached or is not responding, or a problem with the configuration of the DHCP server itself.

The main troubleshooting tools available to the administrator include the following actions:

➤ Run the server process in debug mode (detailed in the preceding section).

➤ Run the client process (dhcpagent) in debug mode to view additional messages.

➤ Run snoop to capture network traffic between the DHCP client and the server.

Run the DHCP Client in Debug Mode to View Messages

To see more detailed messages about the client IP allocation process, you can run the client DHCP daemon, dhcpagent, in debug mode. The following session proceeds through these steps:

➤ Releases the current IP address assigned to the DHCP client.

➤ Stops the client DHCP process, dhcpagent.

➤ Starts the client DHCP process in debug mode.

➤ Enables the network interface so that it requests an IP address from the DHCP server.

➤ Releases the current IP address assigned to the DHCP client and stops the client DHCP process, dhcpagent.

The lines of interest appear in bold.

```
ultra5# ifconfig hme0 dhcp release

ultra5# pkill dhcpagent
ultra5# /sbin/dhcpagent -d1 -f &
ultra5# ifconfig hme0 dhcp start

/sbin/dhcpagent: debug: set_packet_filter: set filter 0x2e648
➥(DHCP filter)
/sbin/dhcpagent: debug: init_ifs: initted interface hme0
/sbin/dhcpagent: debug: insert_ifs: hme0: sdumax 1500, optmax 1260, \
hwtype 1, hwlen 6
/sbin/dhcpagent: debug: insert_ifs: inserted interface hme0
/sbin/dhcpagent: debug: set_packet_filter: set filter 0x2e648
➥(DHCP filter)
/sbin/dhcpagent: debug: init_ifs: initted interface hme0
/sbin/dhcpagent: debug: dhcp_selecting: DF_REQUEST_HOSTNAME
/sbin/dhcpagent: debug: select_best: OFFER had 42 points
/sbin/dhcpagent: debug: select_best: most points: 42
/sbin/dhcpagent: debug: register_acknak: registered acknak id 5
/sbin/dhcpagent: debug: unregister_acknak: unregistered acknak id 5
/sbin/dhcpagent: debug: set_packet_filter: set filter 0x2c640 (ARP reply
➥filter)
/sbin/dhcpagent: info: setting IP netmask on hme0 to 255.255.255.0
/sbin/dhcpagent: info: setting IP address on hme0 to 192.168.28.32
/sbin/dhcpagent: info: setting broadcast address on hme0 to
➥192.168.28.255
/sbin/dhcpagent: info: added default router 192.168.28.28 on hme0
/sbin/dhcpagent: debug: set_packet_filter: set filter 0x2e6d4 (blackhole
➥filter)
```

```
/sbin/dhcpagent: debug: configure_if: bound ifsp->if_sock_ip_fd
/sbin/dhcpagent: info: hme0 acquired lease, expires Tue Jun 24 00:59: 09
➡2003
/sbin/dhcpagent: info: hme0 begins renewal at Tue Jun 24 00:29:46 2003
/sbin/dhcpagent: info: hme0 begins rebinding at Tue Jun 24 00:50:33 2003

ultra5# ifconfig hme0 dhcp release
/sbin/dhcpagent: info: releasing interface hme0
/sbin/dhcpagent: debug: free_ifs: freeing interface hme0

ultra5# pkill dhcpagent
/sbin/dhcpagent: info: received SIGTERM, shutting down...
```

The following options to dhcpagent were used in the preceding example:

> -d1—Debug level 1. This value can be set to 1 or 2. Level 2 provides the most verbose output.

> -f—Instructs the process to run in the foreground, rather than in the background as a daemon process. This option means that messages are written to the standard output, instead of via syslog, making the output readily available.

The example debug session shows a successful IP address being obtained by a client. You can see that the client assesses the offer of an address, scores it (42 points), and then selects it. The network mask, IP address, broadcast address, and default router are also set from the DHCP server and finally the lease is acquired.

snoop

Use the snoop command to monitor network traffic between the DHCP client and the server. It can often provide useful information when you are trying to diagnose a problem. The following snapshot from snoop captures packets when a client requests an IP address. Note that only the DHCP protocol items are shown here:

```
ultra10# snoop -i /tmp/sn.log
DHCP: ----- Dynamic Host Configuration Protocol -----
DHCP:
DHCP: Hardware address type (htype) =  1 (Ethernet (10Mb))
DHCP: Hardware address length (hlen) = 6 octets
DHCP: Relay agent hops = 0
DHCP: Transaction ID = 0x6372d201
DHCP: Time since boot = 0 seconds
DHCP: Flags = 0x0000
DHCP: Client address (ciaddr) = 0.0.0.0
DHCP: Your client address (yiaddr) = 0.0.0.0
DHCP: Next server address (siaddr) = 0.0.0.0
DHCP: Relay agent address (giaddr) = 0.0.0.0
DHCP: Client hardware address (chaddr) = 08:00:20:8E:48:CE
DHCP:
```

```
DHCP: ----- (Options) field options -----
DHCP:
DHCP: Message type = DHCPDISCOVER
DHCP: Maximum DHCP Message Size = 1472 bytes
DHCP: IP Address Lease Time = -1 seconds
DHCP: Client Class Identifier =   "SUNW.SPARCstation-5"
DHCP: Requested Options:
DHCP:    1 (Subnet Mask)
DHCP:    3 (Router)
DHCP:   12 (Client Hostname)
DHCP:   43 (Vendor Specific Options)


DHCP: ----- Dynamic Host Configuration Protocol -----
DHCP:
DHCP: Hardware address type (htype) =  1 (Ethernet (10Mb))
DHCP: Hardware address length (hlen) = 6 octets
DHCP: Relay agent hops = 0
DHCP: Transaction ID = 0x6372d201
DHCP: Time since boot = 0 seconds
DHCP: Flags = 0x0000
DHCP: Client address (ciaddr) = 0.0.0.0
DHCP: Your client address (yiaddr) = 192.168.28.40
DHCP: Next server address (siaddr) = 0.0.0.0
DHCP: Relay agent address (giaddr) = 0.0.0.0
DHCP: Client hardware address (chaddr) = 08:00:20:8E:48:CE
DHCP:
DHCP: ----- (Options) field options -----
DHCP:
DHCP: Message type = DHCPOFFER
DHCP: DHCP Server Identifier = 192.168.28.28
DHCP: UTC Time Offset = 0 seconds
DHCP: RFC868 Time Servers at = 192.168.28.28
DHCP: IP Address Lease Time = 86400 seconds
DHCP: DNS Domain Name = xyz.com
DHCP: DNS Servers at = 192.168.28.28
DHCP: TFTP Server Name = 192.168.28.28
DHCP: Broadcast Address = 192.168.28.255
DHCP: Router at = 192.168.28.28
DHCP: Subnet Mask = 255.255.255.0
DHCP: Client Hostname = ultra10-40


DHCP: ----- Dynamic Host Configuration Protocol -----
DHCP:
DHCP: Hardware address type (htype) =  1 (Ethernet (10Mb))
DHCP: Hardware address length (hlen) = 6 octets
DHCP: Relay agent hops = 0
DHCP: Transaction ID = 0x180271a2
DHCP: Time since boot = 0 seconds
DHCP: Flags = 0x0000
DHCP: Client address (ciaddr) = 0.0.0. 0
DHCP: Your client address (yiaddr) = 0.0.0.0
DHCP: Next server address (siaddr) = 0.0.0.0
DHCP: Relay agent address (giaddr) = 0.0.0.0
DHCP: Client hardware address (chaddr) = 08:00:20:8E:48:CE
DHCP:
DHCP: ----- (Options) field options -----
DHCP:
DHCP: Message type = DHCPREQUEST
DHCP: IP Address Lease Time = 86400 seconds
DHCP: Maximum DHCP Message Size = 1472 bytes
DHCP: Requested IP Address = 192.168.28.40
```

```
DHCP: DHCP Server Identifier = 192.168.28.28
DHCP: Client Class Identifier =   "SUNW.SPARCstation-5"
DHCP: Requested Options:
DHCP:    1 (Subnet Mask)
DHCP:    3 (Router)
DHCP:   12 (Client Hostname)
DHCP:   43 (Vendor Specific Options)

DHCP: ----- Dynamic Host Configuration Protocol -----
DHCP:
DHCP: Hardware address type (htype) =  1 (Ethernet (10Mb))
DHCP: Hardware address length (hlen) = 6 octets
DHCP: Relay agent hops = 0
DHCP: Transaction ID = 0x180271a2
DHCP: Time since boot = 0 seconds
DHCP: Flags = 0x0000
DHCP: Client address (ciaddr) = 0.0.0.0
DHCP: Your client address (yiaddr) = 192.168.28.40
DHCP: Next server address (siaddr) = 0.0.0.0
DHCP: Relay agent address (giaddr) = 0.0.0.0
DHCP: Client hardware address (chaddr) = 08:00:20:8E:48:CE
DHCP:
DHCP: ----- (Options) field options -----
DHCP:
DHCP: Message type = DHCPACK
DHCP: DHCP Server Identifier = 192.168.28.28
DHCP: UTC Time Offset = 0 seconds
DHCP: RFC868 Time Servers at = 192.168.28.28
DHCP: IP Address Lease Time = 86400 seconds
DHCP: DNS Domain Name = xyz.com
DHCP: DNS Servers at = 192.168.28.28
DHCP: TFTP Server Name = 192.168.28.28
DHCP: Broadcast Address = 192.168.28.255
DHCP: Router at = 192.168.28.28
DHCP: Subnet Mask = 255.255.255.0
DHCP: Client Hostname = ultra10-40
```

Notice how each of the message types is present, namely:

➤ DHCPDISCOVER—The client locates a DHCP server and requests an IP address.

➤ DHCPOFFER—The server responds with an IP address (192.168.28.40).

➤ DHCPREQUEST—The client accepts the offer by confirming the requested IP address (192.168.28.40).

➤ DHCPACK—The server confirms the allocation of the IP address and the hostname.

Problems Acquiring Hostnames

The majority of problems with clients trying to acquire hostnames involve the use of DNS. Table 12.3 identifies some of the more common problems and their resolutions.

Table 12.3 Common Hostname Acquisition Problems	
Problem Description	**Problem Resolution**
The requested hostname has not been configured in the network table for the required network.	Use **dhcpmgr** or **pntadm** to check the network table and, if necessary, add the required hostname.
The DNS server has not been configured to receive updates from the DHCP server.	Check the DNS configuration file, **/etc/ named.conf**. There should be an **allow-update** statement with the DHCP server's IP address.
The DHCP server that has offered an IP address does not know the DNS domain name.	On the DHCP server, check the macro that is processed. The **DNSdmain** symbol should contain the correct domain name.
The client is specifying the hostname in FQDN format.	Solaris 9 DHCP does not support FQDN format for hostnames. Modify the hostname request to a short name.

Obtaining a Lease Manually

When a client is unable to use the normal dynamic mechanism to obtain a lease for an IP address, it is worthwhile trying to obtain a lease manually. Use the following ifconfig command to do this for a client with an hme0 interface:

```
ultra10# ifconfig hme0 dhcp
```

Verify that a lease has been obtained by using the ifconfig command to view the interface status. There should now be an IP address assigned to the interface.

Checking Client Status

At any time you can check the current status of the DHCP client by using the ifconfig command on the network interface being managed by DHCP. Execute the following command to examine the status of the hme0 interface:

```
ultra5# ifconfig hme0 dhcp status
Interface  State       Sent  Recv  Declined  Flags
hme0       BOUND          2     2         0
(Began, Expires, Renew) = (06/24/2003 00:41, 06/25/2003 00:41, 06/24/2003 \
13:03)
```

The state field shows that the interface is BOUND to an address. The lease information gives details of when the lease for the IP address was assigned, when it will expire, and when it can be renewed.

Exam Prep Questions

Question 1

> Which of the following commands runs the DHCP client process in debug mode and provides the most verbose output?
>
> ○ A. **dhcpagent -f**
> ○ B. **dhcpagent -d**
> ○ C. **dhcpagent -d1**
> ○ D. **dhcpagent -d2**

Answer D is correct because the dhcpagent -d2 command provides the most verbose debug output. Answer A is incorrect because the -f option makes the process run in the foreground, rather than in the background as a daemon process. This, in turn, writes messages to the standard output rather than to syslog. Answer B is incorrect because the -d option requires a numeric value, either 1 or 2. Answer C is incorrect because the -d1 option provides less verbose output than -d2.

Question 2

> Which boot command would you enter to initiate a JumpStart client using DHCP?
>
> ○ A. **boot net**
> ○ B. **boot net - install**
> ○ C. **boot net:dhcp - install**
> ○ D. **boot dhcp - install**

Answer C is correct because the boot command boot net:dhcp - install initiates a JumpStart client that uses DHCP. Answer A is incorrect because boot net merely performs a network boot from a remote server, as carried out by diskless clients. Answer B is incorrect because boot net - install is the command to use to initiate a JumpStart client without using DHCP. Answer D is incorrect because the syntax is wrong for the boot command.

Question 3

What function does the **SinstPTH** symbol have when configuring a DHCP server to support JumpStart clients?

- ○ A. It is the IP address of the JumpStart install server.
- ○ B. It is the path to the installation image on the install server.
- ○ C. It is the hostname of the JumpStart install server.
- ○ D. It is the path to the JumpStart configuration file.

Answer B is correct because the SinstPTH symbol contains the path to the installation image on the install server. Answer A is incorrect because this refers to the SinstIP4 symbol. Answer C is incorrect because this refers to the SinstNM symbol. Answer D is incorrect because this refers to the SjumpsCF symbol.

Question 4

When a DHCP client boots up, it sends a message to locate a DHCP server and request an IP address. What type of message is this?

- ○ A. **DHCPDISCOVER**
- ○ B. **DHCPOFFER**
- ○ C. **DHCPREQUEST**
- ○ D. **DHCPACK**

Answer A is correct because a DHCPDISCOVER message is sent by a DHCP client to locate a DHCP server and request an IP address. Answer B is incorrect because the DHCPOFFER message is sent by the DHCP server in response to a DHCPDISCOVER message. It includes the offer of an IP address for the client to lease. Answer C is incorrect because the DHCPREQUEST message is sent by the DHCP client to accept an offer made by a DHCP server. Answer D is incorrect because the DHCPACK message is sent by the DHCP server to the client to confirm the leasing of an IP address.

Question 5

> Which command identifies the platform class of a DHCP client?
>
> ○ A. **uname -r**
> ○ B. **uname -p**
> ○ C. **uname -i**
> ○ D. **uname -s**

Answer C is correct because uname -i displays a host's platform class. Answer A is incorrect because uname -r displays the operating system release level, for example 5.9. Answer B is incorrect because uname -p displays a host's processor type, for example sparc. Answer D is incorrect because uname -s displays the name of the operating system, for example SunOS.

Question 6

> You have been running **snoop** to capture network packets to aid problem resolution with the DHCP server. The data was saved to the file **/tmp/snoop.log**. Which command reads from this file and displays verbose output on the screen?
>
> ○ A. **snoop -v**
> ○ B. **snoop -v -i /tmp/snoop.log**
> ○ C. **snoop -o /tmp/snoop.log**
> ○ D. **snoop /tmp/snoop.log**

Answer B is correct because snoop -v -i /tmp/snoop.log reads records saved to this file and displays them on the screen using the most verbose output. Answer A is incorrect because snoop -v simply displays verbose output on the screen; it does not read any data from a file. Answer C is incorrect because this command saves the data to the file /tmp/snoop.log. This command would have been used to create the file to be read back in. Answer D is incorrect because the snoop command with no arguments produces real-time summary output of network traffic; it does not read any data from a saved file.

Need to Know More?

 Sun Microsystems technical whitepaper, *"DHCP."* Available on the Internet at www.sun.com/software/whitepapers/solaris9/dhcp.pdf.

 Sun Microsystems, *Solaris 9 System Administrator Collection—System Administration Guide: IP Services.* Available in printed form, on the Web at http://docs.sun.com, and from the online documentation provided with the Solaris 9 operating system.

 Sun Microsystems, *System Reference Manual, Section 1M—"System Administration Commands."* Available in printed form, on the Web at http://docs.sun.com, and from the online documentation provided with the Solaris 9 operating system.

Network Time Protocol (NTP)

Terms you'll need to understand:

✓ /etc/inet/ntp.conf
✓ Drift
✓ NTP client
✓ NTP peer server
✓ NTP time server
✓ Reference clock
✓ Strata
✓ Stratum levels

Concepts you'll need to master:

✓ Describe the purpose, features, and functions of NTP, and define NTP terms.
✓ Explain how to configure an NTP server and an NTP client.
✓ Explain how to view logs and use snoop to troubleshoot an NTP problem.

Time is a critical part of operating in a networked environment, particularly when so many time-critical applications are in operation. This chapter describes the Network Time Protocol (NTP), which achieves the best possible time synchronization among machines connected to a network.

NTP Fundamentals

Computers have to maintain a clocking mechanism to be able to maintain the time, although it's not very accurate. In a Sun system, the non-volatile RAM (NVRAM) chip keeps time when Solaris is not running, and when the system starts up, the time value is copied into a counter that the Solaris 9 kernel uses. For most Ultra-based systems, the counter is 64 bits in length. The clock is not very accurate because it relies on an oscillator generating regular interrupts that need to be processed by the CPU, so if the CPU is very busy, this could be delayed and cause *drift* (explained later).

 The 32-bit counter present in older systems is scheduled to reach its limit of values in the year 2038. The 64-bit counter will not reach its limit of values for about another 300 million years. Unix time started at midnight, January 1, 1970.

It is commonly thought that NTP is used to synchronize the system clock on different hosts in a network. This is not what NTP does; it is the end result. NTP is actually the mechanism by which all systems on a network try to get as close as possible to having the correct time. For example, if there are three NTP servers on the network, all acting as peers to each other, they calculate, between them, which is the best time source—having agreed, all three servers synchronize to that source.

NTP operates in a hierarchy, called *strata*, with *stratum* levels ranging from 1–15, where a *stratum-1* server is the most accurate and reliable, and is connected to a reference source, such as a GPS signal, or a UTC (coordinated universal time) source (based on GMT). A few servers provide the time for many clients, some of which may be servers for other clients and so on.

 A time reference source, such as a GPS signal clock, is referred to as a *stratum-0* server. Clients do not synchronize to these servers; they synchronize to the *stratum-1* server that is connected to the reference clock.

NTP has a wide variety of uses within the Solaris operating environment. The following are instances of where it is used:

➤ *System logs*—The `syslog` function needs to log accurately when events occur; the clock needs to be as accurate as possible so that the system administrator can analyze problems later.

➤ *File system times*—When a file is created or modified, an accurate time-stamp is needed to know when it happened. This is particularly important in shared file systems.

➤ *Network management tools*—These need accurate timestamping to report the exact time an event occurred. The network management master system might also be a remote computer, so the time needs to be synchronized.

➤ *Security breaches*—To track and investigate a security breach on a computer network, accurate time recording is essential to identify exactly when specific events occurred so that a complete chronological audit can be made.

➤ *Billing applications*—The time is critical when an application is billing a customer based on time, such as for telephone usage.

➤ *Financial applications*—Some financial services have a legal responsibility for extremely accurate timekeeping.

➤ *Encryption and key management*—Secure applications often use a time value to create part of the key used to encrypt the data. This value has to be accurate so that the receiving host can decrypt the data, again based on the time.

NTP uses the User Datagram Protocol (UDP) to communicate between servers and clients and uses well-known port number 123. Using UDP is preferable with NTP because there are no retries if a synchronization fails (as there would be if TCP was used), which could flood a network with traffic if a number of clients went down.

A number of terms need to be described before you configure NTP:

➤ *Reference clock*—A clock that is known to be accurate because it follows a respected signal, such as GPS, or a UTC clock.

➤ *Resolution*—This is the smallest time increment a clock can make (compare to a domestic watch, where the resolution is one second).

➤ *Precision*—This is the smallest time increase that a computer program can make.

➤ *Accuracy*—This refers to how closely a clock follows a time reference, such as a GPS signal, or UTC reference clock.

➤ *Reliability*—This refers to the length of time that a clock can remain accurate.

➤ *Drift*—This refers to the variations in frequency that make clocks have different time. NTP contains a standard location for a drift file, `/var/ntp/ntp.drift`, which stores the offset for the oscillator, allowing it to be taken into account to produce more accurate time.

➤ *Jitter*—This refers to the fact that different oscillators have different frequencies and produce discrepancies when time is measured repeatedly. Jitter is effectively the difference in drift between a number of oscillators. Jitter is also the condition that database administrators experience when the time is not synchronized across the environment, particularly with distributed databases.

NTP Configuration

The main NTP daemon, `xntpd`, reads its configuration file, `/etc/inet/ntp.conf`, when it starts up. The contents of the configuration file determine whether the system is a client or a server and also the address of the time server. This section describes the configuration options, as well as how to configure an NTP server and an NTP client.

NTP can be configured in a number of ways:

➤ The local system can be used as the reference time source.

➤ Another server on the local network can be used as the reference time source. This is preferred if you need to have all systems on the local network synchronized—it might not be to the correct time, but all the systems can be synchronized at the same time.

➤ A server on the Internet can be used as the reference time source. A list of publicly available NTP servers can be found on the Web at `www.ntp.org`.

➤ A broadcast time signal, such as a GPS signal, can be used as the reference time source. This requires the installation of an interface card in the host to be configured. The IP address of the server, specified in the configuration file is of the form `127.127.t.u`, where `t` is an integer that represents the clock type and `u` is an integer that indicates the unit number within the clock type.

The next two sections show how to set up an NTP server and an NTP client. Table 13.1 shows the current list of available clock types that can be used.

Table 13.1	Available Clock Types		
Type	**Device**	**ID**	**Description**
1	local	LCL	Undisciplined Local Clock
2	trak	GPS	TRAK 8820 GPS Receiver
3	pst	WWV	PSTI/Traconex WWV/WWVH Receiver
4	wwvb	WWVB	Spectracom WWVB Receiver
5	true	TRUE	TrueTime GPS/GOES Receivers
6	irig	IRIG	IRIG Audio Decoder
7	chu	CHU	Scratchbuilt CHU Receiver
8	parse	----	Generic Reference Clock Driver
9	mx4200	GPS	Magnavox MX4200 GPS Receiver
10	as2201	GPS	Austron 2201A GPS Receiver
11	arbiter	GPS	Arbiter 1088A/B GPS Receiver
12	tpro	IRIG	KSI/Odetics TPRO/S IRIG Interface
13	leitch	ATOM	Leitch CSD 5300 Master Clock Controller
15	*	*	TrueTime GPS/TM-TMD Receiver
17	datum	DATM	Datum Precision Time System
18	acts	ACTS	NIST Automated Computer Time Service
19	heath	WWV	Heath WWV/WWVH Receiver
20	nmea	GPS	Generic NMEA GPS Receiver
22	atom	PPS	PPS Clock Discipline
23	ptb	TPTB	PTB Automated Computer Time Service
24	usno	USNO	USNO Modem Time Service
25	*	*	TrueTime generic receivers
26	hpgps	GPS	Hewlett Packard 58503A GPS Receiver
27	arc	MSFa	Arcron MSF Receiver

Values in Table 13.1 with * or ---- indicate generic types that do not use specific devices or IDs; they represent a number of devices.

As an example, it can be seen from Table 13.1 that a server with an IP address of 127.127.11.0 indicates that an Arbiter 1088A/B GPS Receiver is being used and is installed as unit 0.

The clock types are listed in the template server configuration file **/etc/inet/ntp.server**.

Setting Up an NTP Server

To configure a system as an NTP server, the configuration file template /etc/inet/ntp.server needs to be copied to /etc/inet/ntp.conf. This file should be edited to suit your own configuration requirements. /etc/inet/ntp.server contains a valid list of clock types as well as server configuration parameters. The parameters are shown in the following example:

```
# cat /etc/inet/ntp.server
# ident "@(#)ntp.server 1.6      00/07/17 SMI"
#
# /etc/inet/ntp.server
#
# An example file that could be copied over to /etc/inet/ntp.conf and
# edited; it provides a configuration template for a server that
# listens to an external hardware clock, synchronizes the local clock,
# and announces itself on the NTP multicast net.
#

# This is the external clock device.  The following devices are
# recognized by xntpd 3-5.93e:
#
# XType Device    RefID         Description
# -------------------------------------------------------
# 1    local      LCL           Undisciplined Local Clock
... (Truncated output)
#
# * All TrueTime receivers are now supported by one driver, type 5.
#   Types 15 and 25 will be retained only for a limited time and may
#   be reassigned in future.
#
# Some of the devices benefit from "fudge" factors.  See the xntpd
# documentation.

server 127.127.XType.0 prefer
fudge 127.127.XType.0 stratum 0

broadcast 224.0.1.1 ttl 4

enable auth monitor
driftfile /var/ntp/ntp.drift
statsdir /var/ntp/ntpstats/
filegen peerstats file peerstats type day enable
filegen loopstats file loopstats type day enable
filegen clockstats file clockstats type day enable
keys /etc/inet/ntp.keys
trustedkey 0
requestkey 0
controlkey 0
```

The parameters of interest are described here:

➤ `server 127.127.Xtype.0 prefer`—The IP address of the preferred NTP server. To configure a local undisciplined clock as the server, you would change this to `127.127.1.0`. The `prefer` option is used when multiple servers are defined, to define a preference weighting for the order in which servers are referenced. An undisciplined clock is one that does not get its time from a reliable time source, such as a GPS signal. It is used to synchronize systems on a network with the same time, which is not necessarily absolutely correct.

➤ `fudge 127.127.Xtype.0 stratum 0`—The `fudge` option is used for special configuration options. For example, it can be used to change the stratum level of a reference clock: The lower the stratum level, the more reliable the source.

➤ `broadcast 224.0.1.1 ttl 4`—This is the multicast address that the server uses to broadcast to the network. The `ttl 4` parameter specifies that the broadcast will time out in 4 seconds.

➤ `enable auth monitor`—Enables the authentication and monitoring facility.

➤ `driftfile /var/ntp/ntp.drift`—The default location of the drift file.

➤ `statsdir /var/ntp/ntpstats/`—This is the default location of the directory containing NTP statistics.

➤ `filegen entries`—These (optional) three entries generate daily NTP statistics and are as follows:

> ➤ *loopstats*—Each update of the local clock is recorded.

> ➤ *peerstats*—Enables the recording of NTP peer server statistics and logs updates from peer NTP servers.

> ➤ *clockstats*—Collects statistics from the clock driver, that is, the software controlling a reference clock.

➤ `keys /etc/inet/ntp.keys`—The default location for the key file if authentication is used.

➤ key entries—These three entries define secure identifiers providing a mechanism for NTP clients and servers to authenticate each other (this is described fully in RFC 1305). The three entries are as follows:

> ➤ *controlkey*—Specifies a key identifier between 1 and 65535 that is used to authenticate commands issued to the `ntpq` program.

> ➤ *requestkey*—Specifies a key identifier between 1 and 65535 that is used to authenticate commands issued to the `xntpdc` program.

> *trustedkey*—Specifies the key identifiers that are trusted for commands issued to the ntpq and xntpdc commands. The values in this entry should be the same as those for the controlkey and requestkey entries.

After you have configured the ntp.conf file, create an empty drift file at the location specified in the configuration file and then start the xntpd daemon as follows:

```
# /etc/init.d/xntpd start
```

Setting Up an NTP Client

To configure a system as an NTP client, the configuration file template /etc/inet/ntp.client needs to be copied to /etc/inet/ntp.conf. This file doesn't normally need to be edited, as shown here:

```
# cat /etc/inet/ntp.client
# ident "@(#)ntp.client 1.3     00/07/17 SMI"
#
# /etc/inet/ntp.client
#
# An example file that could be copied over to /etc/inet/ntp.conf; it
# provides a configuration for a host that passively waits for a server
# to provide NTP packets on the ntp multicast net.
#

multicastclient 224.0.1.1
```

The file contains only one entry by default, which uses the default multicast address to find NTP servers.

After you have configured the ntp.conf file, start the xntpd daemon as follows:

```
# /etc/init.d/xntpd start
```

When the **/etc/init.d/xntpd** script is run to start the NTP daemon, the **ntpdate** command is run to set the time initially. See the online manual page for **ntpdate** for a detailed description of this command.

The NTP Daemon

The daemon that controls NTP is xntpd and is started via the startup script /etc/rc2.d/S74xntpd.

The startup script for NTP resides in the /etc/rc2.d directory, so it is started when the system enters run level 2. The file /etc/init.d/xntpd is the same file, as the two are hard linked. This is confirmed by listing the inode of both files as shown in the following:

```
# ls -i /etc/rc2.d/S74xntpd /etc/init.d/xntpd
   90358 /etc/init.d/xntpd        90358 /etc/rc2.d/S74xntpd
```

Notice that both of the files have the same inode number of 90358. Either of these two scripts can be used to start and stop the xntpd daemon.

When the daemon is started, it reads from a configuration file /etc/inet/ntp.conf, which contains a number of configuration options and also determines whether the machine is a client or a server.

 The **xntpd** daemon starts only if the configuration file **/etc/inet/ntp.conf** exists.

The xntpd daemon functions like this:

1. NTP servers advertise on the network every 64 seconds, using the multicast address 224.0.1.1. The advertisement lets other systems know that this system is an NTP server.

2. When a server receives a request packet from a client, which also contains the client's time, it replies by inserting the correct time into the packet and returns it to the client.

3. The client compares this packet with what it has received and adjusts its clock accordingly. A client waits for several responses from a server (or a number of servers) before synchronizing its clock, so it can take up to about five minutes for an NTP client to synchronize with an NTP server.

Using **ntpq** to Identify Other NTP Servers

The ntpq command is an NTP query program that can be used to determine whether any NTP peer servers are on the network. The following example shows how to run the command:

```
# ntpq
ntpq> peers
*LOCAL(0)        LOCAL(0)         3 l   64   64  377    0.00    0.000
➥10.03
 224.0.1.1       0.0.0.0         16 -    -   64    0    0.00    0.000
➥16000.0
```

```
+sparc5          LOCAL(0)          4 u   27   64  377    0.02  391.027
➥10.22
ntpq> quit
#
```

In the example, there are two servers: One is the local system that is acting as an NTP server, and the other is the host named sparc5.

Troubleshooting NTP

Problems with NTP, such as when a server is not responding to client requests, are best diagnosed by viewing log messages and using the snoop utility. Also, the xntpdc and ntpq programs can aid you in troubleshooting NTP, especially by examining the current status of the NTP server process (xntpd) and the NTP server itself. Each of these is described in the following sections.

Log Messages

NTP logs messages via syslog and writes them to /var/adm/messages. Look in this file for NTP-related messages. The following extract of messages shows what happens when a client starts up and runs ntpdate to set the initial time, and then synchronizes with a time server:

```
Apr 16 15:22:31 ultra5 ntpdate[432]: [ID 318594 daemon.notice] \
no server suitable for synchronization found yet
Apr 16 15:22:31 ultra5 ntpdate[432]: [ID 147394 daemon.notice] \
trying ttl 1for multicast server synchronization
Apr 16 15:24:22 ultra5 ntpdate[440]: [ID 558275 daemon.notice] \
adjust time server 192.168.28.28 offset 0.048177 sec
Apr 16 15:24:24 ultra5 xntpd[442]: [ID 702911 daemon.notice] \
xntpd 3-5.93e Mon Sep 20 15:47:11 PDT 1999 (1)
Apr 16 15:24:24 ultra5 xntpd[442]: [ID 301315 daemon.notice] \
tickadj = 5, tick = 10000, tvu_maxslew = 495, est. hz = 100
Apr 16 15:24:24 ultra5 xntpd[442]: [ID 798731 daemon.notice] \
using kernel phase-lock loop 0041
```

From this sample output, you can see that the initial line does not find an NTP server; that is, the client has not received a response to its request for the correct time. Subsequently, a server is found and the client's clock is adjusted to show the correct time, as displayed by the server.

snoop

The snoop utility can be used to capture NTP-related packets. An example of an NTP packet is shown in the following code sample. Some of the interesting fields appear in bold.

```
# snoop -v -d hme0
ETHER:   ----- Ether Header -----
ETHER:
ETHER:   Packet 156 arrived at 15:23:54.60
ETHER:   Packet size = 90 bytes
ETHER:   Destination = 1:0:5e:0:1:1, (multicast)
ETHER:   Source      = 8:0:20:b3:41:53, Sun
ETHER:   Ethertype = 0800 (IP)
ETHER:
IP:   ----- IP Header -----
IP:
IP:   Version = 4
IP:   Header length = 20 bytes
IP:   Type of service = 0x00
IP:         xxx. .... = 0 (precedence)
IP:         ...0 .... = normal delay
IP:         .... 0... = normal throughput
IP:         .... .0.. = normal reliability
IP:         .... ..0. = not ECN capable transport
IP:         .... ...0 = no ECN congestion experienced
IP:   Total length = 76 bytes
IP:   Identification = 61371
IP:   Flags = 0x0
IP:         .0.. .... = may fragment
IP:         ..0. .... = last fragment
IP:   Fragment offset = 0 bytes
IP:   Time to live = 4 seconds/hops
IP:   Protocol = 17 (UDP)
IP:   Header checksum = 0920
IP:   Source address = 192.168.28.28, ultra10
IP:   Destination address = 224.0.1.1, 224.0.1.1
IP:   No options
IP:
UDP:   ----- UDP Header -----
UDP:
UDP:   Source port = 123
UDP:   Destination port = 123 (NTP)
UDP:   Length = 56
UDP:   Checksum = 70E0
UDP:
NTP:   ----- Network Time Protocol -----
NTP:
NTP:   Leap = 0x0 (OK)
NTP:   Version = 3
NTP:   Mode     = 5 (broadcast)
NTP:   Stratum = 4 (secondary reference)
NTP:   Poll = 6
NTP:   Precision = 241 seconds
NTP:   Synchronizing distance   = 0x0000.0000  (0.000000)
NTP:   Synchronizing dispersion = 0x0000.56b6  (0.338715)
NTP:   Reference clock = 127.127.1.0 (127.127.1.0)
NTP:   Reference time = 0xc247e5f9.9a18f000 (Wed Apr 16 15:23:53 2003)
NTP:   Originate time = 0x00000000.00000000 (Thu Feb  7 06:28:16 2036)
NTP:   Receive  time = 0x00000000.00000000 (Thu Feb  7 06:28:16 2036)
NTP:   Transmit time = 0xc247e5fa.9a186000 (Wed Apr 16 15:23:54 2003)
```

Notice from the previous code that you can see

➤ The IP destination address is a multicast address.

➤ NTP is using port 123.

➤ This packet is a broadcast packet from the NTP server—Mode = 5 (broadcast).

➤ The reference clock is local—Reference clock = 127.127.1.0 (127.127.1.0).

xntpdc and ntpq

xntpdc is used to query the daemon process xntpd, such as the current status and the current configuration options in use, whereas ntpq is used to query an NTP server, such as testing an NTP server by manually polling it for a response. Both of these commands have a sub prompt that is displayed when they are run. You can use the help command at this prompt to see the available options. The following example shows how to run xntpdc to turn on debugging for the xntpd process to provide additional messaging and display the system information:

```
# xntpdc

xntpdc> help
Commands available:
addpeer        addrefclock    addserver      addtrap        authinfo
broadcast      clkbug         clockstat      clrtrap        controlkey
ctlstats       debug          delay          delrestrict    disable
dmpeers        enable         exit           fudge          help
host           hostnames      iostats        kerninfo       keyid
keytype        leapinfo       listpeers      loopinfo       memstats
monlist        passwd         peers          preset         pstats
quit           readkeys       requestkey     reset          reslist
restrict       showpeer       sysinfo        sysstats       timeout
timerstats     traps          trustedkey     unconfig       unrestrict
untrustedkey   version
xntpdc> debug
debug level is 0
xntpdc> debug more
debug level set to 1
xntpdc> debug more
debug level set to 2
xntpdc> sysinfo
system peer:         LOCAL(0)
system peer mode:    client
leap indicator:      00
stratum:             4
precision:           -15
root distance:       0.00000 s
root dispersion:     0.54124 s
reference ID:        [127.127.1.0]
reference time:      c247f2f9.9a18c000  Wed, Apr 16 2003 16:19:21.601
```

```
system flags:       auth monitor pll stats kernel_sync
frequency:          0.000 ppm
stability:          0.000 ppm
broadcastdelay:     0.003906 s
authdelay:          0.000122 s
xntpdc>q
#
```

Exam Prep Questions

Question 1

> How often do NTP servers advertise on the network?
>
> ○ A. Every minute
> ○ B. Every 5 seconds
> ○ C. Every 15 seconds
> ○ D. Every 64 seconds

Answer D is correct because NTP servers advertise every 64 seconds. This obviously makes A, B, and C incorrect.

Question 2

> You are configuring an NTP client. Which template file will you copy to become your configuration file?
>
> ○ A. **/etc/inet/ntp.keys**
> ○ B. **/etc/inet/ntp.client**
> ○ C. **/var/ntp/ntp.drift**
> ○ D. **/etc/inet/ntp.conf**

Answer B is correct because `/etc/inet/ntp.client` is the template file that you would copy to create the configuration file. Answer A is incorrect because `/etc/inet/ntp.keys` is the file used to contain authentication entries and is not a template file for NTP client configuration. Answer C is incorrect because `/var/ntp/ntp.drift` is the default location for the drift file. Answer D is incorrect because the `/etc/inet/ntp.conf` file is the location of the configuration file, that is, where the template file is copied to, by default. This file does not exist until the correct template file is copied to create it.

Question 3

Which of the following are valid uses for NTP? Choose 2.

- ❑ A. A billing system
- ❑ B. Encryption and key management
- ❑ C. A personnel database
- ❑ D. Creating a new user account

Answers A and B are correct because a billing system might be charging customers by the second (or less) and needs to be very accurate. Also, NTP is used in encryption because the timestamp is often used as part of the key to encrypt a message. Answers C and D are incorrect because they are not time-critical applications and do not rely on accurate clocks as part of their functionality.

Question 4

What is the name of the NTP daemon that runs on NTP servers and clients?

- ○ A. **ntpq**
- ○ B. **xntpdc**
- ○ C. **xntpd**
- ○ D. **/etc/init.d/xntpd**

Answer C is correct because xntpd is the daemon process that controls NTP. Answer A is incorrect because ntpq is a utility used to query NTP servers. Answer B is incorrect because xntpdc is a utility used to query the xntpd daemon. Answer D is incorrect because /etc/init.d/xntpd is the startup script that starts and stops xntpd.

Question 5

On a running NTP server, which file would you edit to change the location of the drift file?

- ○ A. **/etc/inet/ntp.server**
- ○ B. **/etc/inet/ntp.conf**
- ○ C. **/var/ntp/ntp.drift**
- ○ D. **/etc/inet/ntp.client**

Answer B is correct because the file /etc/inet/ntp.conf is the configuration file that is created when the NTP server is initially configured and contains an entry that defines the drift file's location. Of course, after changing the file, the NTP server would have to be restarted. Answer A is incorrect because /etc/inet/ntp.server is the template file that is copied to /etc/inet/ntp.conf to configure an NTP server. Answer C is incorrect because /var/ntp/ntp.drift is the default location for the drift file, which is specified in the configuration file. Answer D is incorrect because /etc/inet/ntp.client is the template file that is copied to /etc/inet/ntp.conf to configure an NTP client.

Question 6

At which run level does NTP get started?

○ A. S

○ B. 1

○ C. 2

○ D. 3

Answer C is correct because NTP is started at run level 2. The startup script is located in /etc/rc2.d/S74xntpd.

Question 7

Which command is used to query the NTP process and can also turn on the debugging facility?

○ A. **ntpq**

○ B. **xntpdc**

○ C. **xntpd**

○ D. **ntpdate**

Answer B is correct because the xntpdc command is used to query the NTP daemon process, xntpd. Answer A is incorrect because the ntpq command is used to query an NTP server, not the running daemon process for a particular server. Answer C is incorrect because xntpd is the NTP daemon process that is queried when you run xntpdc. Answer D is incorrect because ntpdate is used by an NTP client to initially obtain the time from an NTP server when the client starts up.

Question 8

> There are four NTP servers present on your network, and each is configured
> with a different stratum level between 1 and 4. Which stratum level is deemed
> the most reliable?
>
> ○ A. 1
> ○ B. 2
> ○ C. 3
> ○ D. 4

Answer A is correct because the lower the stratum level, the more reliable the
clock. Stratum level 0 servers are normally reference sources, such as a GPS
signal. A stratum level 1 server would normally be directly connected to a
reference source.

Need to Know More?

 Sun Microsystems Blueprints Online, *Using NTP to Control and Synchronize System Clocks—Part I: Introduction to NTP*. Available on the Web at www.sun.com/solutions/blueprints/0701/NTP.pdf.

 Sun Microsystems Blueprints Online, *Using NTP to Control and Synchronize System Clocks—Part II: Basic NTP Administration and Architecture*. Available on the Web at www.sun.com/solutions/blueprints/0801/NTPpt2.pdf.

 Sun Microsystems Blueprints Online, *Using NTP to Control and Synchronize System Clocks—Part III: Monitoring and Troubleshooting*. Available on the Web at www.sun.com/solutions/blueprints/0901/NTPpt3.pdf.

 Sun Microsystems, *Solaris 9 System Administrator Collection—System Administration Guide: Resource Management and Network Services*. Available in printed form, on the Web at http://docs.sun.com, and from the online documentation provided with the Solaris 9 operating system.

 Sun Microsystems, *System Reference Manual, Section 1M—"System Administration Commands."* Available in printed form, on the Web at http://docs.sun.com, and from the online documentation provided with the Solaris 9 operating system.

Practice Exam #1

Don't read Chapters 14 to 17 until you have learned and practiced all the material presented in the earlier chapters of this book. These chapters serve a special purpose. They are designed to test whether you are ready to take Exam 310-044, "Sun Certified Network Administrator for the Solaris 9 Operating Environment." In this chapter and Chapter 16 you will find two sample exams. An answer key and a brief explanation of correct answers along with explanations for why the wrong answers are incorrect appear in the chapters following each one—15 and 17, respectively. Reading these chapters before other chapters is like reading the climax of a story and then going back to find out how the story arrived at that ending. Of course, you don't want to spoil the excitement, do you?

How to Take the Practice Exams

After you have prepared the material presented in the earlier chapters of this book, you should take Practice Exam #1 to check how well you are prepared. After the sample exam is complete, evaluate yourself by using the answer key in the following chapter, "Practice Exam 1 Answer Key." When you evaluate yourself, note the questions, which you answered wrong, identify their corresponding chapters in the book, and then read and understand that material before taking Practice Exam #2. After taking Practice Exam #2, evaluate yourself again and reread the material corresponding to any wrong answers. Finally, repeat both the sample exams until you correctly answer all the questions. Information in the following sections helps you in taking the sample exams and then evaluating yourself.

Exam-Taking Tips

You take these sample exams under your own circumstances, but I strongly suggest that when you take them, you treat them just as you would the actual exam at the test center. Use the following tips to get maximum benefit from the sample exams:

➤ Before you start, create a quiet, secluded environment where you are not disturbed for the duration of the exam.

➤ Provide yourself a few empty sheets of paper before you start. Use some of these sheets to write your answers, and use the others to organize your thoughts. At the end of the exam, use your answer sheet to evaluate your exam with the help of the answer key that follows the sample exam.

➤ Don't use any reference material during the exam.

➤ Some of the questions may be vague and require you to make deductions to come up with the best possible answer from the possibilities given. Others may be verbose, requiring you to read and process a lot of information before you reach the actual question.

➤ As you progress, keep track of the elapsed time and make sure that you'll be able to answer all the questions in the given time limit.

This chapter provides 64 questions on the topics that pertain to Exam 310-044, "Sun Certified Network Administrator for the Solaris 9 Operating Environment." The exam must be completed in 105 minutes. The pass mark for this exam is 70%.

Question 1

These two files are used by the RARP process to map a 48-bit ethernet address to a 32-bit IP address. Which files are involved? Choose 2.

- ❑ A. **/etc/inet/netmasks**
- ❑ B. **/etc/inet/hosts**
- ❑ C. **/etc/ethers**
- ❑ D. **/etc/bootparams**

Question 2

In the TCP/IP model, which of the following are application layer protocols? Choose 3.

- ❑ A. TCP
- ❑ B. HTTP
- ❑ C. DHCP
- ❑ D. Telnet
- ❑ E. ICMP
- ❑ F. PPP

Question 3

You are setting up a network of servers that will be communicating to each other on gigabit networks. Fiber optic cabling is being used and the servers can be as far apart as 3000 meters from each other. Choose the type of LAN media that is suited for this network.

- ○ A. 1000BASE-CX
- ○ B. 1000BASE-LX
- ○ C. 1000BASE-SX
- ○ D. 1000BASE-T

Question 4

Which type of IP address is used when a system needs to communicate with all other nodes on a network?

- ○ A. Broadcast
- ○ B. Ethernet
- ○ C. Multicast
- ○ D. Unicast

Question 5

Which two methods can be used to split an assigned network address into a number of smaller networks? Choose 2.

- ❏ A. Fragmentation
- ❏ B. Encapsulation
- ❏ C. Variable Length Subnet Masks (VLSM)
- ❏ D. Subnetting
- ❏ E. Supernetting

Question 6

Your system is using multipathing over a number of IPv4 network interfaces. Which daemon monitors the status of these interfaces and detects failures?

- ○ A. **in.routed**
- ○ B. **in.rdisc**
- ○ C. **inetd**
- ○ D. **in.mpathd**

Question 7

Which file is used to associate network names and network numbers?

- ○ A. **/etc/inet/netmasks**
- ○ B. **/etc/inet/networks**
- ○ C. **/etc/inet/hosts**
- ○ D. **/etc/ethers**

Question 8

Which type of addressing is used at the Network Interface layer of the TCP/IP model for one-to-one communication?

- ○ A. Broadcast
- ○ B. IP Address
- ○ C. Multicast
- ○ D. Unicast

Question 9

The file **/etc/nsswitch.conf** contains the following entry:

```
hosts:        files  nis    dns
```

Which of the following options describes how a hostname will be resolved?

- ○ A. Only the local **/etc** files will be consulted.
- ○ B. The **dns** servers will be consulted first; then, if unsuccessful, the name service file, and finally the local **/etc** files.
- ○ C. Name service files will be consulted first; then, if unsuccessful, the local **/etc** files will be consulted, and finally the **dns** servers.
- ○ D. The local **/etc** files will be consulted first; then, if unsuccessful, the name service files will be consulted, and finally the **dns** servers.

Question 10

The Interface Identifier calculation results in an end-unit identifier-64, which makes up 64 bits of a 128-bit IPv6 address. Which option shows the correct steps to calculate the Interface Identifier?

- ○ A. With the MAC address in hexadecimal, toggle bit 8 and insert two additional octets (0xFF and 0xFF) between the CID and VID.
- ○ B. Convert the MAC address to binary, toggle bit 7, insert two additional octets (0xFE and 0xFE) between the VID and CID, and then convert to hexadecimal.
- ○ C. Convert the MAC address to binary, toggle bit 7, insert two additional octets (0xFF and 0xFE) between the CID and VID, and convert the address to hexadecimal.
- ○ D. Convert the MAC address to binary, toggle bit 8, insert two additional octets (0xFF and 0xFE) between the CID and VID, and convert the address to hexadecimal.

Question 11

In IPv6, you need to route an address via the Internet. Which type of IPv6 Unicast address would you use?

○ A. Aggregatable Global Unicast Address

○ B. Link-Local Address

○ C. Loopback Address

○ D. Site-Local Address

Question 12

Which protocol is used by a custom JumpStart client to obtain its IP Address when booting?

○ A. RARP

○ B. ARP

○ C. IP

○ D. TCP

Question 13

Which command would be used to configure and enable IPv6 on the **hme0** network interface?

○ A. **ifconfig hme0 up**

○ B. **ifconfig -interface hme0 inet6 up**

○ C. **ifconfig hme0 inet6 plumb up**

○ D. **ifconfig inet6 hme0 up**

Question 14

Which file is updated to add a static route manually?

○ A. **/etc/inet/networks**

○ B. **/etc/defaultrouter**

○ C. **/etc/rc2.d/S69inet**

○ D. **/etc/inet/hosts**

Question 15

Which two protocols are used in the Transport layer of the TCP/IP model? Choose 2.

❏ A. ARP

❏ B. TCP

❏ C. ICMP

❏ D. UDP

❏ E. IP

Question 16

You are setting up a gigabit network of servers that will all be within 50 meters of each other. To utilize existing twisted-pair CAT 5 cable, which type of LAN media would be used?

○ A. 1000BASE-CX

○ B. 1000BASE-LX

○ C. 1000BASE-SX

○ D. 1000BASE-T

Question 17

With reference to DNS record types, the type **AAAA** refers to which type of record?

○ A. IPv4

○ B. IPv6

○ C. Start of Authority

○ D. Canonical Name

Question 18

Which NTP daemon sets and maintains the time of day in agreement with Internet standard time servers?

○ A. **xntpd**

○ B. **inetd**

○ C. **ntpq**

○ D. **xntpdc**

Question 19

Which file provides IP address to hostname mapping?

○ A. **/etc/inet/netmasks**

○ B. **/etc/hosts**

○ C. **/etc/inet/networks**

○ D. **/etc/nsswitch.conf**

Question 20

Your system has a primary network interface, named **hme0**, with an IP address of **192.168.0.33**. You need to change the IP address to **192.168.1.55**. Which two files need to be changed to effect this? Choose 2.

❑ A. **/etc/inet/netmasks**

❑ B. **/etc/inet/hosts**

❑ C. **/etc/system**

❑ D. **/etc/hostname.hme0**

❑ E. **/etc/nodename**

Question 21

To assist you with troubleshooting your DHCP server, you want to run the DHCP server in debug mode for the primary network interface, **hme0**. Which command will achieve this?

○ A. **/usr/lib/inet/dhcpd**

○ B. **/usr/lib/inet/dhcpd -i hme0 -d -v**

○ C. **dhcpconfig -d**

○ D. **ifconfig hme0 dhcp status**

Question 22

Which system startup script is used to start the NTP daemon on an NTP client?

○ A. **/etc/init.d/xntpd**

○ B. **/etc/init.d/ntpclient**

○ C. **/etc/init.d/ntpc**

○ D. **/etc/rcS.d/S30network.sh**

Question 23

Which statement describes static routes?

○ A. Static routes are permanent entries in the route table.

○ B. Static routes are added or removed by various processes.

○ C. Static routes are automatically updated as new routes are advertised.

○ D. Static routes are temporary entries in the route table.

Question 24

TCP is a reliable, connection-oriented protocol. Which statement describes this kind of protocol?

- ○ A. No connection is made prior to data transmission and no acknowledgements are sent.
- ○ B. A connection is made prior to data transmission and acknowledgements are also sent.
- ○ C. A connection is made prior to data transmission, but acknowledgements are not sent.
- ○ D. No connection is made prior to data transmission, but acknowledgements are sent.

Question 25

What is the value of the MTU of an Ethernet II frame?

- ○ A. 1518 bytes
- ○ B. 1500 bytes
- ○ C. 64 bytes
- ○ D. 46 bytes

Question 26

Which system startup script automatically configures the primary network interface?

- ○ A. **/etc/hostname.hme0**
- ○ B. **/etc/hostname.qfe0**
- ○ C. **/etc/rc2.d/S72inetsvc**
- ○ D. **/etc/rcS.d/S30network.sh**

Question 27

The DNS name server daemon starts only if which file exists?

- ○ A. **/etc/nsswitch.conf**
- ○ B. **/etc/named.conf**
- ○ C. **/etc/default/named**
- ○ D. **/etc/inet/named**

Question 28

Which routing protocol is a distance vector protocol, which exchanges route information between IP routers within an autonomous system?

- ○ A. EGP
- ○ B. BGP
- ○ C. OSPF
- ○ D. RIP

Question 29

Which of the following IPv6 addresses is not a valid address?

- ○ A. **fe80:0:0:0:ba1:10fc:be55:4222**
- ○ B. **fe80:0000:0000:0000:0ba1:10fc:be55:4222**
- ○ C. **fe80::ba1:10fc:be55:4222**
- ○ D. **fe80::0000::ba1:10fc:be55:4222**

Question 30

You've configured a JumpStart client to use DHCP. What command will the client system use to initiate the correct boot method?

- ○ A. **boot net - install**
- ○ B. **boot net**
- ○ C. **boot net:dhcp - install**
- ○ D. **boot net:dhcp**

Question 31

Match the following terms with the correct description:

- ○ A. Bridge
- ○ B. Router
- ○ C. Gateway
- ○ D. Repeater

- ○ 1. Also known as a protocol converter, this device connects networks that use different protocols.
- ○ 2. This device connects network segments together and acts as a "booster" for electrical signals.
- ○ 3. This device connects networks together and forwards packets based on the MAC Address.
- ○ 4. This device connects networks together and forwards packets based on the IP Address.

Question 32

Which option to the **in.rarpd** command would you use to provide debug output to assist with troubleshooting?

- ○ A. **-a**
- ○ B. **-d**
- ○ C. **-s**
- ○ D. **-g**

Question 33

What is the MTU value for a loopback interface?

- ○ A. 1500 bytes
- ○ B. 8232 bytes
- ○ C. 1518 bytes
- ○ D. 64 bytes

Question 34

Your LAN is configured in a star topology, but you are getting a higher than expected collision rate. Which central device could be used to reduce collision rates by forwarding packets to only the port containing the destination node, instead of forwarding packets to all ports?

○ A. Shared hub

○ B. Switch

○ C. Router

○ D. Network interface card

Question 35

Which two statements describe IPv6 addresses? Choose 2.

❑ A. An IPv6 address can contain an embedded IPv4 address.

❑ B. IPv6 addresses are 32 bits long and the octets are separated by dots.

❑ C. IPv6 addresses are 128 bits long and the octets are separated by dots.

❑ D. IPv6 addresses are 128 bits long and the octets are separated by colons.

❑ E. IPv4 addresses are incompatible with IPv6 and the two cannot be present on the same network.

Question 36

CIDR uses classless addresses. Which of the following describes a classless address?

○ A. The first 16 bits identify the network, and the remaining 16 bits identify the host.

○ B. The first 18 bits identify the network, and the remaining 14 bits identify the host.

○ C. The first 8 bits identify the network, and the remaining 24 bits identify the host.

○ D. The first 24 bits identify the network, and the remaining 8 bits identify the host.

Question 37

Your hosts file contains the following entry:

```
127.0.0.1          localhost
```

What does this entry mean?

- ○ A. This is the hostname of the system.
- ○ B. This shows the IP address that is assigned to the primary network interface.
- ○ C. This is the loopback entry, allowing the system to send packets to itself.
- ○ D. This is a test entry and is never used.

Question 38

Which of the following IP addresses represents a Class B IP address?

- ○ A. **127.0.0.1**
- ○ B. **146.100.20.5**
- ○ C. **192.168.9.45**
- ○ D. **84.11.4.8**

Question 39

Your system has a primary network interface, named **hme0**, and an IP address of **192.168.3.3**. You need to configure a logical network interface to support an additional IP address of **192.168.5.8**. Which command will achieve this?

- ○ A. **ifconfig hme0 192.168.5.8**
- ○ B. **ifconfig hme0:1 192.168.5.8 up**
- ○ C. **ifconfig hme0:1 plumb 192.168.5.8 up**
- ○ D. **ifconfig hme0 192.168.3.3 192.168.5.8 up**

Question 40

You want to monitor NTP traffic on the network by using the **snoop** command. Which port are you going to be interested in for this kind of network traffic?

- ○ A. 23
- ○ B. 123
- ○ C. 21
- ○ D. 25

Question 41

Which signal would you send to the DNS name service daemon to force it to reread its configuration file?

- ○ A. **INT**
- ○ B. **USR2**
- ○ C. **USR1**
- ○ D. **HUP**

Question 42

Enter the command that is used to capture packets on the network for analysis purposes.

Question 43

In NTP terminology, what does the term "Resolution" refer to?

- ○ A. The smallest time increase that a computer program can use
- ○ B. The smallest increment that a clock can use
- ○ C. How closely a clock follows a time source
- ○ D. How long a clock can remain accurate

Question 44

You're running DHCP on a client system with a primary network interface, **hme0**, but you are having problems obtaining an IP address. As part of the troubleshooting, you can try to obtain a lease for an IP address manually. Which command will achieve this?

○ A. **ifconfig hme0 dhcp**

○ B. **ifconfig hme0 down** followed by **ifconfig hme0 up**

○ C. **/etc/init.d/dhcp stop** followed by **/etc/init.d/dhcp start**

○ D. **ifconfig hme0 dhcp start**

Question 45

While troubleshooting your DNS server, which file do you check to see whether there are any error messages?

○ A. **/var/named/messages**

○ B. **/var/adm/messages**

○ C. **/var/log/named**

○ D. **/var/log/messages**

Question 46

Which statement describes the difference between the TCP and UDP protocols?

○ A. TCP is a reliable, connection-oriented protocol and UDP is unreliable and connectionless.

○ B. UDP is a reliable, connection-oriented protocol and TCP is unreliable and connectionless.

○ C. TCP is a reliable, connectionless protocol and UDP is unreliable and connection-oriented.

○ D. UDP is a reliable, connectionless protocol and TCP is unreliable and connection-oriented.

Question 47

When entering the **ifconfig -a** command as a non-root user, which item of information is not displayed?

- ○ A. IP address
- ○ B. Network mask
- ○ C. Ethernet address
- ○ D. Broadcast address

Question 48

Your JumpStart client is going to use DHCP when installing Solaris 9. Which of the following are requirements that must be satisfied? Choose 2.

- ❑ A. The JumpStart Client must be a Sun Ultra system.
- ❑ B. The JumpStart Server must be a Sun Ultra system.
- ❑ C. The JumpStart Client's boot PROM version must be at least 3.25.
- ❑ D. The JumpStart Server's boot PROM version must be at least 3.25.
- ❑ E. The JumpStart Server and JumpStart Client must be physically on the same subnet.

Question 49

Which statement describes the ARP protocol?

- ○ A. Maps a 32-bit IP address to a 48-bit ethernet address
- ○ B. Maps a 48-bit IP address to a 32-bit ethernet address
- ○ C. Maps a 48-bit ethernet address to a 32-bit IP address
- ○ D. Maps a 32-bit ethernet address to a 48-bit IP address

Question 50

Which of the following statements are features of the Sun Trunking product? Choose 2.

- ❑ A. Enables more than one IP address to be assigned to a single network interface

- ❑ B. Provides load balancing on outbound network traffic when using multiple destinations

- ❑ C. Allows up to two QFE network adapters to be used to obtain a throughput of 800Mbps

- ❑ D. Allows up to four QFE network adapters to be used to obtain a throughput of 1600Mbps

- ❑ E. Provides load balancing on inbound network traffic when using multiple destinations

Question 51

Which command will correctly remove the logical network interface **hme0:1** without the risk of losing any data?

- ○ A. **ifconfig hme0:1 unplumb down**
- ○ B. **ifconfig hme0:1 down**
- ○ C. **ifconfig hme0:1 down unplumb**
- ○ D. **ifconfig hme0:1 unplumb**

Question 52

Which IPv6 process manages routing?

- ○ A. **in.ndpd**
- ○ B. **in.mpathd**
- ○ C. **inetd**
- ○ D. **in.ripngd**

Question 53

Which command will display the IPv4 routing table?

- ○ A. **ifconfig -a**
- ○ B. **netstat -r**
- ○ C. **netstat -i**
- ○ D. **ndd**
- ○ E. **route print**

Question 54

Which layer in the TCP/IP model uses ethernet addresses as its basis for addressing?

- ○ A. Internet
- ○ B. Application
- ○ C. Network Interface
- ○ D. Transport

Question 55

Which two utilities can be used to configure a DHCP server? Choose 2.

- ❑ A. **dhcpconfig**
- ❑ B. **dhcpmgr**
- ❑ C. **dhtadm**
- ❑ D. **pntadm**

Question 56

How often do NTP servers advertise on the network?

- ○ A. Every 5 minutes
- ○ B. Every minute
- ○ C. Every 64 seconds
- ○ D. Every 30 seconds

Question 57

At which layer of the TCP/IP model does ARP operate?

○ A. Between the Transport and Internet layers

○ B. The Network Interface layer

○ C. Between the Network Interface and Internet layers

○ D. The Internet layer

Question 58

You have been troubleshooting your DNS server, running in debug mode. Which signal do you send to the DNS server process to turn off debugging?

○ A. **INT**

○ B. **HUP**

○ C. **USR1**

○ D. **USR2**

Question 59

Which statement is true about IPv6 autoconfiguration?

○ A. Stateful and stateless autoconfigurations cannot co-exist.

○ B. The duplicate address detection software automatically assigns an alternate address if the proposed address is in use.

○ C. Autoconfiguration tests for a duplicate address before assigning an address to a network interface.

○ D. Stateful autoconfiguration is the recommended method to use because it is the easiest to set up.

Question 60

A receiving host, using the TCP protocol, sends an acknowledgement and a window advertisement. The window advertisement contains what information?

○ A. Confirmation of the number of bytes received

○ B. The number of retransmissions that have been received

○ C. The number of additional bytes that can be sent

○ D. The amount of data received so far

Question 61

Enter the command (without any parameters) that would be used to verify the speed of your network interface card.

Question 62

An IPv6 datagram is sent to a group of hosts, but instead of the datagram being delivered to all of the hosts in the group, it is delivered to the nearest host. Which IPv6 address type is being described?

○ A. Anycast

○ B. Broadcast

○ C. Multicast

○ D. Unicast

Question 63

Which of the following are features of DHCP? Choose 2.

❑ A. DHCP automatically assigns an ethernet address to a host.

❑ B. DHCP automatically assigns an IP address to a host.

❑ C. DHCP makes it easier to renumber the network if the ISP changes.

❑ D. DHCP addresses are static and cannot be changed.

Question 64

You are configuring your DHCP server and you need to select an option for the datastore. Which of the following are valid options for the datastore? Choose 2.

❑ A. **SUNWfiles**

❑ B. **SUNWldap**

❑ C. **SUNWbinfiles**

❑ D. **SUNWdhcp**

❑ E. **SUNWdns**

Practice Exam #1
Answer Key

1. B, C

2. B, C, D

3. B

4. A

5. C, D

6. D

7. B

8. D

9. D

10. C

11. A

12. A

13. C

14. B

15. B, D

16. D

17. B

18. A

19. B

20. B, D

21. B

22. A

23. A

24. B

25. B

26. D

27. B

28. D

29. D

30. C

31. A matches 3

B matches 4

C matches 1

D matches 2

32. B

33. B

34. B

35. A, D

36. B

37. C

38. B

39. C

40. B

41. D

42. snoop

43. B

44. A

45. B

46. A

47. C

48. A, C

49. A

50. B, C

51. C

52. D

53. B

54. C

55. A, B

56. C

57. C

58. D

59. C

60. C

61. ndd

62. A

63. B, C

64. A, C

Answer Key Explanations

Question 1

Answers B and C are correct because a RARP request supplies only an ethernet address. The lookup in `/etc/ethers` provides the hostname, which is then used in the lookup of `/etc/inet/hosts` to ultimately return the IP address. Answer A is incorrect because `/etc/inet/netmasks` is used to associate network masks with network numbers. Answer D is incorrect because `/etc/bootparams` is used to provide boot information for diskless clients.

Question 2

Answers B, C, and D are correct. HTTP, DHCP, and Telnet are all Application layer protocols. Answer A (TCP) is a Transport layer protocol, Answer E (ICMP) is an Internet layer protocol, and Answer F (PPP) is a Network Interface layer protocol.

Question 3

Answer B is correct. Sun's implementation of the 1000BASE-LX standard supports distances up to 3000 meters, using fiber optic cable. Answer A is incorrect because 1000BASE-CX uses copper cable up to a distance of 25 meters and is primarily used within wiring cabinets. Answer C is incorrect because even though it uses fiber optic cable, the maximum distance is 550 meters. Answer D is incorrect because 1000BASE-T uses UTP Cat 5 cabling and supports distances of up to 100 meters.

Question 4

Answer A is correct because the broadcast address is used to communicate with all hosts on the network. Answer B is incorrect because an ethernet address is not a type of IP address. Answer C is incorrect because the multicast type is used to communicate with a specific group of hosts on a network. Answer D is incorrect because the unicast type is used to communicate with a single host on a network.

Question 5

Answers C and D are correct. Variable length subnet masks (VLSM) and subnetting are two methods for splitting up a single network address into a number of smaller networks. Answer A is incorrect because fragmentation is used to split up ethernet frames when the amount of data to be transmitted is larger than the MTU. Answer B is incorrect because encapsulation is used in the TCP/IP model whereby each layer adds its own header information before passing the resulting packet on to the next layer. Answer E is incorrect because supernetting is the reverse of subnetting, where a number of smaller networks are combined into one larger network.

Question 6

The correct answer is D; the `in.mpathd` daemon is used to monitor multipath interfaces and to detect failures. Answer A is incorrect because `in.routed` is a routing daemon. Answer B is incorrect because `in.rdisc` is used to dynamically discover routers on the network. Answer C is incorrect because `inetd` is the daemon that manages network services and it does not affect multipathing.

Question 7

The correct answer is B. The file `/etc/inet/networks` is used to associate networks' names with network numbers. Answer A is incorrect because this file is used to specify network masks for the networks listed. Answer C is incorrect because this file provides the IP address to hostname mapping. Answer D is incorrect because this file provides the ethernet address-to-hostname mapping.

Question 8

The correct answer is D. Unicast addressing is used for one-to-one communication. Answer A is incorrect because this type of addressing is used to communicate with all nodes on a network. Answer B is incorrect because IP is not a type of address; it is a protocol. Answer C is incorrect because this type of addressing is used to communicate with a group of nodes on a network.

Question 9

The correct answer is D. The search order is determined by this entry in the /etc/nsswitch.conf file. In this case, files is the first entry, so the local /etc files are referenced initially. If this search is unsuccessful, the next entry in the list will be used, nis. The naming service hosts table is referenced and if unsuccessful, then the final entry, dns, is consulted. This will cause a dns search to be initiated. If the search is still unsuccessful, then an unknown host error message will be displayed. Answer A is incorrect because the entry would have to contain only the word files to search the local /etc files. Answer B is incorrect because the search order is from left to right and the entry would have been dns nis files. Answer C is incorrect because the entry would have been nis files dns.

Question 10

The correct answer is C. The correct method for calculating the Interface Identifier is to first convert the MAC address to binary. Next, toggle bit 7 and add the two octets (0xFF and 0xFE) between the CID and VID. Finally, convert the address back to hexadecimal. Answer A is incorrect because the conversion to binary is not included. Also, it is bit 7 that is toggled, not bit 8. Answer B is incorrect because the two inserted octets (0xFE and 0xFE) are wrong. The two inserted octets need to be 0xFF and 0xFE. Answer D is incorrect because it is bit 7 that is toggled, not bit 8.

Question 11

The correct answer is A. The Aggregatable Global Unicast address is used if you need to route an IPv6 address across the Internet. Answer B is wrong because this address type is intended for single, local network links. Answer C is wrong because this type of address is used by an IPv6 system to send datagrams to itself. Answer D is wrong because this type of address is used within an intranet.

Question 12

The correct answer is A. The custom JumpStart client uses RARP to identify itself by its ethernet address. The boot server looks up the ethernet address in its local /etc/ethers file to find out the IP address. Answer B is incorrect because ARP is used to map a 32-bit IP address to a 48-bit ethernet address. Answer C is incorrect because the IP protocol is not used at boot time for a system to determine its IP address. Answer D is incorrect because TCP is a transport protocol that is not used at boot time for a system to determine its IP address.

Question 13

The correct answer is C. The command `ifconfig hme0 inet6 plumb up` would correctly configure and enable IPv6 on the `hme0` interface. Answer A is incorrect because this would merely enable an existing IPv4 interface. Answer B is incorrect because the command syntax is invalid. Answer D is incorrect because the first argument to `ifconfig` should be the network interface, not the keyword `inet6`—the syntax is invalid.

Question 14

The correct answer is B. The file `/etc/defaultrouter` is referenced at boot-time to add any static routes that have been defined. Answer A is incorrect because `/etc/inet/networks` is used to associate network numbers with network names. Answer C is incorrect because `/etc/rc2.d/S69inet` is a system startup script used to initialize networking processes. The file `/etc/defaultrouter` is referenced in this script to check whether the routing daemon should be started. Answer D is incorrect because `/etc/inet/hosts` is a file that is used to map IP addresses to hostnames.

Question 15

The correct answers are B and D because TCP and UDP are both Transport layer protocols. Answers A, C, and E are incorrect because they are Internet layer protocols.

Question 16

The correct answer is D. 1000BASE-T supports distances of up to 100 meters using CAT-5 cabling. Answer A is incorrect because 1000BASE-CX uses copper cable. Answers B and C are incorrect because these types use fiber optic cable.

Question 17

The correct answer is B because the record type AAAA denotes an IPv6 record. Answer A is incorrect because the type would be A. Answer C is incorrect because the type would be SOA. Answer D is incorrect because the type would be CNAME.

Question 18

The correct answer is A because the xntpd daemon sets and maintains the time of day, in agreement with Internet standard time-servers. Answer B is incorrect because inetd is the daemon that manages network services. Answer C is incorrect because ntpq is used to query NTP servers. Answer D is incorrect because xntpdc is used to query the NTP daemon.

Question 19

The correct answer is B. The file /etc/hosts is linked to /etc/inet/hosts and provides IP address to hostname mapping. Answer A is incorrect because this file is used to identify the network mask for the listed networks. Answer C is incorrect because this file maps network numbers to network names. Answer D is incorrect because this file determines the search order, depending on whether local files, a name service, or DNS is used.

Question 20

The correct answers are B and D. To change the IP address on the network interface hme0, you would need to edit the two files, /etc/hostname.hme0 and /etc/inet/hosts. Answer A is incorrect because /etc/inet/netmasks is used to associate network masks with network numbers. Answer C is incorrect because /etc/system is used to set and modify system and kernel parameters. Answer E is incorrect because /etc/nodename contains the canonical name for the system. This file would be modified if you were manually changing a system's hostname.

Question 21

The correct answer is B. The command /usr/lib/inet/dhcpd -i hme0 -d -v would start the DHCP server daemon in debug mode with verbose output so that additional messages would be displayed. Answer A is incorrect because this command simply runs the daemon in normal mode. Answer C is incorrect because dhcpconfig is used to configure a DHCP server and the -d option is a sub-option used to define the DNS domain name. Answer D is incorrect because this command displays the status of an interface that is under DHCP control; it does not run the dhcpd daemon.

Question 22

The correct answer is A. The startup script /etc/init.d/xntpd is used to start the NTP daemon on an NTP client. Answers B and C are incorrect because they don't exist. Answer D is incorrect because this script is used to configure the network interface.

Question 23

The correct answer is A. Static routes are permanent entries in the route table. Answers B, C, and D are incorrect because they describe dynamic routing entries.

Question 24

The correct answer is B because TCP makes a connection prior to data transmission. TCP also utilizes acknowledgements as part of its provision of a guaranteed delivery mechanism. Answer A is incorrect because this describes a connectionless, unreliable protocol, such as UDP. Answer C is incorrect because TCP utilizes acknowledgements as part of its provision of a guaranteed delivery mechanism. Answer D is incorrect because TCP is connection oriented and establishes a connection prior to data transmission.

Question 25

The correct answer is B. The maximum amount of data that can be included in a single Ethernet II frame is 1500 bytes. Answer A is incorrect because this is the maximum length of an Ethernet II frame, including the data. Answer C is incorrect because this is the minimum length of an Ethernet II frame, including the minimum amount of data. Answer D is incorrect because this is the smallest value that the data field can be.

Question 26

The correct answer is D. The startup script /etc/rcS.d/S30network.sh automatically configures the IP address of the primary network interface. Answers A and B are incorrect because these are not system startup scripts. Answer C is incorrect because this script is executed at run level 2—the network interface is configured at run level S.

Question 27

The correct answer is B. The DNS name server daemon, in.named, starts only if the configuration file /etc/named.conf exists. Answer A is incorrect because /etc/nsswitch.conf contains information on lookups and the order in which data sources are searched. It does not affect the startup of the DNS name server daemon, in.named. Answers C and D are incorrect because these filenames do not exist.

Question 28

The correct answer is D. RIP is a distance-vector routing protocol that exchanges route information between IP routers within an autonomous system. Answers A and B are incorrect because they exchange routes between autonomous systems. Answer C is incorrect because OSPF is a link-state protocol that maintains a map of the network topology instead of working out route paths.

Question 29

The correct answer is D. The double colon (::) can appear only once in an IPv6 address.

Question 30

The correct answer is C. The command `boot net:dhcp - install` boots the JumpStart client to install using the DHCP protocol. Answer A is incorrect because this option would perform a normal JumpStart boot without invoking DHCP. Answer B is incorrect because this option performs just a network boot, such as that done by a diskless client—again, without invoking DHCP. Answer D is incorrect because this option performs a DHCP boot, but does not invoke the JumpStart installation facility.

Question 31

A matches 3 because this device does forward packets based on the MAC Address. B matches 4 because a router forwards packets based on the IP Address. C matches 1 because a gateway connects networks running different protocols, unlike bridges and routers. D matches 2 because a repeater merely "repeats" the electrical signal. A repeater does not route signals to a number of ports, or specific ports; its function is to extend a network segment.

Question 32

The correct answer is B. The `-d` option to the `in.rarpd` command initiates the daemon in debug mode, providing additional messages. Answer A is incorrect because this option merely starts `in.rarpd` for all network interfaces. Answers C and D are incorrect because they are invalid arguments.

Question 33

The correct answer is B. The MTU value for a loopback interface is 8232 bytes. Answer A is incorrect because this is the MTU value for an ethernet interface. Answer C is incorrect because this value is the maximum size of an Ethernet II frame, including data. Answer D is incorrect because this is the minimum size of an Ethernet II frame, including the smallest data size that can be sent.

Question 34

The correct answer is B. A switch is the device that could reduce collisions by reducing the network traffic. A switch only forwards packets to the port containing the destination address. Answer A is incorrect because the hub forwards packets to all ports and does not reduce network traffic or collisions. Answer C is incorrect because this device connects networks together. Answer D is incorrect because the NIC is installed to enable a host to connect to a network.

Question 35

Answers A and D are correct, because IPv6 addresses can contain embedded IPv4 addresses and IPv6 addresses are 128 bits long, with octets separated by a colon character. Answer B is incorrect because this describes an IPv4 address. Answer C is incorrect because, although IPv6 addresses are 128 bits long, the octets are separated by a colon character. Answer E is incorrect because a system can have both IPv4 and IPv6 addresses—it is called a dual stack.

Question 36

The correct answer is B. A classless address consists of the first 18 bits to identify the network and the remaining 14 bits to identify the host. Answer A is incorrect because this describes a class B IP address. Answer C is incorrect because this describes a class A IP address. Answer D is incorrect because this describes a class C IP address.

Question 37

The correct answer is C. The IP address 127.0.0.1 is used as a loopback address, enabling the host to send packets to itself. Answer A is incorrect because the hostname is assigned to the IP address of the primary network interface, not the loopback entry. Answer B is incorrect because the IP address 127.0.0.1 is a reserved address for loopback communication, not for the primary network interface. Answer D is incorrect because the loopback entry is not a test entry and it is used by the system to send packets to itself. It could be used, for example, where both the server and client portions of an application reside on the same physical host.

Question 38

The correct answer is B. A class B IP address contains network addresses where the first octet can be between 128 and 191—the IP address 146.100.20.5 falls within this range. Answer A is incorrect because this is the loopback address. Answer C is incorrect because this is a class C IP address. Answer D is incorrect because this is a class A IP address.

Question 39

The correct answer is C. The command ifconfig hme0:1 plumb 192.168.5.8 up will correctly configure and enable a logical interface on the primary network interface, hme0. Answer A is incorrect because the logical interface (hme0:1) is not specified—the interface also needs to be configured using the plumb option. Answer B is incorrect because the logical interface needs to be configured using the plumb option. Answer D is incorrect because the IP address of the current primary interface should not be specified in addition to the logical interface IP address; the plumb option is also missing.

Question 40

The correct answer is B because NTP uses port 123. Answer A is incorrect because Telnet uses port 23. Answer C is incorrect because FTP uses port 21. Answer D is incorrect because SMTP uses port 25.

Question 41

The correct answer is D. The HUP signal causes the DNS daemon to reread its configuration file. Answer A is incorrect because this signal causes the DNS daemon to take a snapshot of its in-memory cached data. Answer B is incorrect because this signal turns off the debugging option. Answer C is incorrect because this signal increases the debug level by 1.

Question 42

The correct answer is snoop, because this command is used to capture packets on the network.

Question 43

The correct answer is B. *Resolution* is the term used to describe the smallest increment a clock can use. Answer A is incorrect because this describes *precision*. Answer C is incorrect because this describes *accuracy*. Answer D is incorrect because this describes *reliability*.

Question 44

The correct answer is A. The command ifconfig hme0 dhcp tries to obtain a lease manually. Answer B is incorrect because this would only disable and then enable the network interface. It would have no effect on DHCP. Answer C is incorrect because this would stop and start the DHCP server. Answer D is incorrect because this starts the normal process of automatically obtaining an IP address; it would not try to acquire a lease manually.

Question 45

The correct answer is B. The /var/adm/messages file contains error messages produced by the DNS server. Answers A, C, and D are incorrect because these files do not exist.

Question 46

The correct answer is A. TCP is a reliable, connection-oriented protocol and UDP is an unreliable, connectionless protocol. Answer B is incorrect because TCP is a reliable, connection-oriented protocol, not UDP. Also it is UDP that is unreliable and connectionless, not TCP. Answer C is incorrect because TCP is connection-oriented, not connectionless. Also UDP is not connection-oriented, it is connectionless. Answer D is incorrect because UDP is unreliable; TCP is the reliable protocol.

Question 47

The correct answer is C because you need to be root to see the ethernet address. Answers A, B, and D are incorrect because the IP address, network mask, and broadcast address are all displayed if you enter the `ifconfig -a` command as a non-root user.

Question 48

The correct answers are A and C. The JumpStart client must be of the ultra architecture—that is, `sun4u`—and must also have its boot PROM version at 3.25 or greater. Answer B is incorrect because the JumpStart server can be any architecture that is supported in Solaris 9. Answer D is incorrect because it is the JumpStart client that must have its boot PROM version at 3.25 or greater, not the server. Answer E is incorrect because the server and the client do not need to be on the same subnet. That is only necessary for JumpStart clients and boot servers when using the RARP protocol to boot; the DHCP protocol can boot across subnetworks.

Question 49

The correct answer is A. ARP is used to map a 32-bit IP address to a 48-bit ethernet address. Answers B and D are incorrect because they are invalid: IP addresses are 32 bits long and ethernet addresses are 48 bits long. Answer C is incorrect because this describes the function of the RARP protocol.

Question 50

The correct answers are B and C. Sun Trunking provides outbound load balancing when more than one destination is involved (there must be multiple destinations). It also allows up to two Quad Fast Ethernet cards (providing a maximum of eight network ports) to be combined to form a single "trunk" running at 800Mbps. Answer A is incorrect because this describes a logical network interface. Answers D and E are incorrect because these are not features of Sun Trunking.

Question 51

The correct answer is C. The command `ifconfig hme0:1 down unplumb` will successfully remove the logical interface `hme0:1`. Answer A is incorrect because the interface must be marked `down` before the `unplumb` option can be used to remove it. Answer B is incorrect because this only disables the network interface, it does not remove it. Answer D is incorrect because the interface has not been marked `down`. This needs to happen before the interface can be removed; otherwise, there is a risk that data might be lost.

Question 52

The correct answer is D. The `in.ripngd` is a routing daemon used in IPv6. Answer A is incorrect because this command is an IPv6 daemon used with autoconfiguration. Answer B is incorrect because the `in.mpathd` daemon monitors IPv6 multipath interfaces. Answer C is incorrect because `inetd` is the Internet services daemon and is not related to multipathing.

Question 53

The correct answer is B. The `netstat -r` command displays the routing table entries. Answer A is incorrect because this command displays the status of all installed network interfaces. Answer C is incorrect because this command displays network interface statistics. Answer D is incorrect because this command is used to inspect and modify network parameters. Answer E is incorrect because `print` is an invalid option to the `route` command in the Solaris operating environment.

Question 54

The correct answer is C. The Network Interface layer uses ethernet addresses as its basis for addressing. Answer A is incorrect because the Internet layer uses IP addresses as its basis for addressing. Answer B is incorrect because the Application layer uses application-to-application communications to address its peer. Answer D is incorrect because the Transport layer uses ports as its basis for addressing.

Question 55

The correct answers are A and B. The dhcpconfig utility is used to configure a DHCP server from the command line, whereas the dhcpmgr utility is used to configure a DHCP server in a graphical interface. Answer C is incorrect because dhtadm is used to manage configuration tables within DHCP and not to configure the DHCP server. Answer D is incorrect because pntadm is used to manage network tables within DHCP and not to configure the DHCP server.

Question 56

The correct answer is C. NTP servers advertise every 64 seconds on the network.

Question 57

The correct answer is C. Even though ARP has traditionally been listed as an Internet layer protocol, it actually operates between the Network Interface and Internet layers.

Question 58

The correct answer is D. The USR2 signal is used to reset the debugging level to 0—that is, to turn off debugging. Answer A is incorrect because the INT signal is used to cause the DNS daemon to take a snapshot of its in-memory cached data. Answer B is incorrect because the HUP signal causes the DNS daemon to reread its configuration file. Answer C is incorrect because the USR1 signal increases the debug level by 1 each time, providing more debug information to be displayed.

Question 59

The correct answer is C. Before assigning an IPv6 address to a network interface, the autoconfiguration utility checks to see whether the address is a duplicate. It does this by sending a solicitation message and checks for a response. If no response is received, then it is assumed that the address is unique and it is assigned to the interface; otherwise a message is issued and no further action is taken. Answer A is incorrect because addresses can be obtained by using a combination of both stateless and stateful autoconfiguration. Answer B is incorrect because manual intervention is required if a duplicate address is detected. Answer D is incorrect because stateful autoconfiguration is not the recommended method because it requires an additional means of providing hostname-to-IP address resolution.

Question 60

The correct answer is C. The window advertisement contains the number of additional bytes that can be sent. The window advertisement is part of the flow control available with TCP. Answers A, B, and D are incorrect because they are not contained within a window advertisement.

Question 61

The correct answer is ndd. This command is used to inspect and modify network parameters, such as the speed of the network interface. For a system with an hme network interface, the speed of the interface is viewed by entering the following command: ndd /dev/hme link_speed. A value of 0 indicates the interface is running at 10Mbps, whereas a value of 1 indicates the interface is running at 100Mbps.

Question 62

The correct answer is A. When a datagram is sent to an anycast address, only the nearest host that is a member of a multicast group receives the datagram. Answer B is incorrect because this type is used to communicate with all hosts on the network. Answer C is incorrect because this type is used to communicate with a specific group of hosts on the network. Answer D is incorrect because this type is used to communicate with a single host on the network.

Question 63

Answers B and C are correct. DHCP is used to automatically assign IP addresses to hosts. Using DHCP makes it much easier to renumber the network if the ISP changes. Answer A is incorrect because DHCP does not assign ethernet addresses; it assigns IP addresses. Answer D is incorrect because IP addresses assigned by DHCP are not static and can be changed easily.

Question 64

Answers A and C are correct. SUNWfiles and SUNWbinfiles are both valid locations for the datastore. The other valid option for the datastore (not shown in this question) is SUNWnisplus. Answers B, D, and E are not valid entries for the datastore location.

16

Practice Exam #2

This chapter provides another 64 questions on the topics that pertain to Exam 310-044, "Sun Certified Network Administrator for the Solaris 9 Operating Environment." Like the first practice exam, this exam must be completed in 105 minutes. The pass mark for this practice exam is also 70%.

Question 1

Match the following protocols with the correct layer at which each operates.

○ A. TCP

○ B. FTP

○ C. ICMP

○ D. PPP

○ 1. Network Interface layer

○ 2. Internet layer

○ 3. Transport layer

○ 4. Application layer

Question 2

This DHCP configuration file is created when you run the configuration utilities, **dhcpconfig** or **dhcpmgr**. The file should never be manually edited. In previous versions of Solaris, the file was **/etc/default/dhcp**. What is this filename in Solaris 9?

○ A. **/etc/default/dhcpsvc.conf**

○ B. **/etc/inet/dhcpsvc.conf**

○ C. **/etc/dhcp/dhcpsvc.conf**

○ D. **/var/dhcp/dhcpsvc.conf**

Question 3

You have a primary network interface, **hme0**, and you run the command to find out the speed at which the interface is running by typing **ndd /dev/hme link_speed**. The value returned is **1**. What does this tell you about the speed of the network interface?

○ A. The interface is running at 10Mbps.

○ B. The interface can negotiate the correct speed from the network.

○ C. The interface is running at 100Mbps.

○ D. The interface is running at 1000Mbps.

Question 4

When using multipathing, the **in.mpathd** daemon detects failures on monitored network interfaces. Which file, containing a number of settings, is referenced when the daemon starts?

○ A. **/etc/default/mpathd**

○ B. **/etc/inet/mpathd**

○ C. **/etc/default/inetd**

○ D. **/etc/default/init**

Question 5

When a diskless client boots, what is the only piece of information it is able to provide to a server to continue?

○ A. The hostname

○ B. The IP Address

○ C. The Ethernet Address

○ D. The IP Address of its boot server

Question 6

Which file specifies the canonical name for a system?

○ A. **/etc/inet/hosts**

○ B. **/etc/inet/networks**

○ C. **/etc/nodename**

○ D. **/etc/system**

Question 7

When trying to contact a remote host, you get the message:

Destination unreachable

Which protocol would initiate this error message?

○ A. IP

○ B. ARP

○ C. TCP

○ D. ICMP

Question 8

To find out whether your system is using DNS as part of the name-resolution search order, which file would you consult?

- ○ A. **/etc/inet/hosts**
- ○ B. **/etc/resolv.conf**
- ○ C. **/etc/nsswitch.conf**
- ○ D. **/etc/named.conf**

Question 9

Which IEEE standard identifier is used to represent ethernet?

- ○ A. 802.3
- ○ B. 802.4
- ○ C. 802.5
- ○ D. 802.2

Question 10

Which of the following are features of the UDP protocol? Choose 2.

- ❑ A. UDP has a low overhead.
- ❑ B. UDP has a high overhead.
- ❑ C. UDP is a connectionless, stateless, and unreliable protocol.
- ❑ D. UDP is a connection-oriented, stateful, and reliable protocol.
- ❑ E. UDP requires acknowledgement messages from the receiving host.

Question 11

Which command allows you to continuously view changes to the routing table?

- ○ A. **route monitor**
- ○ B. **route flush**
- ○ C. **netstat -r**
- ○ D. **netstat -i**

Question 12

What is the default network mask for a class B network?

○ A. **255.0.0.0**

○ B. **255.255.0.0**

○ C. **255.255.255.0**

○ D. **255.255.255.240**

Question 13

When configuring your DHCP server, you decide that your datastore option is going to be **SUNWnisplus**. For this option, the location is going to be which of the following?

○ A. An absolute pathname

○ B. A relative pathname

○ C. The root (/) directory

○ D. An NIS+ table name

Question 14

The Point-to-Point protocol operates at which layer of the TCP/IP model?

○ A. Application layer

○ B. Internet layer

○ C. Network Interface layer

○ D. Transport layer

Question 15

The **pntadm** utility is used to manage DHCP network tables. Which of the following can be achieved using **pntadm**? Choose 2.

❑ A. Add networks that are under DHCP management.

❑ B. Remove networks that are under DHCP management.

❑ C. Create alias names for networks under DHCP management.

❑ D. Modify the DHCP datastore type.

Question 16

Which of the following are reasons why many network applications need time synchronization to work properly? Choose 2.

- ❑ A. Many encryption algorithms use time as part of the encryption key.
- ❑ B. DHCP clients must be time synchronized with the DHCP server when they request a lease.
- ❑ C. Time stamps are used on Ethernet II frames, requiring the sender and the receiver to be time synchronized.
- ❑ D. Files and directories are time stamped by applications when they are created or modified

Question 17

Which two utilities should be used to manage the **dhcptab** table? Choose 2.

- ❑ A. **dhcpmgr**
- ❑ B. **pntadm**
- ❑ C. **dhcpconfig**
- ❑ D. **dhtadm**

Question 18

You have a system with a primary network interface **hme0** and a logical network interface configured with the IP address **192.168.7.4**. You do not know to which logical interface the IP address is assigned, but the logical interface is no longer required. Which command will successfully remove this logical interface?

- ○ A. **ifconfig hme0 down**
- ○ B. **ifconfig hme0 removeif 192.168.7.4**
- ○ C. **ifconfig hme0 192.168.7.4 down**
- ○ D. **ifconfig 192.168.7.4 hme0 removeif**

Question 19

When you run the **netstat -i** command, you notice a high number of output errors occurring on the primary interface. Which two scenarios could be the cause of this?

- ❑ A. A duplicate IP address is on the same network.
- ❑ B. Several hosts are trying to send data at the same time.
- ❑ C. The system has a faulty network adapter.
- ❑ D. A remote host on the network has a hardware problem.

Question 20

Which options of the **ifconfig** command are used to set up a test address for a network interface being used in a multipath environment? Choose 2.

- ❑ A. **deprecated**
- ❑ B. **-failover**
- ❑ C. **failover**
- ❑ D. **-deprecated**
- ❑ E. **unplumb**

Question 21

Which of the following are true about DNS zones of authority? Choose 2.

- ❑ A. Zones can cross one or more domains.
- ❑ B. Zones are restricted to a single domain.
- ❑ C. Zones comprise a domain and the data associated with the domain.
- ❑ D. Zones comprise the domain, but not the associated data within the domain.

Question 22

Which address type was present in IPv4, but is not used in IPv6?

- ○ A. Anycast
- ○ B. Multicast
- ○ C. Unicast
- ○ D. Broadcast

Question 23

NTP servers belong to a hierarchy called *strata*. How many strata are there?

- ○ A. 5
- ○ B. 10
- ○ C. 15
- ○ D. 20

Question 24

Your ultra10 system (hostname **alpha**) has a primary network interface, **hme0**, and a logical interface, **hme0:1**. You want to add a further logical interface with the IP address **192.168.9.9**. Which of the following options will do this correctly? Choose 2.

- ❏ A. **ifconfig hme0 plumb 192.168.9.9 up**
- ❏ B. **ifconfig hme0:2 plumb 192.168.9.9 up**
- ❏ C. **ifconfig hme0 addif 192.168.9.9 up**
- ❏ D. **ifconfig hme0 -add 192.168.9.9 up**
- ❏ E. **ifconfig addif hme0 192.168.9.9 up**

Question 25

Which configuration file does the **in.ndpd** process read on startup?

- ○ A. **/etc/inet/ndpd.conf**
- ○ B. **/etc/ndpd.conf**
- ○ C. **/etc/inet/ipnodes**
- ○ D. **/etc/ipnodes**

Question 26

DNS domains such as **com**, **gov**, **edu**, and **org** belong to which type of domain?

- ○ A. Root domain
- ○ B. Top-level domain
- ○ C. Second-level domain
- ○ D. Fully-qualified domain name

Question 27

TCP uses which kind of connection to provide concurrent data transfer in both directions?

○ A. Full-duplex

○ B. Simplex

○ C. Half-duplex

○ D. Double duplex

Question 28

Output from the **netstat -i** command can be used to compute the collision rate on a network interface. Your output has reported 352 collisions and 16000 output packets. What is the collision rate as a percentage?

○ A. 4.4%

○ B. 2.2%

○ C. 1.1%

○ D. 8.8%

Question 29

You want to remove all entries from the routing table. Which command (and option) will achieve this?

○ A. **route delete default**

○ B. **route flush**

○ C. **init 2**

○ D. **route monitor**

Question 30

The file **/etc/default/mpathd** sets some initial variables that are used by the **in.mpathd** daemon. One of these variables defines how long to wait before marking an interface as having failed. Which variable does this?

- ○ A. **FAILURE_TIMEOUT**
- ○ B. **FAILURE_DELAY**
- ○ C. **FAILURE_DETECT**
- ○ D. **FAILURE_DETECTION_TIME**

Question 31

The Hardware layer of the TCP/IP model is not always identified as a separate layer in its own right. Which layer is described as incorporating the Hardware layer as part of its function?

- ○ A. Network Interface layer
- ○ B. Internet layer
- ○ C. Transport layer
- ○ D. Application layer

Question 32

Which option for the **arp** command is used to delete a static entry from the ARP cache?

- ○ A. **-s**
- ○ B. **-d**
- ○ C. **-a**
- ○ D. **-f**

Question 33

How many bits of a class C IP address are used to denote the network portion of the address, assuming a standard netmask of **255.255.255.0**?

○ A. 8

○ B. 16

○ C. 18

○ D. 24

Question 34

When using IP multipathing, why is it necessary to create a test address for a network interface?

○ A. To provide a failover address that can be used in the event of a failure.

○ B. To allow the **in.mpathd** process to monitor the status of the interface.

○ C. To enable testing while multipathing is being set up.

○ D. To aid outbound load balancing when network traffic is being routed to multiple hosts.

Question 35

At which layer of the TCP/IP model does routing take place?

○ A. Internet layer

○ B. Transport layer

○ C. Application layer

○ D. Network Interface layer

Question 36

Which of the following fields are present in an Ethernet II frame? Choose 3.

- ❑ A. Ethernet address of the destination host
- ❑ B. IP address of the destination host
- ❑ C. Ethernet address of the sending host
- ❑ D. IP address of the sending host
- ❑ E. Acknowledgement number
- ❑ F. Cyclic redundancy check (CRC)

Question 37

Which file is used to assign permanent network mask entries?

- ○ A. **/etc/inet/hosts**
- ○ B. **/etc/inet/netmasks**
- ○ C. **/etc/inet/networks**
- ○ D. **/etc/hosts**

Question 38

The **dhtadm** command is used to manage the DHCP service configuration table. Which option creates the DHCP table?

- ○ A. **-M**
- ○ B. **-C**
- ○ C. **-A**
- ○ D. **-D**

Question 39

Which statement describes unsolicited ARP messages?

- ○ A. Messages where a specific ethernet address was asked for by a host
- ○ B. Messages where a specific IP address was asked for by a host
- ○ C. Messages where the information about a host that issued an ARP request is stored
- ○ D. Messages where the IP address for a host that issued an ARP request is stored

Question 40

Which layer of the TCP/IP model handles flow control?

- ○ A. Transport layer
- ○ B. Network Interface layer
- ○ C. Internet layer
- ○ D. Application layer

Question 41

Which option for the **pntadm** command is used to view changes made to the DHCP table?

- ○ A. **-M**
- ○ B. **-C**
- ○ C. **-A**
- ○ D. **-P**

Question 42

Which of the following are reasons why IPv6 was needed? Choose 2.

- ❑ A. IPv6 provides a solution to the shortfall in IPv4 addresses.
- ❑ B. IPv6 addresses are split according to a number of network classes.
- ❑ C. IPv6 provides simpler routing.
- ❑ D. IPv6 provides greater administrator control through manual assigning of IPv6 addresses.

Question 43

Which file would you create, prior to rebooting the system, to configure an IPv6 address on the **hme0** interface?

○ A. **/etc/hostname6.hme0**

○ B. **/etc/hostname.hme0**

○ C. **/etc/hostname6.hme6**

○ D. **/etc/hostname.hme0:6**

Question 44

NTP servers use a drift file to handle differences between the server and the reference time source. What is the default location of the drift file?

○ A. **/etc/ntp.drift**

○ B. **/var/ntp/ntp.drift**

○ C. **/var/adm/ntp.drift**

○ D. **/etc/ntp/ntp.drift**

Question 45

Which of the following are functions of the client DHCP process **dhcpagent**? Choose 2.

❑ A. Listens for server responses

❑ B. Releases or renews leases

❑ C. Configures the DHCP client

❑ D. Manages the list of available IP addresses

Question 46

Which of the following are cases in which logical network interfaces are used? Choose 2.

- ❏ A. To ease network performance problems by spreading network traffic between the primary and logical interfaces
- ❏ B. With a server running a number of applications that need to appear as separate systems
- ❏ C. With servers using a high-availability failover mechanism, such as IP multipathing
- ❏ D. To provide hardware resilience

Question 47

What is the formula for calculating the collision rate on a network interface?

- ○ A. Multiply the number of collisions by 100 and then divide by the total number of input packets.
- ○ B. Multiply the total number of input packets by 100 and then divide by the number of collisions.
- ○ C. Multiply the total number of output packets by 100 and then divide by the number of collisions.
- ○ D. Multiply the number of collisions by 100 and then divide by the total number of output packets.

Question 48

What type of connection does TCP establish before starting data transmission?

- ○ A. Full-duplex connection
- ○ B. Half-duplex Connection
- ○ C. Virtual circuit connection
- ○ D. Physical connection

Question 49

Solicited ARP messages are held in the ARP cache, by default, for 20 minutes. How long are unsolicited messages held in the cache?

- ○ A. 2 minutes
- ○ B. 5 minutes
- ○ C. 10 minutes
- ○ D. 20 minutes

Question 50

Which file provides IPv6 address-to-hostname mapping, similar to the IPv4 file **/etc/inet/hosts**?

- ○ A. **/etc/ipnodes**
- ○ B. **/etc/inet/ipnodes**
- ○ C. **/etc/ip6hosts**
- ○ D. **/etc/inet/ip6hosts**

Question 51

A **dhcp_network** file is present for each network served by a DHCP server. The **dhcp_network** filename is created from which two items? Choose 2.

- ❑ A. The IP address of the network being supported
- ❑ B. The type of datasource
- ❑ C. The hostname of the DHCP server
- ❑ D. The IP address of the DHCP server

Question 52

Which server startup script starts the DNS daemon **in.named**?

- ○ A. **/etc/rcS.d/S30network.sh**
- ○ B. **/etc/rc2.d/S30sysid.net**
- ○ C. **/etc/rc2.d/S72inetsvc**
- ○ D. **/etc/rc2.d/S69inet**

Question 53

Which of the following are valid representations of the IPv6 loopback address? Choose 3.

- ❑ A. **::1**
- ❑ B. **1**
- ❑ C. **0000:0000:0000:0000:0000:0000:0000:0001**
- ❑ D. **0:0:0:0:0:0:0:1**
- ❑ E. **0000::0000::1**

Question 54

The process of subnetting provides the facility to break down a network into a number of subnetworks. Which of the following are valid uses for subnetting? Choose 3.

- ❑ A. To associate subnetworks with a specific geographical area, or department
- ❑ B. To reduce network contention by separating local subnetworks
- ❑ C. To reduce the number of IP addresses that need to be administered
- ❑ D. To enhance security by restricting access to a subnetwork
- ❑ E. To simplify the management of the network

Question 55

One media type uses four pairs of wires, one pair for sending, one for receiving and two for bi-directional communication. It can be implemented over UTP Cat-3, CAT-4 or Cat-5 cables for distances of up to about 100 meters. Which media type is this?

- ○ A. 100BASE-T4
- ○ B. 100BASE-FX
- ○ C. 100BASE-TX
- ○ D. 100BASE-X

Question 56

In DHCP, what does the **dhcp_network** file contain?

○ A. Configuration information for the **dhcpagent** process

○ B. The range of IP addresses under the DHCP server control, for a single network

○ C. The range of IP addresses under the DHCP server control, for all networks

○ D. Configuration information for the DHCP server

Question 57

An NTP server's configuration file, **/etc/inet/ntp.conf**, is created by copying a template file. Where is the template file located?

○ A. **/etc/inet/ntp.master**

○ B. **/etc/inet/ntp.temp**

○ C. **/etc/inet/ntp.client**

○ D. **/etc/inet/ntp.server**

Question 58

The transition to IPv6 allows IPv4-compatible IPv6 addresses, where an IPv4 address is embedded in the IPv6 address. The IPv6 address **0000:0000:0000:0000:0000:FFFF:C0A8:1507** contains the IPv4 address **192.168.21.7** (represented in hexadecimal). Which part of this IPv6 address indicates that an embedded IPv4 address is present?

○ A. **C0A8**

○ B. **1507**

○ C. **FFFF**

○ D. **0000**

Question 59

The **dhcpmgr** utility provides a graphical interface for easy configuration of a DHCP server. In which directory can this command be found?

- ○ A. **/usr/bin**
- ○ B. **/usr/sadm/bin**
- ○ C. **/usr/sadm/admin**
- ○ D. **/usr/sadm/admin/bin**

Question 60

TCP manages flow control on the sending side by using a congestion window. What does this window do to manage the flow of data?

- ○ A. The congestion window is halved in size when acknowledgements are received and is doubled in size when congestion is detected.
- ○ B. The congestion window is doubled in size when acknowledgements are received and halved in size when congestion is detected.
- ○ C. The congestion window informs the receiving host of the number of packets sent.
- ○ D. The congestion window requests the number of packets that have been received from the receiving host.

Question 61

Which layer of the TCP/IP model handles the conversion and presentation of data?

- ○ A. Application layer
- ○ B. Internet layer
- ○ C. Network Interface layer
- ○ D. Transport layer

Question 62

In this network topology, the output of one node connects to the input of the next. Each host is connected only to its adjacent neighbors on each side. Which topology is being described?

- ○ A. Bus
- ○ B. Ring
- ○ C. Star
- ○ D. VLAN

Question 63

The RARP daemon **in.rarpd** will start at system bootup only if which directory exists?

- ○ A. **/tftpboot**
- ○ B. **/boot**
- ○ C. **/boottftp**
- ○ D. **/tftp**

Question 64

The use of logical network interfaces can have some disadvantages. Which of the following are disadvantages? Choose 2.

- ❏ A. Logical interfaces can create performance bottlenecks as they are all tied to a specific physical ethernet interface.
- ❏ B. Logical interfaces are more expensive.
- ❏ C. Logical interfaces create a significant administration overhead.
- ❏ D. Eash logical interface must be configured at system boot time, which can slow down the overall boot time of a system when multiple logical interfaces are used.

Practice Exam #2
Answer Key

1. A matches 3
   B matches 4
   C matches 2
   D matches 1
2. B
3. C
4. A
5. C
6. C
7. D
8. C
9. A
10. A, C
11. A
12. B
13. D
14. C
15. A, B
16. A, D
17. A, D
18. B
19. A, C
20. A, B
21. A, C
22. D
23. C
24. B, C
25. A
26. B

27. A
28. B
29. B
30. D
31. A
32. B
33. D
34. B
35. A
36. A, C, F
37. B
38. B
39. C
40. A
41. D
42. A, C
43. A
44. B
45. A, B
46. B, C
47. D
48. C
49. B
50. B
51. A, B
52. C
53. A, C, D
54. A, B, D
55. A

56. B
57. D
58. C
59. D
60. B
61. A
62. B
63. A
64. A, D

Answer Key Explanations

Question 1

A matches 3 because TCP is a Transport layer protocol. B matches 4 because FTP is an Application layer protocol. C matches 2 because ICMP is an Internet layer protocol, and D matches 1 because PPP is a Network Interface layer protocol.

Question 2

The correct answer is B, because the DHCP configuration filename that is automatically created when the DHCP server configuration utilities are run is `/etc/inet/dhcpsvc.conf`. Answers A, C, and D are incorrect because these filenames don't exist.

Question 3

The correct answer is C. When you run `ndd /dev/hme link_speed`, and the return value is `1`, it indicates that the interface is running at 100Mbps. Answer A is incorrect because the value would be `0` if the interface was running at 10Mbps. Answer B is incorrect because the auto-negotiation capability is a different parameter of `ndd`, namely `autoneg_cap`. Answer D is incorrect because the `hme0` interface cannot run at 1000Mbps.

Question 4

The correct answer is A, because `/etc/default/mpathd` is the file referenced by `in.mpathd`. Answer B is incorrect because `/etc/inet/mpathd` does not exist. Answer C is incorrect because `/etc/default/inetd` contains default settings for the `inetd` daemon. Answer D is incorrect because `/etc/default/init` is the file that is read by the `init` process when the system boots, to set environment variables.

Question 5

The correct answer is C because a diskless client knows only its own ethernet address. This address is passed in a RARP request to obtain the client's IP address, which, in turn, enables the client to continue the boot process. Answers A and B are incorrect because a diskless client does not possess these items of information—it gets them from the server. Answer D is incorrect because the client does not have the IP address of the boot server—the client sends a RARP message, which is broadcast to all hosts on the network, and the boot server responds with the client's IP address.

Question 6

The correct answer is C. The file /etc/nodename specifies the canonical name for a system. The entry in this file identifies the system name to be used for applications. Answer A is incorrect because /etc/inet/hosts provides IP address-to-hostname mapping. Answer B is incorrect because /etc/inet/ networks associates network numbers with network names. Answer D is incorrect because /etc/system contains essential system kernel settings and configurable kernel variables.

Question 7

The correct answer is D. The ICMP protocol is used to send control or error messages. The destination unreachable error message is one example of a message produced by ICMP. This message is normally produced when there is no defined route to the remote host or network. Answers A, B, and C are incorrect because these protocols are not used to send control or error messages.

Question 8

The correct answer is C because the file /etc/nsswitch.conf shows the search order for name resolution. The relevant line of this file is the hosts: entry. Answer A is incorrect because /etc/inet/hosts contains a mapping of IP addresses to hostnames. Answer B is incorrect because /etc/resolv.conf is the file that lists the search order and addresses of DNS servers. Answer D is incorrect because /etc/named.conf is the configuration file used by the DNS daemon in.named.

Question 9

The correct answer is A. 802.3 is the IEEE identifier for ethernet. Answer B is incorrect because 802.4 is the IEEE identifier for the token bus network access method. Answer C is incorrect because 802.5 is the IEEE identifier for the token ring network access method. Answer D is incorrect because 802.2 is the IEEE identifier for the logical link control (LLC).

Question 10

The correct answers are A and C. UDP has a low overhead and is a connectionless, stateless, and unreliable protocol. Answer B is incorrect because UDP does not have a high overhead; it has a low overhead. Answers D and E are incorrect because these describe TCP, not UDP.

Question 11

The correct answer is A. The route monitor command provides continuous output of any changes that occur in the routing table. Answer B is incorrect because route flush removes all entries from the routing table. Answer C is incorrect because netstat -r simply displays all entries in the routing table. Answer D is incorrect because netstat -i is used to display interface statistics.

Question 12

The correct answer is B. The network mask 255.255.0.0 is the default mask for a class B network. Answer A is incorrect because this is the default netmask for a class A network. Answer C is incorrect because this is the default netmask for a class C network. Answer D is incorrect because this is the netmask for a class C network that uses subnetting.

Question 13

The correct answer is D. When specifying the datastore as type SUNWnisplus, the location must be the name of an NIS+ table. Answer A is incorrect because an absolute pathname must be used for the other two datastore options, SUNWfiles and SUNWbinfiles. Answers B and C are incorrect because they are not valid options for the datastore location.

Question 14

The correct answer is C. The Point-to-Point protocol (PPP) operates at the Network Interface layer of the TCP/IP model and transmits packets over serial point-to-point links. Answers A, B, and D are incorrect because PPP does not operate at these layers; it operates at the Network Interface layer.

Question 15

The correct answers are A and B. The pntadm utility is used to add and remove networks that are under the management of DHCP. Answer C is incorrect because /etc/inet/networks associates network numbers with network names. Answer D is incorrect because the datastore type cannot be changed after it has been created.

Question 16

The correct answers are A and D. Encryption algorithms often use time as part of the encryption key. Time synchronization is also required because files and directories are time stamped when created or modified. Answers B and C are incorrect because they do not have time-critical elements.

Question 17

The correct answers are A and D. The two utilities that should be used to manage the dhcptab table are dhcpmgr and dhtadm. Answer B is incorrect because pntadm is used to manage DHCP network tables. Answer C is incorrect because dhcpconfig is used to configure the DHCP server.

Question 18

The correct answer is B. The command `ifconfig hme0 removeif 192.168.7.4` will successfully remove the logical interface that has the named IP address assigned to it. Answer A is incorrect because `ifconfig hme0 down` will disable only the primary network interface. Answers C and D are incorrect because they both represent invalid use of the syntax of the `ifconfig` command.

Question 19

The correct answers are A and C. A faulty network adapter would cause a high number of output errors on the primary network interface. Additionally, a duplicate IP on the same network would also produce the same result. Answer B is incorrect because this would result in a high number of collisions. Answer D is incorrect because a remote host would have no effect on the number of output errors.

Question 20

The correct answers are A and B. The `deprecated` option ensures that the interface is not used for passing application data and the `-failover` option marks the address so that `in.mpathd` will not use it as a failover address. Answer C is incorrect because the `failover` option enables the interface as a failover address. Answer D is incorrect because the `-deprecated` option marks the interface as not deprecated and uses it for passing data to other applications. Answer E is incorrect because the `unplumb` option is used to remove a network interface.

Question 21

The correct answers are A and C. Zones of authority can cross one or more domains and a zone comprises a domain (or more than one domain), including the data associated with the domain. Answer B is incorrect because zones of authority can cross one or more domains; they are not restricted to a single domain. Answer D is incorrect because a zone comprises a domain as well as the data associated with the domain.

Question 22

The correct answer is D. IPv6 does not use the broadcast address mechanism. Answers A, B, and C are incorrect because anycast, multicast, and unicast are all address types that are used in IPv6.

Question 23

The correct answer is C. There are 15 strata, ranging from 1 to 15. A stratum-1 server is the most accurate and has its own time reference source.

Question 24

The correct answers are B and C. The command `ifconfig hme0:2 plumb 192.168.9.9` will configure and enable the logical interface `hme0:2`. The command `ifconfig hme0 addif 192.168.9.9 up` will also configure and enable the logical interface `hme0:2`; the latter command will automatically select the next available index number to use (because `hme0:1` is already in use). Answer A is incorrect because this command would overwrite the primary network interface address with `192.168.9.9`, which is not required. Answers D and E are incorrect because the syntax for the `ifconfig` command is invalid.

Question 25

The correct answer is A. The configuration file `/etc/inet/ndpd.conf` is read by the `in.ndpd` process on startup. Answer B is incorrect because this file does not exist. Answer C is incorrect because `/etc/inet/ipnodes` is the file used to map IPv6 addresses to IPv6 hostnames, similar to the way in which `/etc/inet/hosts` is used in IPv4. Answer D is incorrect because this file does not exist. Unlike IPv4, where `/etc/hosts` is symbolically linked to `/etc/inet/hosts`, there is no such link for the `ipnodes` file.

Question 26

The correct answer is B. Domains such as `com`, `gov`, `edu`, and `org` are examples of top-level domains. Top-level domains are currently controlled by

ICANN. Geographical domains are also further examples, based on their physical locations. Answer A is incorrect because the root domain is the single top domain in the DNS hierarchy and contains the names and addresses of top-level domains. The root domain is controlled by IANA. Answer C is incorrect because second-level domains are located below top-level domains in the DNS hierarchy. sun.com is an example of a second-level domain, which is controlled by Sun Microsystems. Answer D is incorrect because a fully qualified domain name (FQDN) is the portion of a uniform resource locator (URL) that fully identifies a domain on the Internet, such as www.sun.com.

Question 27

The correct answer is A. TCP uses a full-duplex connection, which allows concurrent data transfer in both directions. Answer B is incorrect because a simplex connection allows data transfer in a single direction—it is one-way. Answer C is incorrect because a half-duplex connection allows data transfer in both directions, but not concurrently. Answer D is incorrect because double duplex does not exist.

Question 28

The correct answer is B. With 352 collisions and 16000 output packets, the collision rate is calculated as follows:

$(100 \times 352) / 16000 = 2.2\%$

Question 29

The correct answer is B. The route flush command is used to empty the routing table of all entries. Answer A is incorrect because route delete default removes only the default route entry (if defined). It does not affect any other entries in the routing table. Answer C is incorrect because init 2 causes the system to change its run level to level 2, and will only disable NFS. It does not remove the routing entries. Answer D is incorrect because route monitor is used to view continuous output of any changes made to the routing table. It does not remove any entries.

Question 30

The correct answer is D because the FAILURE_DETECTION_TIME variable specifies how long to wait before marking an interface as failed. The default setting for this variable is 10,000 milliseconds (or 10 seconds) and can be adjusted in the file /etc/default/mpathd. Answers A, B, and C are incorrect because these variable names do not exist.

Question 31

The correct answer is A. The Network Interface layer often incorporates the Hardware layer as part of its functionality, when the Hardware layer is not identified as a separate layer in its own right. Answers B, C, and D are incorrect because the Hardware layer is often incorporated within the Network Interface layer.

Question 32

The correct answer is B. arp -d <hostname> would delete the entry relating to <hostname> from the ARP cache. Answer A is incorrect because the -s option is used to add a static entry to the ARP cache. Answer C is incorrect because the -a option lists all entries in the ARP cache. Answer D is incorrect because the -f option is used in conjunction with a filename to add multiple entries to the ARP cache.

Question 33

The correct answer is D. A class C IP address uses the first 24 bits of the address to denote the network and the next 8 bits to denote the host address. Answer A is incorrect because this describes a class A IP address. Answer B is incorrect because 16 bits are used to denote the network portion of a class B IP address. Answer C is incorrect because 18 bits are used to denote the network portion of a classless IP address.

Question 34

The correct answer is B because the test address is used by the `in.mpathd` process to monitor the status of the interface. The test address is not used to pass network traffic from any other applications; it is solely used for failure and recovery detection. Answer A is incorrect because the test address is not used as a live failover. Answer C is incorrect because the test address is used all the time for failure and recovery detection. Answer D is incorrect because outbound load balancing is a feature of multipathing and is not applicable to test addresses because they do not pass any network traffic from other applications.

Question 35

The correct answer is A. Routing takes place at the Internet layer of the TCP/IP model. Answers B, C, and D are incorrect because routing does not take place at these layers; it is a function of the Internet layer.

Question 36

The correct answers are A, C, and F. The Ethernet II frame contains the sending and destination ethernet addresses and the cyclic redundancy check (CRC) fields. Answers B and D are incorrect because IP addresses are not contained within Ethernet II frames; they are found in IP datagrams. Answer E is incorrect because the acknowledgment number field is not found within an Ethernet II frame; it is found within a TCP segment header.

Question 37

The correct answer is B. The file `/etc/inet/netmasks` is used to assign permanent network mask entries. Answer A is incorrect because `/etc/inet/hosts` is used to provide IP address to hostname mapping. Answer C is incorrect because `/etc/inet/networks` associates network numbers with network names. Answer D is incorrect because `/etc/hosts` is a symbolic link to `/etc/inet/hosts`.

Question 38

The correct answer is B. The -c option to dhtadm creates the DHCP table. Answer A is incorrect because the -M option is used to modify a symbol or macro definition. Answer C is incorrect because the -A option is used to add a symbol or macro definition. Answer D is incorrect because the -D option is used to delete a symbol or macro definition.

Question 39

The correct answer is C. Unsolicited ARP messages are related to a host that made an ARP request. Information about the host is stored in the ARP cache. Answer A is incorrect because this describes a solicited ARP message. Answers B and D are incorrect because these are not ARP messages.

Question 40

The correct answer is A. Flow control is handled by the Transport Layer of the TCP/IP model. Answer B is incorrect because the Network Interface layer handles the transfer of frames across the network. Answer C is incorrect because the Internet layer handles the routing of packets between destinations as well as fragmentation. Answer D is incorrect because the Application layer interacts with running applications; it does not have anything to do with flow control.

Question 41

The correct answer is D. The -P option to the pntadm command is used to see the changes made to the DHCP table. Answer A is incorrect because the -M option is used to modify an entry that has been made to the DHCP table. Answer B is incorrect because the -c option is used to create the DHCP table. Answer C is incorrect because the -A option is used to add an entry to the DHCP table.

Question 42

The correct answers are A and C. IPv6 addresses the shortfall in IPv4 addresses and also makes routing easier through simplified headers. Answer B is incorrect because IPv6 provides classless addressing. Answer D is incorrect because IPv6 addresses are assigned automatically, with the autoconfiguration facility.

Question 43

The correct answer is A. The file /etc/hostname6.hme0 would configure and enable an IPv6 address on the hme0 network interface, following a reboot of the system. Answer B is incorrect because this would affect the primary IPv4 address. Answer C is incorrect because this would configure an IPv6 address on the hme6 interface. Answer D is incorrect because this would configure an IPv4 logical interface.

Question 44

The correct answer is B. /var/ntp/ntp.drift is the default location for the drift file, as specified in the configuration file, /etc/inet/ntp.conf. Answers A, C, and D are incorrect because they are invalid file names and do not exist.

Question 45

The correct answers are A and B. The dhcpagent process on the client handles the release and renewal of leases and also listens for server responses. Answer C is incorrect because to configure a DHCP client you need to create a specific file relating to a network interface. If you have an hme interface, hme0, then the file to create is /etc/dhcp.hme0. The client will use DHCP when it is rebooted. Answer D is incorrect because it is the server that manages the list of available IP addresses—the pntadm command is used.

Question 46

The correct answers are B and C. Servers that use a high-availability failover mechanism, such as IP multipathing, make use of logical network interfaces. A server running a number of applications that require the system to appear as separate is also a good case for using logical network interfaces. Answer A is incorrect because logical network interfaces do not ease network congestion. The logical interfaces still use the single primary interface, so network throughput is not improved. Answer D is incorrect because the use of logical network interfaces does not improve hardware resilience because they all use the same physical network interface—there is no resilience.

Question 47

The correct answer is D. The collision rate is determined by multiplying the number of collisions by 100 and then dividing by the total number of output packets. Answer A is incorrect because the number of collisions is divided by the total number of output packets, not input packets. Answer B is incorrect because the total number of output packets is used in the calculation, not the total number of input packets. Answer C is incorrect because multiplying the number of output packets by 100 and then dividing by the number of collisions would give the wrong collision rate.

Question 48

The correct answer is C. TCP establishes a virtual circuit connection between the sending and receiving hosts before data transmission can start. Answer A is incorrect because TCP establishes a virtual circuit connection. A characteristic of the connection is that it is full-duplex because it allows concurrent transmission of data in both directions. Answer B is incorrect because TCP establishes a virtual circuit connection and does not use half-duplex communications, which allow data transmission in both directions, but not concurrently. TCP makes use of full-duplex communications. Answer D is incorrect because TCP does not make a physical connection; it establishes a virtual circuit connection.

Question 49

The correct answer is B. Unsolicited ARP messages are held in the ARP cache for 5 minutes.

Question 50

The correct answer is B. The file /etc/inet/ipnodes provides IPv6 address-to-hostname mapping in the same way that /etc/inet/hosts does for IPv4. Answers A, C, and D are incorrect because these files do not exist.

Question 51

The correct answers are A and B. Each dhcp_network filename consists of the type of datastore and the IP address of the network being supported. An example for an ASCII datastore supporting the network 192.168.1.0 is named SUNWfiles1_192_168_1_0. Answers C and D are incorrect because the hostname and IP address of the DHCP server are not items used to create the dhcp_network filename.

Question 52

The correct answer is C. The startup script /etc/rc2.d/S72inetsvc starts the in.named daemon. Answer A is incorrect because /etc/rcS.d/S30network.sh configures the network interface. Answer B is incorrect because /etc/rc2.d/S30sysid.net is the script that completes the configuration of the network. Answer D is incorrect because /etc/rc2.d/S69inet is a script that configures networking aspects, such as routing.

Question 53

The correct answers are A, C, and D. The IPv6 loopback address can be represented in three ways, namely ::1, 0000:0000:0000:0000:0000:0000:0000:0001, or 0:0:0:0:0:0:0:1. Answer B is incorrect because the leading zeros have not been compressed; they have been discarded, making this an invalid IPv6 address. Answer E is incorrect because the :: compression character can be used only once in an IPv6 address.

Question 54

The correct answers are A, B, and D. Subnetting can be used to provide separate subnetworks, according to geographical area or department. It is also used to restrict access to a subnetwork and to reduce network contention by splitting up the network into a number of smaller, local subnetworks. Answer C is incorrect because the number of IP addresses increases with the use of subnetting. Answer E is incorrect because subnetting actually increases the complexity of network management.

Question 55

The correct answer is A. 100BASE-T4 is the media type that uses four pairs of wires: one to send, one to receive, and two bi-directional pairs. It is implemented on unshielded twisted pair cables, can be CAT-3 or CAT-4, but CAT-5 is recommended. 100 BASE-T4 operates over distances of about 100 meters. Answer B is incorrect because 100BASE-FX is implemented on fiber-optic cable, not twisted pair. Answer C is incorrect because 100BASE-TX uses two pairs of wires, not four. Answer D is incorrect because 100BASE-X is a term often used to describe 100BASE-FX and 100BASE-TX.

Question 56

The correct answer is B. The `dhcp_network` file contains the range of IP addresses that can be assigned by the DHCP server, for a single network. Answer A is incorrect because the `dhcpagent` process that runs on a DHCP client obtains default configuration information from the file `/etc/default/dhcpagent`. Answer C is incorrect because the `dhcp_network` file contains the range of IP addresses for a single network, not all networks. Answer D is incorrect because the configuration information for the DHCP server is found in the file `/etc/inet/dhcpsvc.conf`.

Question 57

The correct answer is D. The NTP server configuration file, `/etc/inet/ntp.conf`, is created by copying the file `/etc/inet/ntp.server`. It is then edited to meet the requirements of the local network. Answers A and B are incorrect because these files do not exist. Answer C is incorrect because the file, `/etc/inet/ntp.client`, is the template file used by an NTP client to create its configuration file.

Question 58

The correct answer is C. The sixth octet, `FFFF`, in the address indicates that an embedded IPv4 address is present in the IPv6 address. Answer A is incorrect because `C0A8` is the hexadecimal representation of the first 16 bits of the IPv4 address `192.168`. Answer B is incorrect because `1507` is the hexadecimal representation of the second 16 bits of the IPv4 address `21.7`. The embedded IPv4 address occupies the rightmost 32 bits of the IPv6 address. Answer D is incorrect because `0000` is used as padding.

Question 59

The correct answer is D. The `dhcpmgr` utility can be found in the directory `/usr/sadm/admin/bin`. Answers A and B are incorrect because the `dhcpmgr` utility is not found in these directories. Answer C is incorrect because `/usr/sadm/admin/dhcpmgr` is a directory containing the Java, help, and library files required to run `dhcpmgr`. The utility itself is not found in this directory.

Question 60

The correct answer is B. TCP uses a congestion window on the sending side to manage the flow of data. If congestion is detected, the size of the congestion is halved to reduce the amount of data that is sent across the network. When acknowledgements are received from the receiving host, the congestion window is doubled in size to allow a greater number of packets to be sent across the network. Answer A is incorrect because the congestion window is not halved in size when acknowledgements are received; it is doubled in size. Also, the congestion window is not doubled in size when congestion is detected; it is halved in size. Answers C and D are incorrect because they are not features of the congestion window.

Question 61

The correct answer is A. The application layer handles the formatting of data and any conversions that are necessary. Answer B is incorrect because the Internet layer handles the routing of packets and fragmentation/reassembly. Answer C is incorrect because the Network Interface layer handles the transmission of ethernet frames across the network. Answer D is incorrect because the Transport layer handles the end-to-end communication and does not deal with data formatting.

Question 62

The correct answer is B. The ring network topology is one where hosts are connected in a ring formation, and each host is connected only to its adjacent neighbors. Answer A is incorrect because a bus topology involves all hosts being connected to a single backbone cable. Answer C is incorrect because the star topology involves hosts being connected to a central hub. Answer D is incorrect because a VLAN topology involves the use of a central intelligent hub or switch and functions in a similar way to multiple star topology networks.

Question 63

The correct answer is A. The `in.rarpd` daemon will start at boot time only if the `/tftpboot` directory exists. Answers B, C, and D are incorrect because these directories do not exist.

Question 64

The correct answers are A and D. Logical interfaces can cause performance bottlenecks because they all use the same physical ethernet interface. They can also slow down the system boot process because each logical interface has to be configured at boot time. Answer B is incorrect because logical interfaces provide additional resources at a much lower cost because there is no need to purchase additional physical ethernet interfaces. Answer C is incorrect because logical interfaces are not an administration overhead; they allow central administration on a single host.

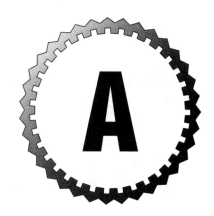

What's on the CD-ROM

This appendix provides a brief summary of what you'll find on the CD-ROM that accompanies this book. For a more detailed description of the *PrepLogic Practice Exams, Preview Edition*, exam simulation software, see Appendix B, "Using the *PrepLogic Practice Exams, Preview Edition*, Software." In addition to the *PrepLogic Practice Exams, Preview Edition*, software, the CD-ROM includes an electronic version of the book, in Portable Document Format (PDF), and the source code used in the book.

The *PrepLogic Practice Exams, Preview Edition*, Software

PrepLogic is a leading provider of certification training tools. Trusted by certification students worldwide, PrepLogic is the best practice exam software available. In addition to providing a means of evaluating your knowledge of this book's material, *PrepLogic Practice Exams, Preview Edition*, features several innovations that help you improve your mastery of the subject matter.

For example, the practice tests allow you to check your score by exam area or domain, to determine which topics you need to study further. Another feature allows you to obtain immediate feedback on your responses, in the form of explanations for the correct and incorrect answers.

PrepLogic Practice Tests, Preview Edition, exhibits all the full-test simulation functionality of the Premium Edition, but offers only a fraction of the total questions. To get the complete set of practice questions, visit www.preplogic.com and order the Premium Edition for this and other challenging exam training guides.

An Exclusive Electronic Version of the Text

As mentioned previously, the CD-ROM that accompanies this book also contains an electronic PDF version of this book. This electronic version comes complete with all figures as they appear in the book. You can use Acrobat's handy search capability for study and review purposes.

Using the *PrepLogic Practice Exams, Preview Edition*, Software

This book includes a special version of the PrepLogic Practice Exams software, a revolutionary test engine designed to give you the best in certification exam preparation. PrepLogic offers sample and practice exams for many of today's most in-demand and challenging technical certifications. A special Preview Edition of the PrepLogic Practice Exams software is included with this book as a tool to use in assessing your knowledge of the training guide material while also providing you with the experience of taking an electronic exam.

This appendix describes in detail what *PrepLogic Practice Exams, Preview Edition*, is, how it works, and what it can do to help you prepare for the exam. Note that although the Preview Edition includes all the test simulation functions of the complete retail version, it contains only a single practice test. The Premium Edition, available at www.preplogic.com, contains a complete set of challenging practice exams designed to optimize your learning experience.

The Exam Simulation

One of the main functions of *PrepLogic Practice Exams, Preview Edition*, is exam simulation. To prepare you to take the actual vendor certification exam, PrepLogic is designed to offer the most effective exam simulation available.

Question Quality

The questions provided in *PrepLogic Practice Exams, Preview Edition*, are written to the highest standards of technical accuracy. The questions tap the content of this book's chapters and help you review and assess your knowledge before you take the actual exam.

The Interface Design

The *PrepLogic Practice Exams, Preview Edition*, exam simulation interface provides you with the experience of taking an electronic exam. This enables you to effectively prepare to take the actual exam by making the test experience familiar. Using this test simulation can help eliminate the sense of surprise or anxiety you might experience in the testing center because you will already be acquainted with computerized testing.

The Effective Learning Environment

The *PrepLogic Practice Exams, Preview Edition*, interface provides a learning environment that not only tests you through the computer but also teaches the material you need to know to pass the certification exam. Each question includes a detailed explanation of the correct answer, and most of these explanations provide reasons as to why the other answers are incorrect. This information helps to reinforce the knowledge you already have and also provides practical information you can use on the job.

Software Requirements

The PrepLogic Practice Exams software requires a computer with the following:

➤ Microsoft Windows 98, Windows Me, Windows NT 4.0, Windows 2000, or Windows XP

➤ A 166MHz or faster processor

➤ A minimum of 32MB of RAM

➤ 10MB of hard drive space

Performance   As with any Windows application, the more memory, the better the performance.

Installing *PrepLogic Practice Exams, Preview Edition*

You install *PrepLogic Practice Exams, Preview Edition*, by following these steps:

1. Insert the CD-ROM that accompanies this book into your CD-ROM drive. The Autorun feature of Windows should launch the software. If you have Autorun disabled, select Start, Run. Go to the root directory of the CD-ROM and select setup.exe. Click Open, and then click OK.

2. The Installation Wizard copies the *PrepLogic Practice Exams, Preview Edition*, files to your hard drive. It then adds *PrepLogic Practice Exams, Preview Edition*, to your Desktop and the Program menu. Finally, it installs test engine components to the appropriate system folders.

Removing *PrepLogic Practice Exams, Preview Edition*, from Your Computer

If you elect to remove the *PrepLogic Practice Exams, Preview Edition*, you can use the included uninstallation process to ensure that it is removed from your system safely and completely. Follow these instructions to remove *PrepLogic Practice Exams, Preview Edition*, from your computer:

1. Select Start, Settings, Control Panel.

2. Double-click the Add/Remove Programs icon. You are presented with a list of software installed on your computer.

3. Select the *PrepLogic Practice Exams, Preview Edition*, title you want to remove. Click the Add/Remove button. The software is removed from your computer.

How to Use the Software

PrepLogic is designed to be user friendly and intuitive. Because the software has a smooth learning curve, your time is maximized because you start practicing with it almost immediately. *PrepLogic Practice Exams, Preview Edition*, has two major modes of study: Practice Exam and Flash Review.

Using Practice Exam mode, you can develop your test-taking abilities as well as your knowledge through the use of the Show Answer option. While you are taking the test, you can expose the answers along with detailed explanations of why answers are right or wrong. This helps you better understand the material presented.

Flash Review mode is designed to reinforce exam topics rather than quiz you. In this mode, you are shown a series of questions but no answer choices. You can click a button that reveals the correct answer to each question and a full explanation for that answer.

Starting a Practice Exam Mode Session

Practice Exam mode enables you to control the exam experience in ways that actual certification exams do not allow. To begin studying in Practice Exam mode, you click the Practice Exam radio button from the main exam customization screen. This enables the following options:

➤ *The Enable Show Answer button*—Clicking this button activates the Show Answer button, which allows you to view the correct answer(s) and a full explanation for each question during the exam. When this option is not enabled, you must wait until after your exam has been graded to view the correct answer(s) and explanation for each question.

➤ *The Enable Item Review button*—Clicking this button activates the Item Review button, which allows you to view your answer choices. This option also facilitates navigation between questions.

➤ *The Randomize Choices option*—You can randomize answer choices from one exam session to the next. This makes memorizing question choices more difficult, thereby keeping questions fresh and challenging longer.

On the left side of the main exam customization screen, you are presented with the option of selecting the preconfigured practice test or creating your own custom test. The preconfigured test has a fixed time limit and number of questions. Custom tests allow you to configure the time limit and the number of questions in your exam.

The Preview Edition on this book's CD-ROM includes a single preconfigured practice test. You can get the compete set of challenging PrepLogic Practice Exams at www.preplogic.com to make certain you're ready for the big exam.

You click the Begin Exam button to begin your exam.

Starting a Flash Review Mode Session

Flash Review mode provides an easy way to reinforce topics covered in the practice questions. To begin studying in Flash Review mode, you click the Flash Review radio button from the main exam customization screen. Then you select either the preconfigured practice test or create your own custom test.

You click the Best Exam button to begin a Flash Review mode session.

Standard *PrepLogic Practice Exams, Preview Edition,* Options

The following list describes the function of each of the buttons you see across the bottom of the screen:

Button Status Depending on the options, some of the buttons will be grayed out and inaccessible—or they might be missing completely. Buttons that are appropriate are active.

➤ *Exhibit*—This button is visible if an exhibit is provided to support the question. An *exhibit* is an image that provides supplemental information necessary to answer a question.

➤ *Item Review*—This button leaves the question window and opens the Item Review screen, from which you can see all questions, your answers, and your marked items. You can also see correct answers listed here, when appropriate.

➤ *Show Answer*—This option displays the correct answer, with an explanation about why it is correct. If you select this option, the current question is not scored.

➤ *Mark Item*—You can check this box to flag a question that you need to review further. You can view and navigate your marked items by clicking the Item Review button (if it is enabled). When your exam is being graded, you are notified if you have any marked items remaining.

➤ *Previous Item*—You can use this option to view the previous question.

➤ *Next Item*—You can use this option to view the next question.

➤ *Grade Exam*—When you have completed your exam, you can click Grade Exam to end your exam and view your detailed score report. If you have unanswered or marked items remaining, you are asked whether you would like to continue taking your exam or view the exam report.

Seeing Time Remaining

If your practice test is timed, the time remaining is displayed on the upper-right corner of the application screen. It counts down the minutes and seconds remaining to complete the test. If you run out of time, you are asked whether you want to continue taking the test or end your exam.

Getting Your Examination Score Report

The Examination Score Report screen appears when the Practice Exam mode ends—as a result of time expiration, completion of all questions, or your decision to terminate early.

This screen provides a graphical display of your test score, with a breakdown of scores by topic domain. The graphical display at the top of the screen compares your overall score with the PrepLogic Exam Competency Score. The *PrepLogic Exam Competency Score* reflects the level of subject competency required to pass the particular vendor's exam. Although this score does not directly translate to a passing score, consistently matching or exceeding this score does suggest that you possess the knowledge needed to pass the actual vendor exam.

Reviewing Your Exam

From the Your Score Report screen, you can review the exam that you just completed by clicking the View Items button. You can navigate through the items, viewing the questions, your answers, the correct answers, and the explanations for those questions. You can return to your score report by clicking the View Items button.

Contacting PrepLogic

If you would like to contact PrepLogic for any reason, including to get information about its extensive line of certification practice tests, you can do so online at www.preplogic.com.

Customer Service

If you have a damaged product and need to contact customer service, please call

800-858-7674

Product Suggestions and Comments

PrepLogic values your input! Please email your suggestions and comments to feedback@preplogic.com.

License Agreement

YOU MUST AGREE TO THE TERMS AND CONDITIONS OUT-LINED IN THE END USER LICENSE AGREEMENT ("EULA") PRESENTED TO YOU DURING THE INSTALLATION PROCESS. IF YOU DO NOT AGREE TO THESE TERMS, DO NOT INSTALL THE SOFTWARE.

Glossary

. . . .

A (Address) Resource Record

Resource record used in the
Domain Name System (DNS) zone
file to map IPv4 addresses to hostnames, like the entries in the
`/etc/inet/hosts` file.

AAAA (Address) Resource Record

Resource record used in the
Domain Name System (DNS) zone
file to map IPv6 addresses to hostnames—similar in functionality to
the local `/etc/inet/ipnodes` file.

Address Resolution Protocol (ARP)

A protocol in the TCP/IP model
that operates between the network
interface and Internet layers. It is
used to map a 32-bit IP address to
a 48-bit Ethernet or MAC address.

anycast address

An IPv6 address type, similar to a
multicast address, where a message
is sent to a specific group of hosts
on a network. A message sent to an
anycast address is received only by
the nearest host that is a member
of the group.

bandwidth

The maximum capacity at which
data can be transferred across a
communication medium.

baseband

Communication uses the entire
bandwidth of the medium exclu-
sively. An error (collision) occurs if
there is more than one signal
present.

Berkeley Software Distribution (BSD)

A variant of Unix developed at the
University of California at
Berkeley. Solaris contains some
historical links to files for BSD
compatibility. Prior to Solaris 2.0,
SunOS was based on the BSD variant of Unix.

broadband

Multiple signals existing concurrently on the same communication media, allowing more information to be transmitted in a given time.

broadcast address

The IP address used to send a message to all computers connected to a network.

client

A networked computer that makes use of services provided by a *server*.

Common Desktop Environment (CDE)

The standard graphical user interface (GUI) supplied with the Solaris 9 operating environment.

Company Identifier (CID)

The first (leftmost) 24 bits of an Ethernet address that are assigned to a company, or organization, by the Institute of Electronic and Electrical Engineers (IEEE). The CID is used with a *vendor identifier (VID)* to form an *Ethernet address*. The CID is also known as an organizationally unique identifier (OUI).

connection-oriented protocol

A protocol that establishes a virtual connection prior to any data transmission taking place. The *Transmission Control Protocol (TCP)* is an example of a connection-oriented protocol.

connectionless protocol

A protocol that does not establish any connection prior to data transmission taking place. The *User Datagram Protocol (UDP)* is an example of a connectionless protocol.

DHCP lease time

The time that an IP address being managed by DHCP is valid. At the end of the lease time, the lease expires and is no longer available to the DHCP client unless it is renewed.

DHCP scope

The range of IP addresses being managed by a DHCP server.

diskless client

A computer connected to a network that does not have any local storage capability and retrieves its network configuration information from a remote server on the network. All file systems and swap space reside on remote file servers.

DNS primary name server

The master server for a DNS domain. Changes and updates to the data held in the DNS domain are made on this server. A serial number that is incremented on the primary server is used by secondary DNS servers to detect updates and synchronize the data files. The Solaris versions of DNS have a single primary DNS server per domain.

DNS secondary name server

A slave server for a DNS domain. There can be multiple secondary name servers in a DNS domain and they act as a backup for the primary name server. A secondary name server is synchronized at regular intervals through *zone transfers* from the primary name server.

Domain Name System (DNS)

A service providing domain name–to–IP address resolution, and vice versa, primarily on the Internet.

Dynamic Host Configuration Protocol (DHCP)

A protocol used to automatically provide IP address and other network configuration information to clients.

encapsulation

The process of adding protocol header information to the data packet at each layer of the TCP/IP model before the packet is passed to the next layer. Each layer's header information is interpreted only by its peer layer at the destination; the other layers handle this information as part of the data.

Ethernet address

A 48-bit unique address that identifies a network interface. The address comprises a company identifier (CID) and a vendor identifier (VID). It is also known as a MAC address and is hard-coded by the manufacturer.

Ethernet frame

The basic unit of transfer on Ethernet networks, comprising the sender address, the destination address, control information, and the actual data to be transferred.

Fully Qualified Domain Name (FQDN)

The absolute path to a domain, such as www.sun.com.

Fully Qualified Host Name (FQHN)

The absolute path to a hostname, which includes the short hostname itself, as well as the domain name in which it resides, such as sales.sun.com.

Hop count

A means of measuring distance between two hosts on a network, used in network routing. It identifies the number of routers, or hosts, that a data packet passes through to reach its destination. Each router, or host, constitutes a hop.

host

A computer, or other device, that is connected to a network.

Internet Control Message Protocol (ICMP)

An integral part of the Internet Protocol (IP) that is used to send error and control messages to other hosts on the network. It is often used in network problem diagnosis. The ping command uses ICMP to send ECHO REQUEST messages.

Internet Engineering Task Force (IETF)

The body that defines standards for protocols. The standards are released as Requests For Comments (RFCs).

Internet Protocol (IP)

Part of the TCP/IP suite that is responsible for the delivery of datagrams across a network and any fragmentation/reassembly of data required.

IP forwarding

The process of forwarding IP datagrams from one network to another. This is only enabled on routers, or systems acting as routers.

IPng

Synonymous with *IPv6*, ng stands for next generation.

IPv4 address

A 32-bit address that uniquely identifies a host on a network.

IPv6

The next version of the Internet Protocol that is being introduced to alleviate the shortfall in IPv4 addresses. IPv6 uses 128-bit IP addresses, providing a vast increase in the number of available addresses. It is also a classless protocol, unlike IPv4.

IPv6-over-IPv4 Tunnel

The feature that enables IPv6 hosts to communicate across an IPv4 network. It was introduced to assist with the transition from IPv4 to IPv6 so that both protocols can co-exist on the same network infrastructure.

JumpStart client

A computer connected to a network that makes use of the Solaris JumpStart feature to automatically install the Solaris operating environment over a network.

JumpStart install server

A server that provides the installation image for a JumpStart client to install the Solaris operating environment automatically over a network.

JumpStart profile server

A server that provides the configuration information for a JumpStart client to install the Solaris operating environment automatically over a network. Also known as a JumpStart configuration server.

local area network (LAN)

A network that spans a small geographical area, normally a site, but can comprise numerous buildings. A LAN is used to interconnect a number of departments in an organization, or a number of systems. A LAN uses private cabling and achieves a high data transmission rate. LAN hardware is much cheaper and easier to install than a *Wide Area Network (WAN)*. Ethernet is an example of a LAN technology.

MAC Address

Synonymous with *Ethernet address*.

Master DNS Server

Synonymous with *primary name server*.

Multicast Address

An IP address that is used to communicate with a specific group of hosts on a network. Messages sent to multicast addresses are received only by hosts belonging to the multicast group.

MX (Mail Exchanger) Resource Record

Resource record used in the Domain Name System (DNS) zone file to identify mail servers to be used for handling electronic mail. A preference value can also be applied to this record to specify a master and slave server.

name server switch

The common name for the switch file /etc/nsswitch.conf, which is used to determine the search order and the name service to use to obtain network information.

network mask

A value that is used to distinguish the network portion of an IP address from the host portion.

network topology

The physical structure of a network—how the hosts, or nodes, on a network are physically wired together.

node

Synonymous with *host*.

NS (Name Server) resource record

Resource record used in the Domain Name System (DNS) zone file to identify other DNS name servers in a domain. This record is also used to show where a sub-domain has been delegated to another DNS server.

Open Shortest Path First (OSPF)

A link-state routing protocol that maintains a complex knowledge of the network topology. When a network change occurs, only the change is exchanged with other routers, unlike *RIP*, where the entire routing table is exchanged. OSPF can process updates to the network configuration more quickly than RIP.

protocol

The defined set of rules that govern how data is transferred between hosts on a network.

PTR (Pointer) Resource Record

Resource record used in the Domain Name System (DNS) zone file for mapping hostnames to IPv4 addresses and for reverse DNS lookups.

reliable protocol

Each exchange of data is acknowledged by the receiving host. The sender knows whether each transmission was successful because of this acknowledgement and resends any data that was not acknowledged. TCP is an example of a reliable protocol.

Reverse Address Resolution Protocol (RARP)

A protocol in the TCP/IP model that operates between the Network Interface and Internet layers. It is used to map a 48-bit Ethernet address to a 32-bit IP address.

Routing Information Protocol (RIP)

A distance-vector routing protocol that determines the path to the destination by the number of hops taken. The entire routing table is passed to the router's neighbor at regular intervals and when a change occurs. The maximum number of hops allowed in a path is 15. If the hop count reaches 16 (deemed to be infinity), the destination is marked as unreachable.

server

A computer system that provides services to other systems on a network.

SOA (Start Of Authority) resource record

Resource record used in the Domain Name System (DNS) zone file to identify the start of the zone data and to define default parameters for the whole zone.

stateful protocol

Both the sending and receiving hosts monitor a connection and exchange status information as part of the data exchange, providing greater reliability, but, because of the extra information, a greater overhead. TCP is an example of a stateful protocol.

stateless protocol

Neither the sending nor receiving hosts monitor the state of a communications link and both operate independently of the other, unlike stateful protocols where there is a clear exchange of control information. Stateless protocols are inherently less reliable than stateful protocols because data packets can be lost, or arrive in any order, but they incur virtually no overhead. Connectionless protocols are also normally stateless. UDP is an example of a stateless protocol.

System V

The variant of Unix developed by AT&T Bell Labs. Solaris is based on System V Unix Release 4.

TCP/IP model

A protocol stack that enables devices to communicate across a network. The TCP/IP model is a four-layer model comprising the Network Interface (including hardware layer), Internet, Transport, and Application layers. The structure is hierarchical, with each layer performing a specific function.

Transmission Control Protocol (TCP)

A connection-oriented, reliable, and stateful protocol that operates at the Transport layer of the TCP/IP model. It is used on networks where a guaranteed delivery service is required. TCP implements a guaranteed delivery service through the use of acknowledgements and error checking/retransmission mechanisms.

unicast address

An IP address used to communicate with a single host on a network.

unreliable protocol

Each exchange of data is not acknowledged, so packets can be lost. Applications using an unreliable protocol normally handle data loss within the application and do not rely on the network. UDP is an example of an unreliable protocol.

User Datagram Protocol (UDP)

A connectionless, unreliable, and stateless protocol that operates at the Transport layer of the TCP/IP model. It was designed for applications that do not require a reliable transport mechanism, primarily because the application itself carries out any error checking and data delivery guarantee.

vendor identifier (VID)

The second (rightmost) 24 bits of an *Ethernet address* that are assigned and managed by the vendor and must be unique within the vendor organization. The VID is used with the *company identifier (CID)* to form an Ethernet address.

wide area network (WAN)

A network that spans a large geographical area and that can be used to interconnect departmental local area networks (LANs), or different locations in a city or state. A WAN makes use of third-party service providers and telecommunications companies to provide the interconnection. Data transfer rates are typically slower than that achieved on a LAN. Frame relay is an example of a WAN technology.

zone

The extent of the authority of a DNS name server.

zone file

A data file used in the domain name system (DNS) relevant to a particular *zone*. The file identifies configuration information and hostname resolution details for domains and systems that come under the authority of the zone.

zone transfer

The process by which secondary DNS name servers are updated from the primary DNS server to synchronize the data.

Index

How can we make this index more useful? Email us at indexes@quepublishing.com

How can we make this index more useful? Email us at indexes@quepublishing.com

J-K

L

LANs (local area networks)
  Connections, bridges, 7
  network access methods, 12-13
  network devices, 6-9
  network media, 9-12
  network topologies, 2-5
layers
  TCP/IP model, 37-40
  Transport, 164
leases
  DHCP clients, 208, 214-215
  IP addresses, obtaining, 251
Length header field (UDP), 169
link-local unicast IPv6 addresses, 135
links, /etc/hosts, 55
link_speed parameter, 27
load balancing
  IPMP (IP multipathing), 92
  Sun Trunking, 100
local area networks. *See* LANs
local ethernet addresses, 19
log messages, NTP (Network Time
  Protocol) troubleshooting, 266
logical interfaces
  IPv4, 78-81
  IPv6, 145
Long frame error, 18
loopback address type unicast IPv6 address,
  137
loopback reverse resolution zones (DNS
  servers), 189

M

MAC (media access control), 6, 100
macros, DHCP, 213, 234-236
Mail Exchanger (MX), 187
management, key, 259
manual configuration, \non-routers (IPv6),
  144
mapping
  32-bit IP addresses, 50
  address-to-hostname (IPv4), 76
Mark Item button, 361
masks. *See* network masks
Max field (vendor symbols), 236
maximum hopcount option, RIPv1 (Routing
  Information Protocol Version 1), 119
maximum transfer unit (MTU), 17-18
media access control (MAC), 6, 100

media. *See* network media
messages. *See also* error messages
  ARP (Address Resolution Protocol), 51
  ICMP (Internet Control Message
    Protocol), 64-65
  neighbor advertisement, 142
  neighbor solicitation, 142
mixed topologies, 4
MMF (multimode fiber), 10
Modify command (Service menu), 225
MTU (maximum transfer unit), 17-18
multicast addresses, 15
multicast IPv4 addresses, 67-68
multicast IPv6 addresses, 137-138
multihomed hosts, 123
multimode fiber (MMF), 10
multipathing (IPv6). *See also* IPMP (IP multipathing)
    command line, 152-154
    configuration files, 152-153
    test addresses, 152
multiport repeaters, 7
MX (Mail Exchanger), 187

N

name resolution, IPv4 route tables, 111
Name Server (NS), 186
named.ca file, 182-185
namespaces, DNS, 176
ndc utility, 196-197
ndd command, 26-28, 51
NDP (neighbor discovery protocol),
  142-143
neighbor advertisement message, 142
neighbor discovery protocol (NDP),
  142-143
neighbor solicitation message, 142
neighbor unreachability detection, 143
netstat –i command, 21
netstat –p command, 21
netstat –r command, 111-112
netstat command, 23, 124
network access methods, 12-13
network Interface layer (TCP/IP model),
  38, 42
network management tools, NTP (Network
  Time Protocol), 259
network masks, IPv4 addresses, 68
  /etc/inet/netmasks file, 69-70
  subnetting, 70-72
  VLSM (variable length subnet mask),
    72-73

How can we make this index more useful? Email us at indexes@quepublishing.com

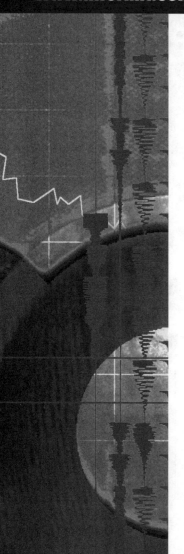